Producing globalisation

MANCHESTER
1824

Manchester University Press

Producing globalisation

Politics of discourse and institutions in Greece and Ireland

Andreas Antoniades

Manchester University Press

Manchester and New York

distributed in the United States exclusively
by Palgrave Macmillan

Published by Manchester University Press
Oxford Road, Manchester M13 9NR, UK
and Room 400, 175 Fifth Avenue, New York, NY 10010, USA
www.manchesteruniversitypress.co.uk

Distributed in the United States exclusively by
Palgrave Macmillan, 175 Fifth Avenue, New York,
NY 10010, USA

Distributed in Canada exclusively by
UBC Press, University of British Columbia, 2029 West Mall,
Vancouver, BC, Canada V6T 1Z2

British Library Cataloguing-in-Publication Data
A catalogue record for this book is available from the British Library
Library of Congress Cataloging-in-Publication Data applied for

ISBN   978 0 7190 7844 6 *hardback*

First published 2009

18 17 16 15 14 13 12 11 10 09   10 9 8 7 6 5 4 3 2 1

Typeset
by Action Publishing Technology Ltd, Gloucester
Printed in Great Britain
by CPI Antony Rowe, Chippenham, Wiltshire

Contents

List of tables and figures

Tables

Figures

Acknowledgements

The longer the writing of a book, the more difficult it is for the author to acknowledge properly the help and support of all those who contributed, directly or indirectly, consciously or unconsciously, to its completion. I guess the same goes for the journeys. The longer they last, the more difficult it is for one to remember at once all things, people, feelings encountered. Still, these all make the journey what it is. This, as an apology for those who are not, although they should have been, mentioned here.

I must acknowledge the input and multifaceted support of my colleagues at the London School of Economics (especially in the Department of International Relations and the European Institute) and the University of Sussex, where I have been working while writing this book. Their help and encouragement shaped the thesis put forward in this book in various ways. I am also grateful to the Bodossaki Foundation for funding part of the research on which this book is based.

A number of friends and colleagues offered generously their time and comments on draft chapters. I am grateful to Kimberley Hutchings, Louiza Odysseos, Stefan Elbe, Nicos Mouzelis, Ben O'Loughlin, Charlotte Epstein, Mary Martin, Bob Hancke, Claudia Aradau, Ben Rosamond, Stella Ladi, Chris Brown, Michael Dillon, Spyros Economides, Theodoros Couloumbis, Panos Kazakos, Michael Tsinisizelis, Dimitris Chryssochoou, Peter Wilson, Costas Constantinou, Diane Stone, Elias Nikolakopoulos, George Pagoulatos, Dimitris Sotiropoulos, Niamh Hardiman, Jennifer Jackson Preece, Pavlos Hatzopoulos, Nelli Kambouri, Fabio Petito, Andreas Gofas, Colin Wight, Julian Reid, David Howarth, David Stasavage, Nicky Short, Evanthia Milingou, Yannis Stavrakakis, Nicki Smith, Panagiota Manoli, Sotiria Theodoropoulou, Diego Muro, Dermot Hodson, Benedicta Marzinotto, Emma Haddad, Peter Bratsis, Nadia Spiliou, Chryssoula Maurokosta, Rania Kommata, Kostas Manios, Dimitris Sofos, Giorgos Voyiatzis, Marietta

Provata, Douglas Bulloch, Jill Stuart, Simon Usherwood, Marco Simoni. Without the long conversations with and guidance of Christopher Hill, and the extensive and thoughtful feedback from Loukas Tsoukalis, Vivien Schmidt, Colin Hay and Kevin Featherstone, this book would not be the same.

I also owe sincere thanks to the people that helped me during my fieldwork in Greece and Ireland. In Greece the help of Nikiforos Diamandouros was more than critical. I am most grateful to him for all his time, encouragement and support. The same goes for Brigid Laffan in Ireland. The time I spent in the Dublin European Institute at University College Dublin proved indeed more productive than what I could have wished for. I am also grateful to Peter Cassells, Garret FitzGerald, Paul Gillespie and Katy Hayward in Ireland, and Dimitris Katsoridas, Pandelis Kapsis, Giorgos Kirtsos, Dimitris Politis, Savvas Robolis and Iason Stratos in Greece, for generously sharing their time and thoughts with me. Many thanks are also due to the political party secretaries in Greece and Ireland for their cooperation and assistance in my search for archival material.

The encouragement and inspiration I draw from my undergraduate and graduate students at the LSE, the University of Essex and the University of Sussex is hard to put in words. To paraphrase and old Irish proverb, if you are lucky enough to have good students, you are lucky enough. They have been the best part in my encounter with the educational process up to now. I thank them from my heart! Special thanks also to Tony Mason, Jenny Howard and the production team at MUP for all their patience, support and encouragement. It has indeed been a pleasure to work with them. Warm thanks also to the MUP anonymous reviewers for all their time, comments and professionalism.

For some debts in life words are not appropriate or enough. Yet I would like to say that without the trust, support, assistance and love of Andreas, Irene, Dimitris, Thodoris, Andy, Aristea and (the newly arrived) Alexios-Andreas nothing of all these would be possible. I dedicate this book to them.

List of Abbreviations

ASEAN	Association of South East Asian Nations
CEEP	European Centre of Employers and Enterprises providing Public Services
CSSBs	Commercial State-Sponsored Bodies
EESC	European Economic and Social Committee
EIHEA	Athens Daily Newspaper Publishers' Association
EPL	employment protection legislation
ETUC	European Trade Union Confederation
EU	European Union
FDI	foreign direct investments
FF	Fianna Fáil
FG	Fine Gael
GI	*A. T. Kearney/Foreign Policy* 'Globalisation Index'
GSEE	Greek General Confederation of Labour
IBEC	Irish Business and Employers Confederation
ICTU	Irish Congress of Trade Unions
ILO	International Labour Organisation
IMF	International Monetary Fund
INE	Institute of Labour [Greece]
IPE	International Political Economy
IR	International Relations
KKE	Communist Party of Greece
LP	Labour Party [Ireland]
MNC	multinational corporations
NAFTA	North American Free Trade Agreement
ND	New Democracy
NESC	National Economic and Social Council
NGO	non-governmental organisation
OECD	Organisation for Economic Cooperation and Development
OKE	Economic and Social Council [Greece]

PASOK	Panhellenic Socialist Movement
PD	Progressive Democrats
PLAC	Pro-Life Amendment Campaign
REC	Report of the Executive Council
SEV	Federation of Greek Industries
SPUC	Society for the Protection of the Unborn Child
Synaspismos	Coalition of the Left and Progress
UN	United Nations
UNICE	Union des Industries de la Communauté Européenne (Union of Industrial and Employers' Confederations of Europe)
WTO	World Trade Organisation

Introduction

Two issues have dominated the agenda of political science over the last decade: on the one hand the importance of *institutions* and on the other the importance of *knowledge, ideas* and *discourse*. The respective bodies of literature have generated important insights in the study and understanding of world politics and economics. This book is based on these theoretical developments. It subscribes to the statement that if one wants to understand international relations/ international political economy, one cannot exclude the study of institutional and ideational factors. But the great challenge is not to recognise the importance of these two sets of factors but rather to develop an analytical framework capable of studying the conditions of their co-existence and the nature of their interaction.

To this end, I propose the concept of hegemonic discourse. A hegemonic discourse is conceptualised as a set of *productive* practices and meanings that dominate world politics and economics during particular historical periods. This book aspires to explicate the conditions of existence of hegemonic discourses and the relationship developed between these discourses and national social milieux. In particular, it has two main research goals: first, to explore the nature of the interplay between hegemonic discourses and national institutional arrangements; second, to shed light on the nature of hegemonic discourses and their validity as an analytical tool for studying change and continuity in world politics and economics.

The issue of hegemonic discourse communication by states is Janus-faced. One face is internal/national, and mainly concentrates on the domestic political arena and the games played therein. The other is external/international, and focuses on actors and interactions that transcend national borders. I will try to exemplify that these two faces are inexorably related and that their subject matter is common: *social life,* and how it is produced, reproduced and changes. It is within this context that the book introduces 'social life' as a key level of analysis that allows the question about the function of hegemonic discourses to be addressed in the context of comparative institutional analysis.

The purpose of the book is to scrutinise the nature of the interplay between hegemonic discourses and national institutional settings. The focus is on globalisation. How did the hegemonic discourse of globalisation emerge into different national politico-economic systems? How did globalisation resonate and/or dominate in different national contexts? What was the role of national political economies and domestic institutions in this process? What role did specific institutional actors play in it? How are we to explain the nature of the interplay between globalisation and states? How can we study globalisation in a way that transcends the material/ideational rift?

To examine these questions I focus on the communication of the hegemonic discourse of globalisation in Greece and Ireland[1] (a Mediterranean and an Anglo-Saxon political economy respectively) during the period 1995–2001. Instead of taking globalisation as granted, my purpose is to explore how political actors produced the phenomenon of globalisation. Thus, my analysis is based on an examination of the discourses, policies and strategies of key national institutional actors (political leaders and political parties, employers, workers, the church, and the press). This analysis has three main aims. First, to make a contribution to the globalisation literature. A great amount of work has tried to clarify the phenomenon of globalisation at a conceptual level. This project, in contrast, aims at shifting the focus from the general, the international, the outside and the top-down to the concrete, the national/comparative, the inside and the bottom-up. My target is to examine in depth the process of domination of the hegemonic discourse of globalisation. To do so, I present and analyse new evidence on how globalisation emerged in the aforementioned two European states. The second aim of the project is to make a contribution to the second wave of institutional analysis (that focuses on *how*, rather than *if*, institutions matter). My aim here is to account for the role of domestic institutions and political economy in the materialisation of globalisation. By materialisation I mean the process through which the set of practices and meanings that define globalisation came to be actualised as new policy debates, new policy initiatives, and more broadly as a new politics at the domestic level.[2] The third and more ambitious aim of the project is to suggest a specific way of approaching and studying the interplay between hegemonic discourses and domestic institutional arrangements. To do so,

I attempt to construct a theoretical framework, a hegemonic discourse approach, that allows the question about the nature and the function of hegemonic discourses to be addressed in the framework of comparative institutional analysis.

In conventional terms, the main theoretical puzzle of the book is as follows. On the one hand, we have the hegemonic discourse of globalisation that in the mid-1990s acquired an independent dynamic and came to dominate the public discourses and politico-economic systems of most countries, at least in the West. On the other hand, we have two states with similar political systems and political cultures, but different political economies (Anglo-Saxon vs. Mediterranean). By the late 1990s, the hegemonic discourse of globalisation dominated in both states. How did this domination take place? What was the impact – if any – of the different domestic institutional arrangements of the two countries in the communication of the hegemonic discourse? What conclusions can be drawn about the nature of hegemonic discourses and the interplay between the hegemonic/international and the public/domestic?

These questions, and in general the study of the nature of the *hegemonic*, have gained additional weight in the post-Cold War period, when the US emerged as the sole superpower. Where do the practices and meanings that dominate world politics and economics come from? How do they succeed in dominating world politics and economics? Do states have a choice with regard to their policy options? What are the (pre)conditions for the reproduction or change of a hegemonic discourse? These questions are important, both conceptually and politically, because they attempt to put under scrutiny the concept of the *hegemonic* and the notion of *hegemony* in international relations, rather than take them for granted. They are questions that attempt to re-examine the ways in which world politics and economics are reproduced and changed. Thus, they are questions that invite new thinking on the social condition of world politics and economics. I can only hope the findings of this project speak to these questions and make a small contribution towards their understanding and answer.

The structure of the book is as follows. The first chapter develops the proposed theoretical framework. Here I define the concept of hegemonic discourse and suggest a hegemonic-discourse-communication model. The proposed framework is based on a synthesis of comparative institutionalism and discourse theory, and is focused on the interaction between the *hegemonic* and the *national public* discourses. The second chapter introduces the case studies of the project, i.e. Greece and Ireland, and discusses the nature of their comparison and its potential in terms of theory advancement. Chapters 3 and 4 focus on the communication of the hegemonic discourse of globalisation in Greece and Ireland. These chapters have a double aim. First, they present in detail the empirical findings of our research, concerning the effect of globalisation discourse in the two countries. Here, rather than assuming globalisation to be everywhere in the late 1990s, we attempt to shed light on when, by whom and how globalisation discourse emerged in the two national contexts. The second aim of these empirical chapters is to offer a concrete example of how hegemonic discourses can be captured and analysed. In this regard, this empirical part of the book has a most important methodological and theoretical standing of its own. It is on the 'empirical details' of these chapters that the proposed conceptualisation of hegemonic discourse is based, and against which its validity and usefulness is tested.

Chapter 5 sums up and juxtaposes the findings from the Greek and Irish cases. Hence, rather than offering separate summaries of findings at the end of the two case-study chapters, the book offers a single, comparative summary. In doing so, I aim to subject the comparison of the two cases to both a vertical and a horizontal angle of analysis. Thus while the main research material in chapters 3 and 4 is organised vertically, i.e. in terms of countries, the recapitulation of this material is organised horizontally, i.e. in terms of domestic institutions (e.g. political parties, employers, workers, etc.). Through this combination of comparative methods I aim to cross-examine and double-check our research material and its interpretation.

The juxtaposition of the two cases reveals that while the same hegemonic discourse prevailed in both countries during the 1990s, the way in which it was materialised at the national level was fundamentally different. Indeed we can talk about two different facets of the hegemonic/globalisation; *political* in the case of Greece, and *apolitical* in the case of Ireland.

On the basis of these findings, chapter 6 evaluates the role of political economy and domestic institutional arrangements in the materialisation of hegemonic discourses, and attempts to elucidate what part of the observed differences in Greece and Ireland was due to these factors (i.e. the nature of political economy and the domestic institutional arrangements) and what part was not. In particular, I examine three research questions: (a) is the nature of political economy sufficient to account for the materialisation process of hegemonic discourses? And in this regard, how useful is the 'goodness-of-fit' hypothesis found in Europeanisation studies?; (b) Is the nature of domestic institutional arrangements sufficient to account for the materialisation process of hegemonic discourses? Here, I focus on the broader socio-political structures of interest representation and state-society relations; (c) can the combination of the above two factors (i.e. the nature of political economy and the nature of interest representation) account for the materialisation process of hegemonic discourses?

Finally, in the Epilogue I try to do two things. First, I elaborate on what general conclusions we can draw with regard to the communication of hegemonic discourses, and the respective approach that was advanced in this project. Second, I attempt to recover the broader and historically enduring sociological and philosophical debates upon which this research project touches.

Notes

1 The island of Ireland includes both 'Northern Ireland', which is part of the UK, and the 'Republic of Ireland', which became independent from the UK in 1922. The use of the name 'Ireland' in this thesis is made for convenience and refers only to the Republic of Ireland.

2 Throughout the book the terms 'materialisation' and 'communication' are used interchangeably. Therefore the same definition would also apply for the concept of 'communication of a hegemonic discourse'. See also chapter 1.

Part I

Theory and agents

1

Hegemonic discourse communication

The aim of this chapter is to offer a theoretical framework for studying and understanding hegemonic discourses and their function and effects. It is suggested that the domination of a hegemonic discourse signifies a complex communication process that directly involves national discursive realities, domestic institutional arrangements and agents/subjects. Therefore what is under scrutiny in this chapter is this communication process itself, in order to illustrate what this process signifies, how it should be conceptualised, what are its constitutive elements, and how concepts such as change and continuity should be interpreted in this context. In real terms the concept of hegemonic discourse is proposed as an analytical framework for studying the conditions of production, reproduction and change of social life within the *international*.

Most political scientists would agree that discourses (loosely defined as sets of policy ideas, e.g. neoliberalism) are diffused into different national politico-economic systems. But what is the nature of this diffusion and how does it take place? For sure, there are international institutions that act as powerful channels for the generation and surveillance of these discourses. But still this does not say very much about how these discourses are introduced and communicated at the national level, or what is the nature of the relationship between these discourses and the public/domestic sphere. This problem becomes even more acute if we shift our focus from sets of policy ideas onto systems of political or politico-economic governance (e.g. liberal democracy and capitalism), or onto what we have referred to in our Introduction as hegemonic discourses. There seems to be a black box in the stage of national communication of either policy ideas or hegemonic discourses which needs to be opened; and indeed it is this observation that constitutes *the point of departure* of this research.

This chapter offers a way of analysing the interplay between hegemonic discourses and national institutional arrangements. The main claim is that the dissemination of hegemonic discourses should be conceptualised as an interaction process between two discursive realities: the *hegemonic discourses* on the one hand, and the *public discourses* on the other. In order to do so two bodies of literature are combined: *comparative institutionalism* and *discourse theory*. The aim is to propose an understanding of hegemonic discourse communication as an integral part of national ideology–production mechanisms. The term integral is crucial here. The aforementioned two discursive realities (the 'hegemonic' and the 'public') are conceptualised as parts of a single discursive ensemble; their relationship is a relationship of mutual presupposition; and their analytical separation aims at stressing and clearly delineating this mutual presupposition, rather than obfuscating or denying it. For, as is analysed below, the hegemonic forms the outside (for the public), but it lies within it.[1]

In the first part I develop the theoretical framework of this project. First I elaborate on the weakness of the existing literature to account for a wide range of discursive phenomena. Then I focus on the concept of hegemonic discourses, and suggest how they should be conceptualised and studied. The second part of the chapter elaborates on how the concept of hegemonic discourses can be operationalised in terms of research strategy and methodology.

The ideas literature, hegemonic discourses and the (re)production of life

Ideas do not float freely vs. discursive formations

The (re-)emergence of the study of ideational factors in international relations/international political economy (IR/IPE) has indeed produced an important body of literature, and generated several hypotheses on how specific ideas and discourses have been disseminated and produced policy changes (among others, see Hall, 1989; Risse, 1991, 1994, 1999; Checkel, 1997; Blyth, 1997, 2002; Campbell, 1998a; Finnemore and Sikkink, 1998; McNamara, 1998; Rosamond, 1999; Schmidt, 2000, 2001, 2002; Hay, 2001a; Kjær and Pedersen, 2001; Blyth, 2002; Schmidt and Radaelli, 2005). Therefore, insightful research – albeit not as extended as one would expect – has been done on the role of particular actors, such as epistemic communities (Haas, 1992), advocacy coalitions (Sabatier, 1998; Sabatier and Jenkins-Smith, 1993), advocacy networks, think tanks (Stone, 1996; Stone and Denham, 2004) and transnational networks (Risse, 1994, 1995; Evangelista, 1995), in the dissemination of specific ideas/discourses. Moreover, substantial research has been done on how and why common 'external' challenges (ideas could also be included here) produce different national responses (among others, Katzenstein, 1977; Hall, 1986, 1989; Ikenberry, 1988; Risse, 1991, 1994; Wittrock and Wagner, 1996; Campbell, 1998a; Garrett and Lange, 1999; Schmidt, 2000, 2001, 2002). Finally, there is a more specialised literature on how particular technical international norms, such as those produced by the International Standardisation Organisation (e.g. ISO 9000), have been internalised into different national contexts (e.g. Casper and Hancke, 1999).

It is within the above debates that *institutions* and *ideational factors* talk to each other within IR/IPE, and even though an integrated framework of analysis remains to be developed, important contributions towards this aim have been made (see for instance Hall, 1989; Risse et al., 1999; Campbell, 1998a; Hay 2001a). It is also within the above debates that the study of discourse managed gradually to acquire attention, leading recently to a new strand of institutional analysis, called discursive institutionalism (see for instance Schmidt, 2000, 2001, 2002; Kjaer and Pedersen, 2001; Schmidt and Radaelli, 2004, 2004a, 2005).

Yet the way in which the study of ideas and discourses has been developed within most of the above literature has important limitations. Laffey and Weldes (1997) have argued that most of the ideas literature reproduces a set of rationalistic bias and assumptions of which it is supposedly a critique. In particular, they argue that the mainstream ideas literature: (a) treats *ideas and interests as rival explanations*. As a result 'the investigation of the social construction of interests is in practice disavowed because it is assumed … that interests are given and can be determined in isolation from 'ideas'' (ibid., 200; see also 199–201); (b) conceptualises ideas *as causal factors* in a conventional neo-positivist sense. As a result, only certain ideational factors 'pass the test' of what is to be studied, while the relationship between ideas and the social context that gives rise to and influences these ideas is not examined. Thus 'the important questions concern not the broad conditions of possibility which are conceptualised in such a way that they do not seem directly to affect or 'cause' policy, but concern instead the impact of the narrower 'causal' beliefs, which do' (ibid., 201; see also 202–205); (c) ideas are treated *as individual possessions* (usually as beliefs or shared beliefs), and their analysis is based on an understanding of 'ideas as commodities'. Thus ideas are constructed as discrete objects, which in order to be causally effective they require political entrepreneurs. In this way, for Laffey and Weldes, social phenomena are treated in individualist terms and are reduced to individual possessions (ibid., 206).

Along similar lines, Campbell (1998, especially 207–225) criticises the mainstream constructivist approaches for reproducing the idealist–materialist dichotomy and its problems, thus failing to engage with the issue of the materiality of discourse. He also criticises the 'positivistic bias' found in these approaches and especially in the way they have appropriated the concepts of 'culture' and 'identity'. Within these approaches, he argues, '"culture" is figured as no more than that which is not material, the ideas and beliefs that make up the domestic domain, which can be isolated as variables possessing at least some causal autonomy' (ibid., 218). On this basis, then, the policymakers either 'are regarded as being engaged in a sort of conscious and deliberate construction of reality', as if they themselves were outside of the domain of social constitution, or, the factor language or culture is treated as 'an omnipotent force so deterministic that "it" acts as the governing subject such that all accounts of human agency are expunged' (ibid., 219). In this chapter we aspire to advance the above critiques of the ideas literature (see also Hay, 2004) by pointing to a whole range of discursive phenomena, that the existing literature ignores or/and does not seem able to address.

An underlying assumption of the ideas literature is that *ideas do not float freely* (Risse, 1994). The discourses of disarmament, of ozone depletion, of Keynesianism, of neoliberalism, of human rights, of globalisation, to mention a few examples found in the literature, had not floated freely, and actually (the argument goes) they could not have done so. For most of this literature, ideas cannot exist beyond agents (even though many studies acknowledge that ideas are not reducible to agents). My aim here is not to disprove this assumption. I want to argue however that this assumption may make harder or impossible the analysis of certain discursive phenomena. The existing literature, in response to the aforementioned underlying assumption (i.e. ideas do not float freely) has tried to find the (potential) 'carriers', the agents that carry the ideas. Such attempts have focused – as already mentioned – on epistemic communities, advocacy coalitions, advocacy networks, think tanks and transnational networks. The idea of the carrier, however, is not the only possible response to the assumption that ideas do not float freely. The diffusion and function of ideational phenomena into societies cannot always be understood and studied in terms of a carrier. I do not mean, here, to simplify the aforementioned approaches nor to downgrade their diversity. In this manner, in most of the aforementioned approaches the carrier is a network (rather than a single agent), and each approach attributes different characteristics to this network. For instance, it can be a knowledge-based network, as the epistemic communities in the case of ozone depletion discourse, or a winning coalition of domestic and transnational actors, as in the case of the arms control discourse. Nevertheless, all the above approaches prescribe and are based on the existence of a critical channel/network/agent in the communication of ideas/discourses.

Yet there is a type of discourses which does not fit in the above model of ideas/discourse communication. The communication/ dissemination of these discourses is not characterised by, and therefore cannot be studied through, the existence of a critical channel, network or agent. These discourses, to which we refer here as *hegemonic*, are productive, open-ended and have an all-pervasive multilevel societal effect on the body of the international. Therefore these discourses are not 'thematic', they are not characterised by *privileged objects*, as, for instance, ozone is in the discourse of ozone depletion, or supply-side economics is in the discourse of neoliberalism. Their general and all-encompassing nature does not allow their communication in societies to have an authoritative sourcing of definition. Rather than being characterised by *privileged objects*, a hegemonic discourse is characterised 'by the way in which it forms objects [processes and practices] that are in fact highly dispersed'; by its capacity to 'give birth simultaneously or successively to mutually exclusive objects [processes and practices], without having to modify itself' (Foucault, 1972: 44; parentheses added). The substance of a hegemonic discourse is not to be found in any single one of these objects, processes, practices and ideas, neither just in their sum. It is the 'common space' that allows these diverse and often antagonistic forces and processes to be produced and transformed in new social totalities, new social orders.

This is a point that is not clearly addressed in the existing literature, and thus there is a gap in the conceptualisation and study of this type of discourses and their communication and materialisation. In these cases the communication type escapes from the *carrier model* and takes a more complex and social-constructivist form (see also Campbell, 1998; Laffey and Weldes, 1997). Therefore the metaphor/ assumption that ideas do not float freely is rather a misleading one.

To study then hegemonic discourses we need to develop new research tools and rationales. We need to focus our research energies not on specific actors and networks as channels of dissemination of certain ideas and discourses, but on how certain discourses and orders of things acquire an independent dynamic and capacity to (in)form social processes. Such a study ceases to be a study of ideas held by individuals, and becomes a study of the role of the discursive in the constitution of society and its subject (for the category of the discursive, see Milliken, 1999; see also Howarth and Stavrakakis, 2000; Howarth, 2000). The remaining of this first part of this chapter attempts to develop an analytical framework able to capture and scrutinise the nature and communication of hegemonic discourses.

From biopolitics and biopower to the definition of hegemonic discourses
How should we define these phenomena that form new objects and processes, create a 'unity' out of antagonistic forces, and have an all-pervasive effect on the social body as a whole (in our case the *international*)? Taking into consideration that in substance hegemonic discourses concern the production of social orders and social subjects, an obvious place to start from is the biopolitical approach to the study of the social and the political, first developed by Michel Foucault (1978) and rearticulated in 2000 by Michael Hardt and Antonio Negri (2000). Before therefore defining the concept of hegemonic discourse, we should make a brief reference to this biopolitical approach.

The concepts of biopolitics and biopower constitute central themes in Michel Foucault's archaeology of subject, i.e. his attempt to discover and analyse how the modern subject has come to constitute itself as such. In this regard in the first volume of his work on the history of sexuality, Foucault (1978) argues:

> For a long time ... [t]he sovereign exercised his right of life only by exercising his right to kill, or by refraining from killing ... The right which was formulated as the 'power of life and death' was in reality the right to *take* life or *let* live ... Since the classical age [however] the West has undergone a very profound transformation ... Now it is over life, throughout its unfolding, that power establishes its dominion; death is power's limit, the moment that escapes it ... The old power of death that symbolised sovereign power was now carefully supplanted by the administration of bodies and the calculated management of life ... marking the beginning of an era of 'bio-power'. (pp. 135–136, 138, 139–140)

Foucault's analysis of biopower created a biopolitical tradition of thought in social sciences and humanities, followed in different ways (and among others) by Deleuze and Guattari (1987), Agamben (1998), and Hardt and Negri (2000, 2004) (see also Rose and Miller, 1992; Rose, 1999, 2006; Dean, 1999).[2] Despite the differences that exist (see for instance Rabinow and Rose, 2003), the main unifying element of this tradition is the concept of biopower itself, i.e. a specific understanding of the way in which power operates on human beings and in human societies. On this, Hardt and Negri (2000, 23–24) note:

> Biopower is a form of power that regulates social life from its interior, following it, interpreting it, absorbing it, and rearticulating it. Power can achieve an effective command over the entire life of the population only when it becomes an integral, vital function that every individual embraces and reactivates of his or her own accord ... *Biopower thus refers to the situation in which what is directly at stake in power is the production and reproduction of life itself*. (emphasis added)

Following the above tradition and conceptualisation of power, hegemonic discourses may be conceptualised as historically specific sets of practices and meanings that dominate in the (re)production of social life in the international. These 'sets' have productive power, they (re)define and (re)articulate the way in which social life is produced and organised, and thus they (re)articulate 'from within' the way in which social subjects understand their environment and their selves. In this manner, a hegemonic discourse does not form objects and processes from a 'zero point', but rather (re)orders dispersed phenomena towards a dynamic new unity which empowers its own identity as a unity, and (trans)forms the social reality in its own terms. It is in this sense that hegemonic discourses are intrinsically *bio-political* phenomena. Their ultimate stake is the production and reproduction of life itself – the purpose and the way in which we live and change individually and collectively. On this basis we define hegemonic discourses as *historically specific, overarching social technologies, concerning the (re)production of (social) life within the international*.

Three clarifications on the above definition are important here. First, I use the concept of '(re)production' to signify that social life is a dynamic process that leads to social change and transformation. Therefore, the reproduction of social life should be thought of as a process of diversification and change, i.e. a process of ever anew activated productions. Second, we bracket the term 'social' in order to signify that the reproduction of social life and the production of social subjects are not two separate processes. We want thus to underline the fact that, in essence, hegemonic discourses concern the production of social subjects. Third, the term *social technology* is used to signify *sets of meanings and practices* concerning the organisation of social life (Foucault, 1972: 49).

My emphasis on the biopolitical nature of hegemonic discourses serves two purposes. First, to stress the point that what is at stake in these discourses is the (re)production of social life, i.e. hegemonic discourses are not only about the production of wealth and power relationships, but also about the production of subjects, people and societies. Second, to stress the fact that the reproduction or change of these discourses depends on the actions or reactions of social subjects, i.e. hegemonic discourses produce subjects and societies, but are also produced by them. In this manner, the *biopolitical* helps us to bring everyday life and the subject to the forefront of the analysis of world politics and economics.

In order to strengthen our understanding of hegemonic discourses we should also ask the question what makes a discourse hegemonic? Is it the scale of its dissemination, or are there structural elements, specific properties of the discourse itself? The transformation of a discourse to hegemonic discourse is not related to the degree of its dissemination but to its structural relationship with particular interests and modes of social organisation and production. Thus, a discourse becomes hegemonic on the basis of its relationship with dominant 'material' forces. On this basis, the emergence of globalisation discourse, for instance, cannot be separated by the internationalisation of production by multinational enterprises after the mid-1970s and the strengthening of the role and power of financial capital after the early 1980s. Additionally, historically specific material and technological factors and forces constrain and/or enable the development of specific hegemonic discourses. To continue the example of globalisation discourse, the integration of financial markets at an international level would hardly become possible without new technological breakthroughs, such as the Internet.

Yet, the fact that hegemonic discourses have their roots in specific interests, social conditions and material forces does not mean that hegemonic discourses themselves and their impact can be reduced to any specific interests or conditions (for instance MNCs, the USA, financial capital). The emergence of a hegemonic discourse should be understood as a process that acquires an independent dynamic which not only cannot be reduced to, but in fact transforms the initial interests and 'material' conditions which gave birth to it in the first place.

Finally, each hegemonic discourse meets a condition of *universality* (Butler *et al.*, 2000), in the sense that it constitutes the necessary condition, and it functions as the means, for the articulation and expression of all *the particulars* that define a certain social historical reality. As a result of this universality, hegemonic discourses cannot exist and function but only within and through the particular, the specific, the local/national, the non-universal (ibid.).

Thus, in order to understand the nature of hegemonic discourses one has to move from the question of *origins,* i.e. what are the specific interests and material forces that give birth to a hegemonic discourse, to the question of *function,* i.e. what does a hegemonic discourse do. Hence, a discourse is hegemonic when its practices and meanings start to enforce their terms and nature on the reproduction of social life within the international. The term hegemonic, in substance, signifies this power of rearticulating and restructuring life in the international.

Such a conceptualisation of hegemonic discourses problematises the established dichotomy between the 'material' and the 'ideational' in the study of political phenomena. So far as the focus of the analysis is on the reproduction of social life, at no point in time, is any 'material', in terms of interests, power or technological breakthroughs, extra-discursive, that is, outside, beyond or independent from the 'social'. The interests and power relationships that are found at the point of origin of each hegemonic discourse are not externally formed but are both a part and a product of the process through which social life reproduces itself. To use Foucault (1972: 45), the 'material'[3] 'exists under the positive conditions of a complex group of relations ... These relations are established between institutions, economic and social processes, behavioural patterns, systems of norms, techniques, types of classification, modes of characterization; and these relations ... do not define its [i.e. hegemonic discourse's] internal constitution, but what enables it to appear'. In a paradoxical manner then, the more successful a hegemonic discourse is, i.e. the more it succeeds in enforcing its own terms in the reproduction of social life, the closer it gets to its change and transcendence. The redefinition of preferences, interests, identities, practices, rules that a hegemonic discourse carries with it create new dynamics and new relationships which create the conditions for new hegemonic configurations. In this sense, the *being* of each hegemonic discourse should be understood as an integral part of the ever-evolving *becoming* of the international.

By emphasising the biopolitical nature of hegemonic discourses, the aim is not to ignore their more 'traditional' political aspects and elements. In order to understand the nature and impact of hegemonic discourses we need to combine both these approaches to politics. On the one hand, traditional approaches to politics focus on powerful states and specific interests. They inquire who has the power to determine the structures and the rules of the game of world politics and economics. By focusing on who gets what, when and how they locate the core of *hegemony* in powerful states and dominant interests, thus uncovering power relations at play in the international. On the other hand biopolitical approaches to politics emphasise that, to focus on how *power* structures the 'game' (e.g. the social universe, world politics, life itself, etc.), is to externalise power from the 'game'. Thus, before and beyond the structuring of the rules of the game, one has to consider the concept of the game itself, and the conditions of its existence. Within this perspective the game does not exist beyond the subject; and change in the game and its terms can only be conceptualised as part of the process of subject's reproduction, part of the process of the reproduction of social life. Therefore this biopolitical tradition of thought locates 'hegemony' at the level of the (re)production of life itself; locates *hegemony* at the level of the subject.

It is my contention that in order to study hegemonic discourses one has to consider and build upon both of these approaches. The question of 'who gets what when and how' must open itself to the question of what are the conditions of existence, reproduction and change of this who-gets-what system. Put more abstractly, the question who *gets* what hegemonic discourse, when and how, must open itself to the question who *is* what part of a hegemonic discourse, when and how. In this way, 'politics' and 'life' are equal components of the materialisation of hegemonic discourses. I hope the proposed theoretical framework moves towards this direction, even if it does not offer a conclusive solution in terms of a solid framework that integrates these two approaches to politics.

Hegemonic discourses in the post-Second World War era

Referring to some examples of hegemonic discourses would be helpful here. Let us focus first on the Cold War and then on globalisation. The period of the Cold War was characterised by a number of different competing discourses and projects: capitalism, socialism, communism, development, dependency, disarmament, mutual assured destruction, the peace movement, the new international economic order, neutrality, the non-aligned movement, to mention some examples. The Cold War was not and was not determined by any single of these discourses. The concept of hegemonic discourse would be useful then in analysing this period because it allows us to study the conditions of co-existence and the dynamics that governed the co-evolution of these multiple and complex processes, ideas and practices. Through the prism of hegemonic discourses the Cold War was the set of practices and meanings that was consisted of *and* regulated the relationship between all these different and competing projects/discourses. Thus the struggle between the two superpowers (USA and USSR) gave rise to a new social technology that determined the conditions of production of all social, political, economic and cultural identities, projects or visions within the international system and world politics. In this manner, the hegemonic discourse of the Cold War was not only about politics or economics, neither was it only about the 'West' or the 'East'. It literally came to reorder the way in which social life was produced in the international.

Reading the Cold War as a hegemonic discourse would then be to stress four things: first, that the Cold War was historically specific; second, that it emerged as a social technology (as a set of practices and meanings) that came to dominate and define the way in which politics, economics and, in general, life were organised and produced within the international; third, that it was a war of competing models of 'how to live' – competing models of social life, i.e. it had social life as its main stake; and fourth, that it 'started' from the river Elbe in 1945 and, either through inclusion (spheres of influence) or through exclusion (spheres of indifference) it tended towards the incorporation of the entire globe.

The same can be said to be the case for *globalisation* that replaced the Cold War in the 1990s, and which constitutes the subject matter of this book. The emergence of this new hegemonic discourse was certainly a gradual process, and its origins can be traced back to the late 1970s. Key dynamics in this regard were the gradual internationalisation of production by multinational enterprises and the integration of financial markets after the early 1980s. As in the case of the Cold War, globalisation embodied a new social technology, a new set of dominant practices and meanings, that changed the conditions of reproduction of the international system and defined a new way of living and being at the international. States no longer had to position themselves in relation to two dominant superpowers. The new choice to be made (or at least, the states perceived they had to make) was the following: to connect (or remain connected) to the world by joining and/or 'adapting' themselves to the new global economy, or to deny this connection, thus cutting themselves out from the 'outside world'. Thus the compass, the main determinant of policy choices at all levels ceased to be the USA–USSR antagonism. The bipolar social technology of the Cold War was replaced by a new singular social technology based on neoliberal economic ideas and a 'world order' which had only one superpower. This shift in the dominant social technology of the international generated of course a huge hegemonic restructuring process reflected among others at the concepts of '*transition* economies', '*transition* policies', and '*structural adjustment* programmes'. Indicative of the domination of this new social technology was the emergence of new private international regimes and in general the strengthening of the role of private authority in global governance (see Hall and Biersteker, 2002), the increase in the coercive and structural power of private actors such as credit-rating agencies (Sinclair, 2005), the increased influence of a number of 'global indices' (on 'openness', on 'transparency', on 'corruption', etc.), and the tendency towards the privatisation of knowledge production (Mytelka, 2000). As in the case of the Cold War a number of diverse discourses and projects came to constitute and define this new technology, including for instance those of liberalisation, deregulation, privatisation, flexibility, globalisation itself, sustainable development, knowledge economy, risk society, Americanisation, Westernisation, new imperialism, empire, cultural annihilation, American cultural imperialism, and so forth. The hegemonic discourse of globalisation is what these different and often antagonistic projects or discourses, and their relations and evolution consisted of and regulate. To use Foucault's terminology it is 'the system that governs their division, the degree to which they depend upon one another, the way in which they interlock or exclude one another, the transformation that they undergo, and the play of their location, arrangement and replacement' (Foucault, 1992: 34).

Having defined hegemonic discourses and discussed their nature, the next part of this chapter turns to how we can operationalise hegemonic discourses in terms of research strategy and methodology.

Operationalising hegemonic discourses

In this project hegemonic discourses are put forward as a way of examining social change and continuity within the international. This hegemonic discourse approach *aims* at explicating how the universe of world politics and economics (what we refer to here as the *international*) is (re)produced and changed. This hegemonic discourse approach is not understood as a theory in its own right. Rather, it is put forward as a mode of social inquiry that offers a method of 'isolating' – in a Foucaultian, archaeological sense – the international, in order to study its conditions of production, reproduction and change. Thus, the hegemonic discourse approach is proposed as an analytical framework for studying the biopolitics of the international, which is ultimately *the power politics of social life*; the study of how social life, having entered 'into the order of knowledge and power' of the international (see Foucault, 1978: 141–142), becomes the main stake of politics.

Within this framework, the basic assumption of the hegemonic discourse approach is that each and every 'international' is characterised by a certain hegemonic, i.e. a specific set of meanings and practices that dominate in the process through which the international is reproduced and changed. It is furthermore suggested that this hegemonic can be thought of and studied as a social technology – a mode of organising and producing societies. Thus it is suggested that in order to study and understand the international we need to study and understand the hegemonic: where it is to be found, how it is structured, how it functions.

This hegemonic discourse approach locates the strategic field of the hegemonic at the level of social life reproduction; in fact it premises that the hegemonic is about the definition of a certain mode of social life, i.e. of a certain way of everyday life reproduction. It is furthermore assumed that this 'act of definition' is not and cannot be based on physical violence or direct imposition. It should be conceptualised as a process of 'making up citizens' (Rose and Miller, 1992); a process that invests in life-in-freedom rather than in life-in-subjugation.[4]

Based on this approach, capturing the hegemonic entails turning to the *domestic*, and comparing and contrasting the reproduction of different societies during the same historical period. To do so we need to scrutinise the social institutions that play a dominant role in the production of ideology at a national level (for instance political parties, religion institutions, organised interests, the press, the army; these institutions differ from case to case, from country to country). Thus the hegemonic discourse communication model proposed here assumes that the mechanisms of the production, reproduction and change of a hegemonic discourse are not different from the mechanisms of the production, reproduction and change of the various national institutional settings and their societies. Thus, the domination of a hegemonic discourse is a process that takes place through –and at the level of – the reproduction of national societies. In this manner, the materialisation of a hegemonic discourse is not understood as a top-down, outside-in phenomenon, based on coercion, but as an inside-out, bottom-up phenomenon that is generated by national institutional settings and societies themselves. As mentioned above, the hegemonic 'forms the outside', but it 'lies within'.

Therefore, in terms of research strategy the main issue is how to study the 'domestic' – how to locate and analyse the ideology and politics production mechanisms at the domestic level. For this aim it is suggested turning to the literature that deals with the role and significance of domestic structures and institutional arrangements (for relevant works by IR and politics scholars, see among others: Katzenstein, 1977; Risse, 1991; Krasner, 1995; Evangelista, 1995; Tsebelis, 1995; Kjær and Pedersen, 2001; Garrett and Lange, 1999; Schmidt, 2000, 2001). This comparative institutionalist literature aims exactly to open up the 'black box' of state, and examine its organisational structure and institutional composition. Therefore this literature, and particularly, where available, its detailed case-study findings, can be used as a general guide for locating the mechanisms, institutions and actors that dominate in the production of politics in different domestic realms. After locating these mechanisms, institutions and actors the research should then focus on the analysis of emerging rationalities, norms and practices; in the creation of new institutions, identities, policies, interests, goals, strategies, and coalitions; and finally in the redistribution of power and the reordering of the organisational basis of the domestic spheres themselves.

The research strategy proposed here attempts to mobilise within a post-positivist research framework (discourse theory and biopolitics), ideas, categories and findings from more mainstream and positivist strands of research (comparative institutionalism). We do not deem such a strategy as *in principle* problematic. Any research methods and findings should not be judged in principle but in practice. The main criterion should be how much they help us to capture and analyse the phenomena we examine. Along these lines, comparative institutionalism is important for this project because it helps us to open the block box of state and examine its mode of production and change. The purpose of this research, however, is not to establish a causal relationship between a cause (the hegemonic discourse) and an effect (changes in national policies, goals or strategies), but to examine the constitution and emergence of hegemonic discourses, through the life, actions and interplay of specific social actors and institutions. In this framework the emphasis is not on *causal* but on *constitutive* relations, and the main issue at stake is not the production of policy but the production of social life itself. The purpose is to capture hegemonic discourses in action, at the stage of their emergence; and not to treat them as end products that are external to domestic social spheres and dynamics. Instead of taking hegemonic discourses as given, the aim is to inquire who is and produces what part of a hegemonic discourse, when and how. This approach attempts to capture and analyse the *hegemonic* and the *global* through the *local* and the *particular*. To this approach, developing rich, case-study-specific material from different countries, and comparing and contrasting this material, is the only way to break into and understand the conditions of production, reproduction and change of social life within the international.

It would be interesting to conclude this section with a story from Cornelious Castoriadis's writings. Castoriadis on many occasions presented to workers his ideas on the centrality of the factory in the reproduction of capitalism (all quotations are from Castoriadis, 1998). He found, however, that the workers 'had little to say and appeared disappointed'. Their main problem was that they were hearing boring and uninteresting things about the importance of their everyday life, rather than things that 'really mattered', such as the dynamics of overproduction/underconsumption and the law of the falling rate of profit. 'It seemed unbelievable to them that the evolution of modern society is determined far more by the daily movements and gestures of millions of workers in factories all over the world than by some great and mysterious hidden laws of the economy discovered by theoreticians.' For Castoriadis, the

> idea that workers have that how they live, what they do, and how they think 'doesn't really matter' is ... *the gravest manifestation of ... [an] ideological enslavement* ... For ... [any hegemonic system][5] can survive only if people are persuaded that what they themselves do and know is a private little matter of their own that does not really matter, and that really important matters are the monopoly of the big shots and specialists in various fields of endeavour. (italics in the original)

On this basis, the hegemonic discourse approach outlined here aspires to put forward an ontological framework that pays particular attention to the role and importance of agents in the reproduction and change of social reality. Instead of treating the phenomenon of hegemony in world politics and economics as something foreign, as something that is decided by a hegemon 'out there', 'in our name', and in the production, reproduction and change of which we have no role or voice, it attempts to bring under the spotlight how hegemonic phenomena exist, dominate and change only through our being and becoming. In this sense we are products of a hegemonic discourse only so far as a hegemonic discourse is our product.

The final section of this chapter presents the way in which the general hegemonic discourse approach discussed here was translated into research strategy for the specific needs of our research project, i.e. the study of the communication of the hegemonic discourse of globalisation in Greece and Ireland.

Globalisation discourse in Greece and Ireland: research strategy

The research strategy employed in this project can be divided into two steps. The first step refers to the identification of actors/institutions to be analysed. As has been argued, the communication of a hegemonic discourse is an integral part of the domestic ideology–production processes. Thus, the identification of the actors engaged in these ideology–production processes is the first and one of the most important steps in the process of capturing hegemonic discourses and studying their materialisation process.

Two general factors determine the selection of these actors.[6] The first factor has to do with the nature of the hegemonic discourse of globalisation. If the latter was a thematic discourse, e.g. the discourse on armaments, then certain social actors and groups would gain primacy in the investigation; for instance the Ministry of Defence, the army, the defence industry, etc. Yet, hegemonic discourses do not have an authoritative source of definition; they are not produced by and limited within an epistemic or otherwise specific community; they concern the reproduction of social life as a whole and thus have an all-pervasive societal effect.

The second factor that determines the selection of actors is the nature of the domestic structures and institutional arrangements of the countries under examination. For instance, one would focus on different actors in the case of a secular–democratic and a theocratic or a military regime; or, a presidential and a parliamentary democracy. In our case, both Greece and Ireland are characterised by stable, secular, democratic regimes based on parliamentary systems. This general consideration of the nature of the domestic regime was then combined with a more focused analysis on the institutional arrangements that define each country's domestic mechanisms of politics and ideology production. The elaboration of these case-specific characteristics takes place in chapter 2, where the cases of Greece and Ireland are analysed. Yet it can be said here that the main criterion in the selection of actors was that of 'inclusion'. That is, an effort has been made to include all the institutional actors with a considerable role in politics and ideology production. These actors include the main political parties and their leaders, the workers, the employers, the church and the press (see Table 1.1). It needs to be stressed here that these actors and their interaction do not by any means exhaust the complexity of politics production within their respective institutional settings. Yet, we consider that the 'signals' one gets from this set of actors, spread as they are through the body politic, are representative of the trends and changes under way in their respective societies. Put differently, the range of the institutional actors examined is significant, for it is wide enough to capture social trends and changes that exceed the confines of elite-level phenomena. To use a metaphor from the natural science world, the methodology proposed here treats the actors under examination (only) as 'meter stations' that record the time, intensity, epicentre and impact of globalisation on the two societies under examination in this project.

Table 1.1 Actors studied

Greece	Ireland
A Political parties	
Panhellenic Socialist Movement (PASOK)	Fianna Fáil (FF)
New Democracy (ND)	Fine Gael (FG)
Communist Party of Greece (KKE)	Labour Party (LP)
Coalition of the Left and Progress (Synaspismos)	Progressive Democrats (PD)
B Main social partners	
The Greek General Confederation of Labour (GSEE)	Irish Congress of Trade Unions (ICTU)
The Federation of Greek Industries (SEV)	Irish Business and Employers Confederation (IBEC)
The Economic and Social Council of Greece (OKE)	National Economic and Social Council (NESC)
C The church	
Greek Orthodox church (Archbishop Christodoulos)	Catholic church (Cardinal Connell)
D Press (a sample)	
TO VIMA (1996–2001)	*The Irish Times* (1996–2001)

The next important step in terms of research strategy is how to study these actors and their involvement in the communication of the hegemonic discourse of globalisation, i.e. how the above-mentioned signals can be collected and 'decoded'?

The main difficulty with the study of hegemonic discourses is that the key actors involved in their communication process are numerous and thus the primary material that could be collected and studied is almost unlimited (including official documents, speeches, interviews, statistical data, etc.). In order to tackle this problem the following strategy was followed.

First, *the research was limited to the period 1995–2001*. The rationale for this choice is as follows. First, in general this is the period in which the 'globalisation of the globalisation discourse' (Beck, 2001) took place in most countries around the world. Two milestones define this period: the creation of the World Trade Organisation (WTO) in 1995 and the anti-globalisation protests in Seattle, during the 'Millennium Round', in winter 1999. This general context was then combined with domestic, country-specific (historical) junctures and events. The purpose was to explore how the globalisation discourse was implicated in the discourses and strategies of domestic forces that attempted to redefine the public discourses of their countries. I expand on this issue in the chapters that focus on Greece and Ireland.

Second, *the research was based on primary material,* mainly official publications and speeches, in which the actors summarised, publicised and/or justified their annual activities and their positions and policies. This does not pretend to be an exhaustive strategy, nor does it apply strictly to all actors (e.g. the press). But it was used as an objective criterion for the collection of the primary material. Chapters 3 and 4 offer specific information on the nature and the rationale of the selected material for each and every actor examined. A number of interviews were also conducted with institutional actors that had a strategic role in the reproduction and change of their domestic discourses e.g. newspapers' editors, presidents of workers' and employers' associations, etc. (in total fourteen interviews). These interviews were used as a means of inquiring how key actors in the ideology and politics production at the national level were themselves thinking about how ideology is produced in their societies, what is globalisation, and how the various social forces at the national level reacted to it. These interviews however were not used or analysed as primary material.

Third, globalisation as a word vs. globalisation as a world and a 'practice' in the analysis of the primary material; i.e. *how do we study hegemonic discourses through documents?* Conceptualising globalisation as a hegemonic discourse, I did not enforce a narrow a priori definition of globalisation on the research project. Thus, I left the actors to speak for themselves, taking globalisation as whatever these actors were referring to, or expressing, when they used the term globalisation. It is *partly* through this methodology that I attempted to trace and capture the hegemonic discourse of globalisation in the examined documents (see also below). The main questions were: when did the term globalisation enter into the vocabulary of the actors? How did the frequency of its usage evolve? What was the context in which it was used? What was the purpose of its usage and what was its content (i.e. positive or negative)? The strongest advantage of this methodology is its 'blind' objectivity. What was, and what was not, globalisation did not rest with the researcher's judgement but with the social actors. Nonetheless, such a research strategy has a number of grey areas. Most importantly, what if the debates, attitudes and practices in one country also existed in the other but appeared absent due to superficial differences in language? And in this context, what difference did the language used make, and how does this difference affect our analysis of hegemonic discourses?

A hegemonic discourse concerns the production of social life. In this regard language is very important. It is through language that reality becomes intelligible; it is through language that practices and meanings come to be constituted as such. Yet, there is a huge gap between these assumptions and an instrumental analysis of language through content analysis, or in the case of this project, between the study of globalisation discourse and a plain study of references to globalisation. I addressed this problem by placing the quantitative methodology of content analysis within a qualitative analytical framework, based on comparative institutionalism and discourse theory. Thus the focus of the research was not on the word globalisation itself but on the (re)production of institutional identities and arrangements, and through them on the production of new meaning, practices and power relations at the national level. This focus allowed us to go beyond the (important in other regards) 'vessel' of the word globalisation. It allowed us for instance to see a non-ideological space in the Irish politico-economic life. It also allowed us to trace and capture the Irish Celtic Tiger discourse (an Irish-specific globalisation discourse) and contrast it with aspects of the globalisation discourse in Greece.

Hence, even though the concept of globalisation was the driving force of this research, every possible effort was made in order: (a) not to impose the concept where it did not exist; and (b) not to reduce the analysis to a meaningless quantification exercise. Three points are of particular importance here. (i) The selection of the sources (i.e. what was taken to be a representative and encapsulating piece of the actors' voices within their societies), was not influenced by the existence or not of references to globalisation. Thus the overall research design was not based on a globalisation-selection bias.[7] (ii) The referent 'globalisation' was used as a tool to trace emerging or changing practices and policies associated with globalisation by the social actors themselves. Thus the concept/word 'globalisation' was used as a means to trace and monitor policies and practices of globalisation. (iii) The reading of the selected material was not exclusively globalisation driven. To this end, a second reading of the material, independent of the term globalisation, was adopted. Thus the question of where the term globalisation was located within the various institutional discourses, and how this term was used, was always balanced/qualified with the question of what were the dominant objects (including themes, practices, policies, rationalities) of these discourses irrespective of the term/concept globalisation.[8] Furthermore, the dominant objects that came to the surface through this second reading were contrasted with the various dominant objects of the globalisation discourse itself (e.g. flexibility, liberalisation, deregulation, speculative capital) to find out whether there was a relationship between them or not. It was through the above strategy that I tried to bring together the 'words' and the 'worlds' of this project, outlining, even faintly, a hegemonic discourse methodology.

To conclude, the purpose of the adopted research strategy was not to find repetitive isolated themes and references, but to capture changing self-conceptualisations, emerging rationalities and identities, changing power relationships and changing organisation structures. This quest was based on the conceptualisation of globalisation as a hegemonic discourse, i.e. as a productive and ordering power that comes 'from below' and/or 'from within' to enforce its terms on the prevailing – in terms of social life organisation – national institutional apparatuses. Thus my aim was not to capture and monitor static institutional discourses, but hegemonic reorderings materialised through the reproduction of social life, and expressed in changing policies, rationalities, vocabularies, identities and societal ordering principles.

Finally, the research design employed for the comparison of the materialisation of globalisation discourse in Greece and Ireland draws from what is known in comparative studies as the method of 'focused', and in particular, 'paired' comparison. This method, as its name implies, is based on an intensive comparison of two ('paired') or three ('triangular') cases/countries, and the emphasis of the analysis is at least as much on the comparison per se, as on each of the different cases (Hague and Harrop, 2001: 73). Such a research design is conducive to the hegemonic discourse approach adopted here. It permits us to reach the desirable depth in the analysis of the case-study-level transformation without losing sight of the comprehensive hegemonic reordering that these case-study level changes materialise.

Furthermore, the 'focused comparison' method has an important function in the production of knowledge in general and in comparative studies in particular. It helps us to test and reconsider established assumptions, generalisations and categorisations, which exist in social and comparative studies. Paired and triangular comparisons, by being focused and intensive, attempt to offer explanations with reference to social interactions (i.e. 'from within'), rather than with reference to pre-existing constructed models and categorisations (i.e. 'from without'). Hence, although their starting point may be based on existing assumptions and models found in comparative institutionalism, the dynamic of focused comparisons allow them to test and problematise these assumptions and models.

Notes

1   For an elaboration of such a relationship, see Deleuze, 1988: 70–93.
2   Recent applications in IR include Edkins, 2000; Dillon and Reid, 2001; Edkins *et al.*, 2004; Reid, 2007; Langley, 2007.
3   Foucault refers to the 'object of the discourse'.
4   Along these lines Rose and Miller (1992) argue in relation to biopower: '[It] is not so much a matter of imposing constraints upon citizens as of 'making up' citizens capable of bearing a kind of regulated freedom. Personal autonomy is not the antithesis of political power, but a key term in its exercise, the more so because most individuals are not merely the subjects of power but play a part in its operations' (174).
5   Here, Castoriadis refers to capitalism.
6   We derive these criteria from the existing literature on ideas communication. See. Hall, 1989a, b.
7   Two exceptions apply here. The 'press sample' and the speeches of party leaders. Yet in these cases a 'selection bias' does not really apply as a problem, as the purpose was to find how these actors understood and communicated the concept of globalisation.
8   The only exception to this 'double-reading methodology' was the analysis of the press sample. Even in this case, however, the quantitative factor (i.e. references to globalisation) was combined with qualitative factors, such as the authors' identity and the section of publication.

2

Greece and Ireland as social agents in the 1990s

Why Greece and Ireland in a pair comparison? There are a number of reasons that make the comparison of these two countries interesting, especially with regard to the communication of globalisation discourse. These factors include their historical evolution, their socio-economic development since their EU membership, their political culture and their contrasting models of political economy. Moreover, the choice of two countries within the same 'regional block' reduces the independent variables which are involved in the communication of globalisation discourse. Regional integration processes, such as the EU, North American Free Trade Agreement (NAFTA) and Association of South East Asian Nations (ASEAN), constitute an important factor in the way in which countries are affected by and affect global trends and incentives. They thus constitute an important intervening variable for any project dealing with the interplay between national institutional settings and global processes. The choice of Greece and Ireland, that is of two member states of the EU, reduces the variables involved in the communication process by keeping the regional dimension 'constant'. The latter, however, does not mean that this 'regional effect' is identical on the two member states under examination. Furthermore, the study of the EU factor in the communication of globalisation discourse is challenging, for the EU is both a part of, and a response to globalisation (Antoniades, 2007). Below we examine the nature of the Greek–Irish comparison, focusing on these two countries as social agents in the 1990s.

Of what are Greece and Ireland cases?

This is a rather static question, as its main point of reference is the established politico-economic models found in European comparative politics and economics literature, i.e. the Anglo-Saxon, the Continental, the Scandinavian and the Mediterranean. In this regard Greece is

classified in the *Southern European* or *Mediterranean model*[1] of polity
and political economy – a model which is usually treated as a sub-
category of the *Continental Model* –[2] and Ireland is classified in the
Anglo-Saxon model of polity and political economy (even if it is not
the most representative case of it.)[3] Yet it should be noted here that
these two models (i.e. the Anglo-Saxon and the Southern European)
signify different things to the different disciplines of political science,
and thus it is hard to draw a clear and definite division line concerning the countries included in each model. In most cases, however, the
United Kingdom and Ireland represent the Anglo-Saxon tradition at
the European level, whereas Greece, Italy, Portugal and Spain constitute the core of the Southern European model.

This classification is also followed by the influential studies of
Rhodes and Mény (1998) and Hall and Soskice (2001a). In particular, Rhodes and Mény (1998) classify European states in three groups
according to the nature of their institutional arrangements and
welfare states:[4] the 'Scandinavian' (Sweden, Finland, Denmark,
Norway), the 'Germanic-Continental' (Germany, France, BENELUX,
Austria, Switzerland) and the 'Anglo-Saxon' (UK, Ireland), and they
refer to Southern Europe (Italy, Spain, Portugal, Greece) as a separate
variant of the 'Continental' group (see also Ferrera, 1998). Similarly,
Hall and Soskice (2001a), based on a well-developed literature in
comparative political economy, have argued that the industrially
advanced OECD (Organisation for Economic Cooperation and Development) countries can be classified into three categories: (a)
organised market economies (e.g. Germany, Japan), where there is an
extensive institutional support for the coordination of politico-
economic agents; (b) liberal market economies (e.g. USA, UK,
Ireland), where there is less institutional support available for non-
market forms of coordination; and (c) a more ambiguous category
associated with Mediterranean capitalism (e.g. Italy, France, Greece).

What follows is a brief presentation of the characteristics with
which the Anglo-Saxon and Southern European models are associated.[5] It is important to stress from the outset that in this project these
models do not serve explanatory purposes, and their accuracy in
describing Greek and Irish politico-economic systems is not taken for
granted. They are rather used as a point of departure. The undertaken
'pair comparison' will test their accuracy and their limits both in
descriptive and analytical terms. Therefore it is important to keep in
mind that the contrast of the two models that follows aims at
constructing an ideal-type axis of analysis, which can be questioned
and problematised by the analysis of the Greek and Irish cases.

Finally, it should be emphasised that the various characteristics of each model are not independent from each other, but interact in multiple ways and complex historically evolved patterns where 'causes' became 'effects' and vice versa.

The Anglo-Saxon model is usually associated with early *democratisation*. Thus, Britain and the USA are the classical examples of the 'first wave' of democratisation, whereas Greece, Portugal and Spain are examples of the 'third wave' (Huntington, 1991). In this classification Ireland would be placed in-between the first (1828–1926) and the second (1943–62) wave of democratisation.

Furthermore, the Anglo-Saxon model is associated with pluralism in the *organisation of societal interests* and *state–society relations*, the Continental model is associated with 'neo-corporatism' (or 'societal' and 'liberal' corporatism), and the Southern European model is associated with 'state corporatism' (or statism).[6] Let us confine ourselves to the following characteristics of each category. Pluralist systems are typically associated with an individualistic social culture, and a clear separation between state and society (Cawson, 1978). Furthermore, the role of the state in these systems is confined to the arbitration of competition among the various societal groups and interests (ibid.). Neo-corporatist systems, on the other hand, are typically associated with a consociational social culture. State and society in these systems are in an 'institutionalised' and 'collaborationist' relationship (Schmitter, 1979), and thus the state, rather than being an arbiter, is a partner which, along with employers and employees, shapes the trajectory of socio-economic development (Lehmbrunch, 1979). Finally, state corporatism signifies the 'from above' compulsory intervention of the state, which aims at the restriction and/or the control of the voice of societal interests, and not the creation of a 'genuine collaboration' between these interests and the state, as in the case of neo-corporatism (Schmitter, 1979). State corporatism is usually associated with conditions of late development and late industrialisation, such as in Southern Europe, the Balkans and Latin America.[7]

Hence the *nature and the function of the state* and its relationship with society are very different in the Anglo-Saxon and the Southern European models. In the former the state is – or is assumed to be – a 'Weberian-type' state; it is small and functional, with a well-developed independent bureaucracy, where formal and transparent rules and practices are dominating, and where meritocracy prevails over patronage and clientelistic relationships. It is a state which is clearly separated from society, and is able to resist particularistic organised interests. Finally, it is a state which exists and functions in interaction with a well-developed civil society. In a stereotypical sense the Southern European state is considered to be the exact opposite. The state can hardly be described as 'Weberian', and it is usually (very) big and dysfunctional. In particular, in most of the countries in this model there is a tradition of a patrimonial structure of state organisation, close to what Max Weber (1978) called 'sultanism'. The bureaucracy is characterised by 'extended politicisation of the top administrative ranks, enduring patronage patterns in recruitment for the public sector, uneven distribution of human resources, and formalism and legalism' (Sotiropoulos, 2004; see also Dashwood, 1983). As a result, informal practices usually prevail over formal rules and procedures (for the Greek case, see Spanou, 1996; Laffan, 2006), and clientelistic practices and patronage infuse society into the state, and undermine 'both the technical capacity ... and legitimacy of public administration' (ibid.: 474; Ferrera, 1998: 87). As Ferrera (ibid.) argues, the 'Southern' state 'is largely infiltrated and easily manipulated by organised interests (and in particular political parties)', and it is exactly this 'low degree of "stateness" of the Latin Systems ... that isolates this family of nations from the others in Europe' (see also Ferrera, 1996). Therefore, society and state are traditionally fused in the Southern model, and civil society – in its Anglo-Saxon and Continental expression – is underdeveloped.

Taking into consideration this brief contrast between the Anglo-Saxon and the Southern European models it would not be an exaggeration to argue that the two models occupy the two extremes of a hypothetical axis concerning the role and nature of state in the political system and its relationship with society. Yet, Ireland is certainly not a classical case of the Anglo-Saxon model. For instance, the Irish political economy is characterised by a strong social part-nership, which is a defining characteristic of the Continental model of political economy (Hardiman, 2002). Furthermore, the state has played a different role in Irish economy in comparison to the ideal type of the Anglo-Saxon model (see O'Riain and O'Connell, 2000). The remainder of this chapter moves on from this abstract discussion on models to the specific characteristics of Greece and Ireland and the factors that make their comparison important for the analysis of the communication of the hegemonic discourse of globalisation.

Political system, political economy, society

By way of introduction, it is worth noticing that both the Greek and Irish republics are based on and function according to their written constitutions. 'The Constitution of Greece' ('Το Σύνταγμα της

Ελλάδας') was enacted in 1975, and the 'Constitution of Ireland' ('Bunreacht na hEireann') was enacted in 1937. The form of government in both Greece and Ireland is that of a *parliamentary republic*,[8] and the Constitutions of both countries recognise *popular sovereignty* as the basis and the source of all powers.[9]

Political system: the triangle of president – government and prime minister – parliament

Democratic regimes are usually classified according to the constitutionally prescribed balance of power between the presidency, the government/prime minister and the parliament. In this regard both the Greek and Irish political systems are highly centralised, and are characterised by a *critical concentration of power* in the hands of the prime minister.[10] The presidency in both systems performs a rather symbolic function, and the parliament is too government dependent to act as counterbalance. Let us consider these issues in some depth.

The Greek 'President of the Republic'[11] and the 'President of Ireland' ('Uachtaran na hEireann')[12] are constitutionally the supreme figures in their polities, but their role and powers are more symbolic than real. In the Greek case the president of the republic is elected with a special majority by the parliament (Article 32), and is constitutionally responsible for the 'function of the institutions of the Republic' (Article 30.1). The powers of the Greek president were curtailed by the constitutional amendment of 1986, when all the actual powers of the president were transferred to the parliamentary majority, and in real terms to the prime minister (Alivizatos, 1993: 68). Yet it should be mentioned that, depending on the person in office, the influence of the institution to the public discourse varies. The case of the president of Ireland is similar. The latter, even though s/he is elected by a direct vote (Article 12.2.1) and according to the constitution takes precedence over all other persons in Ireland (Article 12.1), has no decisive power in the Irish political system (Elgie, 1999). As in the Greek case, the person in office may make a difference in the influence that the institution of presidency exercises on the public discourse, but again this function is/can be confined and/or controlled by the government (see Article 13.7). Hence the presidency in both Greece and Ireland lacks the constitutional means to act as a counterbalance to the powers of prime minister. The same applies to the parliaments of these two countries.

Ireland's parliament ('Oireachtas') is bicameral.[13] It consists of a directly elected House of Representatives, called the Dail, and an indirectly elected Senate, called the Seanad (Article 15.2). The Greek parliament on the contrary is a unicameral one and is called the Vouli.[14] This difference in the two systems, however, should rather be treated as a difference in form and not in substance,[15] in so far as both parliaments are characterised by their inability to exercise any independent or significant control on their governments. There are two main reasons for this. First, is the fact that both the Dail and Vouli are *party dominated* (Gallagher, 1999: 178–179; Alivizatos, 1993: 70). This, along with the high degree of party discipline that is found in both Greek and Irish political systems,[16] reduces significantly any possibilities for an independent role by the parliaments. Second, is the fact that government and parliament cannot in real terms be considered as separate bodies, in a 'check and balance' relationship. As Gallagher (1999: 178) notes for the Irish case, 'it is more realistic to see parliament as wielding power *through* the government that it has elected than to see it as seeking to *check* a government that has come into being independently of it'. This applies to the Greek case too. Moreover, in the latter the existence of majoritarian single-party governments reduces even further the possibilities of an independent role by the Vouli.[17] Therefore, even if the parliaments under examination are not only forums for party confrontation (i.e. talking parliaments) (Alivizatos, 1993), or even if they are not limited to legitimising legislation rather than making it (Gallagher, 1999), they certainly lack the power to counterbalance effectively the role and powers of their governments. As a result, the power in the political systems of both countries is concentrated in the government and in particular in the person of the prime minister.

It can thus be argued that the all-powerful role of the prime minister constitutes the single most important common characteristic of the Greek and Irish political systems.[18] In both cases the prime minister is solely responsible for the formation and composition of the government and the cabinet, and for the policy-making process. S/he is the one who set the agenda for the government and thus for the parliament too, and who supervises and evaluates the policy implementation, and the performance of the various ministries.[19] It can be argued that the only real constraints on the powers of the prime minister in both systems come from internal party politics (see ibid.: 238–245). Furthermore, in the case of Ireland, the emergence of 'coalition politics' since the 1990s (see below) has also had an influence in the role of the prime minister in the political system (see Laffan, 2006). Nevertheless, the latter do not cancel out the high and constitutionally prescribed centralisation of Greek and Irish political systems. This characteristic has justified the term 'prime ministerial government' for the Irish political system (Elgie, 1999), which surely also describes the Greek case.

Up to this point the similarities of the political systems in Greece and Ireland have been outlined. The next section focuses on the differences in the political economy and the structure of interest representation in the two countries.

Political economy and structure of interest representation
A number of economic indicators and characteristics, such as those related to the size of state control domain of economy, the degree of economic regulation and strictness of employment legislation, and the percentage of part-time employment, clearly justify the classification of Greek and Irish economies in different models of political economy. Indicatively, the economic indicators in Figure 2.1 clearly point to two opposite poles/clusters. At one end we have the Anglo-Saxon economies (UK and Ireland) and at the other end we have the Mediterranean economies (including Greece, Italy and Portugal).

Yet, if in the definition of models of political economy we include more factors, such as the nature of the structure of interest representation, then, although the differences between Greece and Ireland remain, the classification of these two countries in the aforemen-

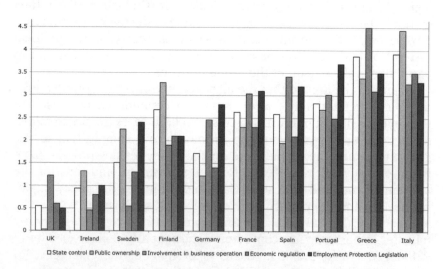

Figure 2.1 Ranking of selected EU countries according to various 'models-of-capitalism' indicators.

Note: 0–6 indicator from least to more state control, or, from least to more restrictive legislation
Source: Nicoletti *et al.* (2000).

tioned models becomes more problematic (especially in the case of Ireland). The remainder of this section deals with this issue.

The contemporary Irish political economy and the structure of interest representation on which it is based are characterised by a high degree of institutionalisation. The latter is expressed through: (a) the institution of social partnership, i.e. the institutionalised cooperation among the government, the employers, the employees, as well as other civil society actors; and (b) the role and function of the National Economic and Social Council (NESC), i.e. the tripartite consultative body, which sets the strategic goals and delineates the parameters for the negotiations among the social partners. As the Irish Congress of Trade Unions' official website declared in 2005, since the revival of the social partnership in 1987 'five three-year pacts have been agreed [see Table 2.1], each building on the success of the previous and attempting more ambitious targets for economic growth; investment in education and health care; social inclusion and action to promote enterprise and employment ... '.

Table 2.1 Social pacts in Ireland

Programme	Period
Programme for National Recovery (PNR)	1987–90
Programme for Economic and Social Progress (PESP)	1990–93
Programme for Competitiveness and Work (PCW)	1994–96
Partnership 2000	1997–2000
Programme for Prosperity and Fairness (PPF)	2000–03
Sustaining Progress (SP)	2003–05
Towards 2016	2006–15

This social partnership evolved as the most distinctive characteristic of Irish political economy in the 1990s, and many analysts contend that it is the successful functioning of this partnership that has led to and sustained the Irish economic miracle[20] (see O'Donnell and O'Reardon, 2000; Hardiman, 2005). In this context the social partnership and NESC can be seen as the central institutions of politico-economic governance in which state and society meet, discuss, co-programme and co-decide in Ireland. The range of civil society organisations that participate in the meetings of social partnership has been indeed impressive and best demonstrates the highly consociational nature of the Irish political economy. For instance in the Partnership 2000 (the agreement reached by social partners in

1997) these organisations included: the Irish National Organisation of the Unemployed, the Conference of Religious of Ireland, the National Women's Council, the National Youth Council of Ireland, the Society of St Vincent de Paul, Protestant Aid and the Community Platform (see Murphy, 1999: 276–277). In the next agreement of the partnership, the Programme for Prosperity and Fairness, the number of these organisations reached approximately thirty-five (Hardiman, 2000: 302). It is also important to underline that many of these voluntary and community sector organisations not only participate in the negotiations of the social partnership but also (since 1998) in the meetings of the NESC (ibid.: 303). In this regard Ireland is a striking exception to the Anglo-Saxon model in which such centralised and consensual mechanisms are unthinkable.

On the other hand, the Greek political economy is characterised by a considerably low degree of institutionalisation and centralisation (Featherstone, 2005a, 2008). The fusion of state and society, a defining characteristic of the Mediterranean model, is also explicit here. For instance, the Greek employee unions are not fully independent from the state, and until recently at least, could hardly be considered as organisations belonging to civil society. Yet, this dependency did not lead, as one might expect, to the control of organised interests by the state. It rather led to a fragmented bargaining system characterised by the antagonistic action of political factions, which had as a result the generation of 'particularistic demands', based on a strong 'guild mentality' (Mavrogordatos, 1993: 61–63; Lavdas, 1997;[21] Pagoulatos, 2003; Kazakos, 2004; Featherstone, 2005a, 2008). This was a dominant characteristic also of the Irish political economy up to the end of the 1980s, when the revival of the institution of social partnership acquired an unprecedented dynamism. In the Greek case various attempts have been made since 1990 to develop an independent and viable social partnership on the basis of the neo-corporatist model (see Ioannou, 1999; Kioukias, 1997). Most importantly, in 1994 an 'Economic and Social Council' was created by law (2232/1994) having as its aim to provide the institutional framework for the development of a social partnership. Nevertheless the Panhellenic Socialist Movement (PASOK) government that created the council in 1994 decided to follow the ad hoc model of a 'National Social Dialogue' in 1997 (Ioannou, 1999). Furthermore, the council was constitutionally recognised as an instrument of social dialogue with the 2001 constitutional amendment. The aim of this provision was to enhance the council's institutional role. Yet in practice it did not have any significant impact. Therefore in contrast to the well-institutionalised social partnership in Ireland, the Greek political economy is characterised by under-institutionalisation and increased –even if diminishing– party domination in the representation of organised interests.

This contrast between the Greek and Irish political economies increases the interest of their comparison in terms of discourse communication. Although both countries have highly centralised political systems (that are characterised by the concentration of power in the person of prime minister), their political economies differ considerably.

The Irish economy is closer to the Anglo-Saxon model in terms of the role of state in the economy, the regulatory framework and the labour market, yet, at the same time, it is based on a highly institutionalised and consensual social partnership. Therefore, in Ireland the energies of actors are 'focused on agreeing amongst themselves and on then persuading their own constituencies that the agreement is acceptable', as Schmidt (2001; see also 2000) would characterise it. On the contrary, the Greek political economy is highly fragmented, with the result that global trends and discourses are not mediated by any thick consociational interest structure (see also Laffan, 2006).

From political economy to civil society
The preceding discussion on political economy and structures of interest representation points to the limits of a 'models approach' (i.e. Anglo-Saxon vs. Mediterranean) as a framework for capturing the social dynamics in the two countries. Several points could be made here. For instance, the aforementioned consociational base of the Irish political economy, which is unknown to the Anglo-Saxon model, is relatively new. Before the late 1980s, although the Irish Congress of Trade Unions (ICTU) may have been able to veto industrial relations reforms, its ability to propose and bring about policy changes was limited (Hardiman, 1988: 207).

Yet, the divergence of Irish political economy from the ideal type of the Anglo-Saxon model is not a phenomenon of the 1980s. Ireland had never had, contrary to the Anglo-Saxon model, a non-party dominated public policy-making process, and an independent civil service (Hardiman, 1988: 205–206). Moreover, Irish political life has traditionally been characterised by 'pervasive localism' and clientelistic relations and, as Hardiman says, rather than mediating, governments were trying to accommodate all these diverse societal interests (Hardiman, 1988: 198–203). Hence, it can be argued that the Irish political economy up (at least) to the beginning of the 1990s

was characterised by fragmentation, and was dominated by particularistic interests – characteristics usually associated with the Southern
European model. Moreover, it can also be argued that Ireland shares
many historical characteristics of the 'externally-centred industrialisation' experienced by Portugal, Spain and Greece (Jacobsen, 1994:
23).[22] It can thus be said that Ireland's divergence from the Anglo-
Saxon model is remarkable both before and after the 1990s.

Nevertheless, the nature of the Irish economy remains closer to the
Anglo-Saxon model. It is characterised by a small state sector and low
involvement of state in economic activities, a flexible labour market
and an Anglo-Saxon corporate governance culture. The latter two
have been enforced to a great extent by the high degree of foreign
direct investments coming from the USA.[23] But these Anglo-Saxon
elements coexist with a (newly born) consociational politico-
economic structure of interest representation, and a (very old)
community – rather than individualist – oriented social culture. All
these elements produce an interesting hybrid model.

Greece and Ireland thus share a number of important socio-political and cultural characteristics. First, the community-oriented culture
–as opposed to the 'individualist orientation' that characterises the
Anglo-Saxon model– can be said to be still dominant in both Greek
and Irish societies (or at least at the self-perceptions of their people).
This community culture creates an invisible social net which is based
on rather personal relationships and traditional social bonds.[24] The
important role that the institution of the family still plays in these two
societies is not unrelated to this community culture. Moreover, with
regard to the issue of public–private sphere division, one should not
ignore the separate developmental trajectory of the 'semi-peripheral'
countries of the EU. Hence in the UK and France for instance, the rise
of a 'private sphere', which supplied the 'vital space' for the development of a 'private/civil society', has been the result of long standing
social struggles. These struggles delineated a space in which private
(economic) interests came together and developed a separate social
sphere of (economic) transactions, in opposition to the state. Hence,
'private/civil society' and 'state' emerged in these societies as two
separate and –to a high degree– oppositional spheres (Tsoukalas,
1993). On the contrary, in many cases in (semi-) peripheral societies,
the emergence of these spheres was not the product of a particular
historical development coming out of social struggles, but the result
of 'models and institutions transferring' from the 'European core'
(ibid.); a fact which created new hybrid models and trajectories.[25]
This 'transplantation process', dominant in colonial and late-

development conditions, has to be kept in mind when we think of categories such as public/private in Greece and Ireland. This is one more factor that brings Ireland closer to the South European model.[26]

A second point with regard to the socio-political culture of the two countries is the existence of a traditionally strong 'underdog culture', which is still (to a lesser degree though) informing and influencing their political culture today. Elements of such a culture can be said to include feelings and attitudes of introvertedness, exceptionalism and cultural insecurity,[27] while this underdog culture is instilled with a distinctive moral gravity and significance. The saying that: 'O my son/We may be a small country/We may be a poor one/But we have our pride'[28] [or, '/But we can hold our head high'],[29] captures one of the traditionally commonest notions to be found in Irish and Greek societies. This notion has many times been accompanied by a tendency to introversion. If cultural heritage and national identity were to be protected, foreign influences and the 'opening' of the society had to be prevented or minimised. Yet, as analysed below, these feelings of insecurity and introvertedness have been challenged in both countries in the 1990s. For economic growth, along with the confidence generated by the EC/EU membership problematised these traditionally negative/defensive self-images (see below).[30]

Moreover, in both Ireland and Greece, the balance of 'knowledge transfer' ceased to be unidirectional in the 1990s. Ireland started to export the experience of its own successful model of growth and social partnership, as well as its experiences with EU membership; and Greece did the same with its own experiences of EU membership and public sector reform, especially towards its Balkan neighbours. These developments increased the pressures on traditional negative self-images and syndromes of inferiority. In this context, Professor O'Donnell, the Director of NESC, wrote in 2000: '[Ireland] is free to walk and run in the century that lies ahead ... It leaves the century free of the two masters that dominated and constrained it – London and Rome. It is now free to reinvent itself' (212). Of course, as is also argued below, this does not mean that the impact of the British legacy on Ireland's socio-political life is – or indeed can be – over. A good example of this is the centrality of the issue of neutrality in the negative referenda on the Nice Treaty in 2001 and the Lisbon Treaty in 2008.[31]

Let us close this section with a short reference to the role of the church in the two countries.[32] Both societies are characterised by a high degree of homogenisation with regard to the religion of their population. In the Republic of Ireland the overwhelming majority of the population is Roman Catholic (91.6%), whereas in Greece the majority of the people is attached to the Greek Orthodox Church (98%).[33] Furthermore, according to various Eurobarometer surveys throughout the period 1990–2001, the Greeks and Irish remained among the most religious people in the European Union. For instance, in 1994, in response to the question: 'Whether you do or you don't follow religious practices, would you say that you are: Religious/Not Religious/Agnostic/Atheist/Don't know ... ', 93% of the Greeks who participated in the survey – the highest percentage in EU12 – replied 'religious', whereas the Irish came fourth with 82% (the Portuguese were second with 89%, and the Italians were third with 82%). The EU12 average was 59% (Eurobarometer 42, 1995). In a similar survey on religious belief among young people two years later, the largest group of 'practising believers' was in Ireland with 49%, followed by Greece with 42%, and Italy with 41%. The EU15 average was 19.4% (Eurobarometer 47.2, 1997).

It is also important to note that religion in both countries is considered by the majority of the population to be an integral part of their national identity; and within this majority a (large) part would consider that 'Greekness' and 'Irishness' as forms of national identity cannot exist without Orthodoxy and Catholicism respectively.[34] At least two points should be mentioned here. First, the church[35] is considered to have played an important role historically in the preservation of national identity and in the fight for national independence.[36] Second, personalities do make a difference in the way in which the church intervenes in political life. This was made clear with the election of Archbishop Christodoulos in Greece in 1998, and Cardinal Desmond Connell in Ireland in 1988, who both adopted an 'interventionist' stance in public affairs (for the Greek case, see Stavrakakis, 2002).

The nature and role of the church in the two countries, however, are considerably different. These differences are not only limited to historico-institutional aspects, such as the fact that the Greek church is a 'national church',[37] whereas the Irish church is a 'global' (and hierarchically structured) one, but also extend to more functional social-specific aspects. Thus it can be argued that traditionally the Greek church depended on and was 'used' by the Greek state for its own purposes, rather than vice versa, which was the case in Ireland. Furthermore, it can be argued that church influence on the public discourse is more centralised in Greece than in Ireland. In the latter one finds a number of powerful interest groups, which, although they advance the church's positions, do not have any formal affiliation to it. Such interest groups include the Pro-Life Amendment Campaign (PLAC), the Society for the Protection of the Unborn Child (SPUC), the Family Solidarity and the Anti-Divorce Campaign (Inglis, 2000: 54–55). In Greece on the other hand, the church's intervention in public discourse remains relatively centralised, and is mainly expressed through the church hierarchy itself.

To sum up, the pair comparison between Ireland and Greece proposed here is based on the characteristics set out in Table 2.2.

Table 2.2 Greece and Ireland: a focused comparison

	Greece	*Ireland*	*Nature of comparison*
Structure of interest representation	Fragmented	Highly institutionalised	Different
Regional dimension	EU	EU	Similar
Political economy	Mediterranean	Anglo-Saxon	Different
Political system	Highly centralised, traditionally clientalistic	Highly centralised, traditionally clientalistic	Similar
Political culture	Late development	Late development	Similar

On the basis of these characteristics the following section compares and contrasts Greece and Ireland as social agents in the 1990s.

Greece and Ireland as social agents

Greece and Ireland as 'extreme stories' in the EU

One could argue that Ireland represents the most 'successful story' in the European Union. A country of the Regional Development Fund, with significant economic and social problems up to the mid/late 1980s, became the 'European tiger', succeeding in having a steadily impressive rate of growth after 1987. Figure 2.2 demonstrates this growth in comparison to Greece, the euro area, and the OECD average in the 1990s.

Indeed, from the 'poorest of the rich' in 1988 (*Economist*, 1988), Ireland became the 'Celtic tiger'[38] (see, among others, Gardiner, 1994: 9–21; Sweeney, 1998; O'Hearn, 1998, 2000; and for critiques, see Allen, 2000; Kirby, 2002) and 'Europe's shining light' (*Economist*, 1997) in the 1990s.[39] Furthermore, the dynamism of Irish development

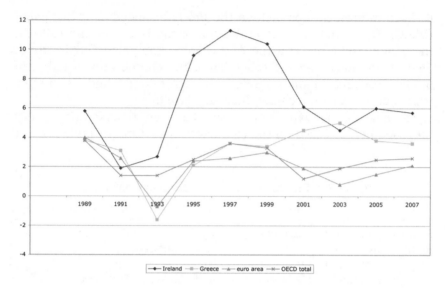

Figure 2.2 Growth in real GDP in Ireland and Greece: a comparative
perspective (percentage change from previous year)

Source: OECD.

was not limited to within the EU borders. It is suggestive that in the
'Globalisation Index' used by the US journal *Foreign Policy* (published by
the Carnegie Endowment for International Peace), Ireland was found to
be the most globalised country in the world throughout the period
2000–02 (*Foreign Policy*, 2002, 2003, 2004; see also Figure 2.7
below).[40] The striking integration of Ireland in the structures of international economy in the 1990s is also evident from the following economic
indicators (Figures 2.3–2.5).

On the other hand, it can be said that Greece in general represents
the least 'successful story' in the European Union. A country of the
Regional Development Fund as well, and a country which entered the
EU in a rather better economic condition than Portugal and Spain, its
Southern European counterparts, it was the only EU member state
which, although it did not opt out, did not manage to fulfil the criteria and participate in the first wave of countries that entered into the
third and final stage of the Economic and Monetary Union (i.e. Eurozone) on 1 January, 1999.[41] Moreover, according to Eurostat,
throughout the period under examination and at least until 2008,
Greece was the country with the second, after Portugal, lowest GDP
per capita among the EU15. Indicatively, according to Eurostat in

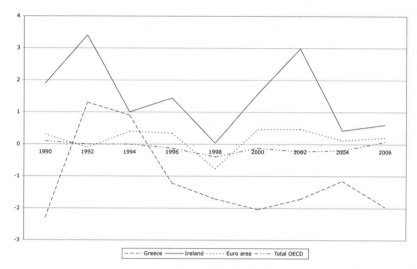

Figure 2.3[a] Foreign balance contributions to changes in real GDP (percentage of real GDP of previous period, seasonally adjusted at annual rates)

Notes: [a]Figure 2.3 shows how payments from abroad (including the price of exports, and the inflows of capital and gold) contributed to Ireland's GDP in comparison to Greece, and the Euro area and OECD average.
Source: OECD.

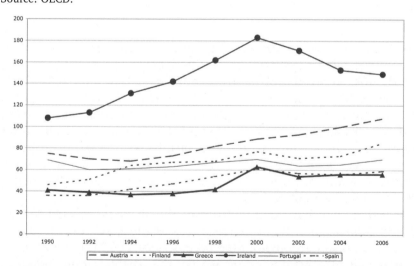

Figure 2.4[a] Trade-to-GDP ratio (total trade) (The sum of exports and imports divided by GDP; current prices, current exchange rates)

Note: [a]The trade-to-GDP ratio measures a country's 'openness' or 'integration' in the world economy.
Source: OECD.

Theory and agents

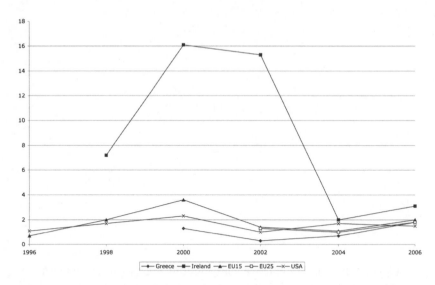

Figure 2.5ᵃ Foreign direct investment intensity (Average value of inward
   and outward FDI flows divided by GDP, multiplied by 100)

Notes: No data were available for Greece during 1996–98, for Ireland for 1996 and
for EU25 during 1996–2000. ᵃThis index measures the intensity of investment
integration within the international economy.
Source: Eurostat.

2004, GDP per capita, expressed in terms of purchasing-power standards, was more than twice the EU25 average in Luxembourg, was
nearly 40% above the EU25 average in Ireland, around 20% above
average in Denmark, Austria, the Netherlands, the United Kingdom
and Belgium, around 15% above average in Sweden and Finland,
around 10% above average in France and Germany, and about 5%
above average in Italy. Spain was just below the EU25 average,
Greece, Cyprus and Slovenia were about 20% below average, while
Portugal, Malta and the Czech Republic were around 30% below
average (see also Figure 2.6).

   It is also suggestive that in terms of the above-mentioned *Foreign
Policy* 'Globalisation Index', Greece was at the bottom of the EU15
countries ranked, throughout the period 1999–2005 (Figure 2.7).

   It would also be interesting to use the 'Globalisation Index' to
compare three indicators of economic globalisation in Greece and
Ireland, in the year 2001 (Table 2.3).

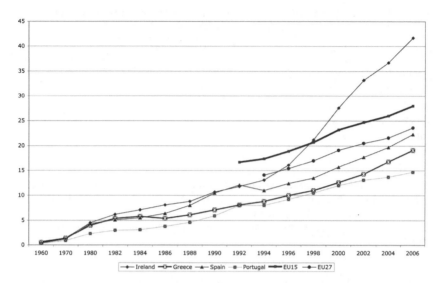

Figure 2.6 Per capita GDP in Greece and Ireland: a comparative perspective (in thousands ECU/Euro; current market prices)

Source: European Commission

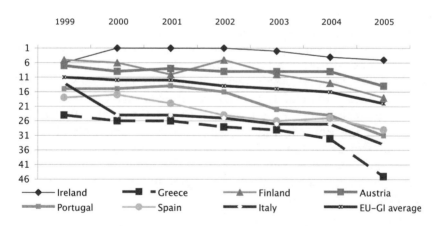

Figure 2.7 The *Foreign Policy* 'Globalisation Index' – selected EU member states (ranking rate: Absolute numbers, from 1 (the most globalised country of the Index) to 62 (the least globalised country of the Index)

Note: EU–GI average includes Austria, Denmark, Finland, France, Germany, Greece, Ireland, Italy, the Netherlands, Portugal, Spain, Sweden and the UK.
Source: the table is based on data from various '*Foreign Policy* – Globalisation Indexes' (see *Foreign Policy*, 2002–07).

Table 2.3[a] Economic globalisation in Greece and Ireland in 2001: a comparative perspective

	Trade	*Foreign direct investments*	*Portfolio capital flows*
Ireland	3	3	1
Finland	30	11	8
Austria	12	29	7
Portugal	29	16	11
Spain	39	14	13
Italy	47	40	21
Greece	45	48	16

Note: [a] The numbers indicate the position of the countries in the various categories of the 'Globalisation Index'. The ranking is from 1 to 62, where 1 indicates the most globalised country and 62 the least globalised
Source: the table is based on the *Foreign Policy* 'Globalisation Index' (see Foreign Policy, 2003).

From Table 2.3 we see that from the sixty-two countries that were ranked in the *Foreign Policy* Globalisation Index, for the year 2001, Ireland was in the third best position in terms of trade and FDIs, and in the first position in terms of portfolio investments, whereas Greece along with Italy were significantly low in the ranking, especially with regard to trade and foreign direct investments (FDIs). These data are indicative of the economic performance of these countries throughout (and beyond) the period under examination here.

This poor economic performance combined with an 'idiosyncratic' foreign policy during the 1980s generated a negative image of Greece in the European press. As a result, during the late 1980s and early 1990s, Greece was widely considered to be 'an awkward partner or indeed a black sheep in the European Union' (Tsoukalis, 1999).

To sum up, one can indeed refer to Greece and Ireland as two 'extreme stories' within the EU, i.e. 'Europe's shining light' on the one hand, and the 'last to join the euro' on the other. Yet this is not the only way to approach the recent developmental trajectories of the two countries.

From 'extreme stories' to 'parallel lives'?
The argument put forward here is as follows. One of the characteristics of Greece and Ireland – at least up to the mid/end 1980s – was the strongly 'traditional' character of their societies (for Ireland, see Coacley, 1999b; for Greece, see Diamandouros, 1994; Tsoukalas, 1993a). The term 'traditional' is used here as opposite to the term 'reflexive'. Put crudely a traditional society is one that does not deeply

question and/or re-examine its beliefs and practices. Identities, national interests and the boundaries of the community are clearly defined, and the way to pursue or protect them is beyond discussion and reflection. It can be argued that as of the late 1980s both Greece and Ireland entered a stage in their history characterised by intensive self-reflection and re-examination of traditionally well-rooted social beliefs and practices. Put sociologically and abstractly, they entered into a period in which the eternal struggle and balance between social *structures* and *agency* became weighted in favour of agency. Such a reading of the modern social change in Greece and Ireland is compatible with Anthony Giddens's conceptualisation of reflexive modernisation.[42] It is also a reading which focuses not only on the level of individuals but also on that of society as a whole. It refers to the re-examination and re-evaluation of beliefs and practices at the level of collective intentionality. It refers to a re-examination of the boundaries and nature of the political community and to a reshuffle of the societal forces that struggle to structure the content of collective intentionality.[43] I would argue that two broad developments played a crucial role in this process of self-reflection in Greece and Ireland.

First, is the accession to the European Community. The 'project EC/EU' had a crucial role in enhancing the aforementioned dynamics in the two societies. Indeed change in modern Greek and Irish polities – along with all the other EU member states – can hardly be studied and understood if the impact of European integration and Europeanisation, as an explanatory factor for change *in* these polities, is neglected.[44] Along these lines it can be argued that in the case of Ireland, the European Community constituted and incarnated an alternative to the dependency on the UK (see also Coakley, 1999b: 47; Garvin, 2000; O'Donnell, 2000: 162–166). Ireland seized the opportunity and found itself in a position to confront its own (new European) future. In the case of Greece, the European Community incarnated a much needed *deus ex machina* for the 'reformist social forces' (Diamandouros, 1994), and a much needed injection of confidence which led Greece to face its well-rooted national insecurities (mainly on the side of Greek-Turkish relations).[45] The Greek–Turkish rapprochement in the late 1990s should rather be interpreted through such a framework. Furthermore, in both countries the financial support of the EC/EU was instrumental in changing the 'material context' experienced in Greece and Ireland (and thus decisive in bringing about the reinvention and redefinition of the boundaries of community discussed below).

The second factor behind the reflexive turn of the two societies refers to a significant – both in real and symbolic terms – disruption between, on the one hand the socio-economic past, and the perceptions that accompanied it, and on the other the socio-economic present and the experiences and images it generates. In the case of Ireland, the 'country of the famine'[46] and the 'poorest of the rich',[47] experienced an 'economic miracle'. Professor Brendan Walsh (2000) refers to this transformation as 'from Rags to Riches'. It is hardly disputable that this economic boom and the influx of FDIs[48] had a significant impact on the way in which Irish people think of themselves. Furthermore and maybe more importantly for the aforementioned reflexive change in Irish self-conceptualisation, was the shift of Irish society from a traditional *emigration* profile to that of *immigration* in the 1990s. Thus Ireland for the first time in its modern history experienced the growth of sizeable immigrant communities (see Mac Einri, 2001). Figure 2.8 is indeed indicative of the change in migration that took place in the 1990s.

The impact of this changing economic and social geography on the self-perception of the Irish should not be underestimated. It would not be an exaggeration to argue that these developments put Irish society in a position to mirror and redefine itself, through the 'new foreigners'.[49]

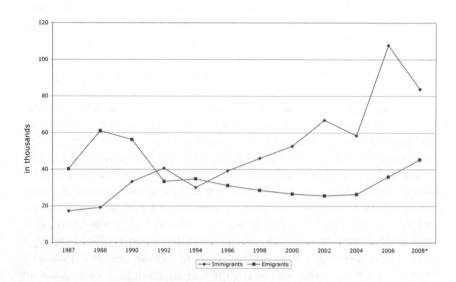

Figure 2.8 Migration in Ireland

Note: [a] The data for 2008 are an estimate.
Source: Central Statistics Office, Ireland, 2008

On the other hand, one can observe a similar disruption between the socio-economic past and present in the Greek case. Greece did not experience an economic miracle. Nevertheless, the economic policies that took place during the 1990s addressed some chronic structural imbalances of the Greek economy, and brought high growth rates and economic stability; developments that generated positive reports in foreign media and international economic institutions.[50] This U-turn in macroeconomic figures and policies was epitomised by the entrance of Greece into the eurozone in January 2001. These developments generated a new sense of confidence in large parts of Greek society, and problematised many traditional negative self-images. Moreover the new economic and political geography of the Balkan region and the significant role of Greece within it, constituted an important factor in the reflexive redefinition of Greek self-understanding. In particular Greece emerged as: (a) a point of entrance to Balkan markets for FDIs; (b) a significant FDI home country itself; and (c) a stabilisation force in the region.[51] Finally and again most interestingly, Greek society also shifted during the 1990s from a traditionally *emigration* society, to one of *immigration*, experiencing for the first time in its post-war history sizeable immigrant and economic refugee communities (Clogg, 2003; Cholezas and Tsakloglou, 2008). In particular, according to official data, in 1991 immigrants in Greece constituted approximately 1.5% of the overall population (1991 census), while in 2001 they constituted approximately 7% of the population (2001 census). Yet most researchers would agree that in the 1980s the immigrant population was closer to 2.5% (see Zavos, 2005: 12), while in the 2000s is approximately 9% of the overall population (see Zavos, 2005; Triandafyllidou, 2005). This phenomenon, as has been argued for the Irish case, led Greek society to look in the mirror and to reflect on its past and future (see also, Diamandouros, 2001).[52]

The U-turn of the early 1990s

Thus until the 1990s both countries had experienced a long period of unfortunate economic management. In the case of Ireland one can observe 'the continuation of protectionism into the late 1950s' and an 'irresponsible fiscal experimentation in the late 1970s' (Walsh, 2000: 121); policies that resulted in a deep economic crisis in the 1980s. It is also worth mentioning that according to surveys, during the period 1979–83 the Greeks and the Irish were prominent among the peoples of the EU in their support for 'classic economic policies of the left' (Coackley, 1999b: 60).

The turning point for Ireland may be put in the second half of the 1980s, when the tripartite approach to national socio-economic development was revived – in a much wider basis and agenda – through the NESC. As Gary Murphy notes, the NESC's Strategy for Development agreed in 1986 formed the basis upon which the new Programme for National Recovery was negotiated by the social partners in 1987 (1999: 274–277). From this point onwards an impressively successful model of consociational socio-economic governance has been functioning in Ireland.[53]

In Greece on the other hand, protectionism with irresponsibly expansionist fiscal policies, was followed up to the end of 1980s, with a small stabilisation parenthesis in 1985–87 (see Katseli, 1990; Kazakos, 1992; Alogoskoufis, 1995). The last years of the 1980s were indeed very formative for the modern Greek politico-economic system. From an economic point of view, a series of events brought the country to the brink of economic disaster. The government of PASOK (elected in 1984) abandoned its 1985–87 economic stabilisation programme and, in a pre-electoral climate, adopted an expansionary economic policy. The two coalition governments that followed (see below), not only failed to reverse the rapid deterioration of macroeconomic indicators but also contributed to the increase of government deficits. When the centre-right party New Democracy (ND) came into power in April 1990 the Greek economy was undergoing its most severe economic crisis since 1974, the date of birth of the fourth Greek Republic. The governmental change of the 1990 can be considered a turning point in the modern Greek politico-economic history. It signified, a shift from *statist* to *deregulation/liberalisation*-oriented policies and discourses (i.e. privatisation, competition, integration into the European and global markets); thus signifying a shift in the dominant economic paradigm (Kazakos, 1992a).[54] It was a moment of transition in which an expansionist and purely clientelistic state started to be transformed into a *stabilisation* (Pagoulatos, 2001) and a *modernisation* state (a transformation that does not seem to have ever been completed).

The beginning of the 1990s can also be considered a turning point for the nature and function of the Greek and Irish political systems. In the case of Greece the turn from the 1980s to the 1990s was marked by the formation of two – if short-lived – unprecedented coalition governments. After eight years in government, the socialist party PASOK was replaced in power in 1989 by a previously unthinkable coalition government, consisting of the centre-right ND party and Synaspismos, a coalition of the Communist and other left-wing parties. After five months in office (June–October 1989), this coalition government was replaced by another, consisting of all three major Greek parties (ND, PASOK and Synaspismos). This all-party government was headed by a widely respected Professor of Economics, Xenophon Zolotas, and also lasted only five months. It was finally replaced by a weak ND government in April 1990.[55] These successive coalition governments marked a historical departure from well-established political cleavages in the Greek political scene;[56] thus constituting the epitome of Greece's democratic consolidation (Pridham and Verney, 1991). Moreover, these coalitions played a significant role in the decline of the (polemical) polarisation that traditionally characterised Greek politics (Pridham and Verney, 1991; Pappas, 2001).[57] This development led to an enhancement of the base and role of civil society in Greek political life.

During the same period, Ireland experienced an equivalent transition in its political system. The turn from the 1980s to the 1990s signified the end of a long-standing, polarised pattern in Irish politics (1948–89): the 'Fianna Fáil versus the rest' system (Mair, 1999). During this period Fianna Fáil was the only party which was in a position to form, and did form, single-party majority governments, whereas Fine Gael and the Labour Party often had to choose between forming a coalition in order to come to power, or stay in opposition. This system came to an end in 1989, when Fianna Fáil, in order to form a government, entered a coalition with the Progressive Democrats.[58] The years that followed were indeed formative for Irish political life. In the elections of 1992 a traditionally unthinkable coalition government was formed out of Fianna Fáil and the Labour Party. In 1994, however, the Labour Party left the government and returned to its 'historical ally', Fine Gael. Thus a new government was formed by Fine Gael and the Labour Party, without general elections being held. Taking into consideration the above, 1989 was indeed a landmark in Irish politics. It gave birth to a 'new politics of coalition-making', initiating a new, compromising style of party politics (Mair, 1999: 148). As the elections of 1997, 2002 and 2007 have demonstrated, the era of single-party governments (and voting behaviour) in Ireland may be over.[59]

Here, one should also mention the different electoral systems of the two countries. The electoral system used in Ireland is proportional representation by means of the single transferable vote (PR–STV) (see Sinnott, 1999), whereas the Greek electoral system is one of reinforced proportional representation. It can be argued that the main difference between the two systems is that the PR–STV in Ireland facilitates proportional representation in the Dail, and therefore creates a greater potential for coalition governments, whereas the Greek electoral system encourages and enhances the formation of single-party majority governments. Yet any generalisations on the effects of any electoral system are rather meaningless without an analysis of the socio-political trajectory, context and culture in which this system is embedded.

Conclusion

This chapter examined the nature and characteristics of the pair comparison between Greece and Ireland. This analysis was further contextualised by contrasting these two countries as social agents in the 1990s, i.e. the period of the materialisation of the hegemonic discourse of globalisation. It was argued that while these countries represented two extreme stories within the EU, at the same time they were undergoing a similar modernisation process. The comparison between Greece and Ireland will allow us to elucidate the material-isation process of the hegemonic discourse of globalisation. It will also allow us to examine how globalisation was materialised in countries with different political economies and what has been the role of different domestic structures of interest representation in this process.

Both Greece and Ireland can be considered 'deviant cases' in the group of political economies to which they belong (i.e. the Mediter-ranean vs. Anglo-Saxon group). The problem with comparing deviant cases is that the research conclusions may not be easily comparable with already existing hypotheses and academic assumptions. Studies of 'deviant cases', however, have the potential to push the limits and widen the horizons of comparative research, and increase the possi-bility for unexpected research findings (see Lijphart, 1971: 65).

There is one important difference between Greece and Ireland: the fact that in Ireland the spoken language is English. This factor is indeed important, considering the global status of the English language, but it does not affect the substance of the research project proposed here. For the issue under examination in this thesis is the actual materialisation process in each country. The language that is spoken in a country does not influence the nature of this materialisa-tion process, nor does it affect the nature of political economy or the domestic structures that are involved in it.

Having developed our theoretical framework in chapter 1, and presented our case studies in chapter 2, Part II turns to the examination of the materialisation of the globalisation discourse in Greece and Ireland.

Notes

1 This model is also referred to as 'Latin'. See for instance Therborn, 1995 and Ferrera, 1998.
2 Referred to also as the 'Germanic' model. See for instance Rhodes and Mény, 1998.
3 Indeed, the use of the term Anglo-Saxon for Ireland sounds rather bizarre, considering its history, culture and relationship with the UK, which will be considered later in this chapter.
4 See also Esping-Andersen's book *The Three Worlds of Welfare Capitalism* (1990), on which the Rhodes and Mény's approach is based.
5 In the comparative studies literature the most frequently employed strategy is the juxtaposition of countries belonging to the Continental and the Anglo-Saxon models. By contrast countries from the Southern European model are less often used in comparisons with Anglo-Saxon or 'orthodox' Continental cases. Arguably, this is so mainly for two reasons: (a) the different developmental trajectory of the countries that belong to the Southern model makes it hard to compare these countries with countries from the other two models; and (b) the 'ambiguous' (see for instance, Hall and Soskice, 2001a) or 'hard to classify' character of the countries in this model. Yet, the different developmental trajectory of the South European countries is an asset for research projects which seek 'to show the robustness of a relationship by demonstrating its validity in a range of contrasting settings' (the 'most different research design' according to Przeworski and Teune, 1970), or which seek to explore how does domestic context matter, in the way in which different states react to common incentives. Moreover, it can be argued that the hard-to-classify character of Southern European countries is rather an advantage, which increases the richness of comparative studies and verifies the diversity and pluralism of European tradition in general. Hence the hard-to-classify character of the Southern model is a problem/threat only for established categorisations and dichotomies, which cannot account for these 'ambiguous' cases, and thus need to reduce difference to particularism.
6 For a classical comparison between pluralism and corporatism, see Schmitter, 1979. In particular according to Schmitter 'pluralism can be defined as a system of interest representation in which the constituent units are organised into an unspecified number of multiple, voluntary, competitive, non-hierarchically ordered and self-determined (as to type or scope of interest) categories which are not specially licensed, recognised, subsidised, created or otherwise controlled in leadership selection or interest articulation by the state and which do not exercise a monopoly of representational activity within their respective categories' (ibid:

15); corporatist is defined as 'a system of interest representation in which the constituent units are organised into a limited number of singular, compulsory, non-competitive, hierarchically ordered and functionally differentiated categories, recognised or licensed (if not created) by the state and granted a deliberate representational monopoly within their respective categories in exchange for observing certain controls on the selection of leaders and articulation of demands and supports' (ibid.: 13). Finally, Schmitter (based on Manoilesco, 1936) distinguishes societal corporatism from state corporatism on the basis that in the latter organised interests 'were created by and kept as auxiliary and dependent organs of the state which founded its legitimacy and effective functioning on other bases' (ibid.: 20).

7 For a comparison of the developmental trajectories of the Balkans and Latin America, see Mouzelis, 1986. In addition, for a Marxist analysis of the 'dependent development' and 'externally centred' industrialisation in Portugal, Greece and Spain, see Poulantzas, 1976.

8 Article 1.1 of the Greek constitution. The Irish constitution lacks an explicit statement about the 'form of government'.

9 For the Greek case: Article 1 paras 2 and 3; for the Irish: Article 6.

10 For the Irish case, see Elgie, 1999; Connolly and O'Halpin, 1999; Ward, 1994; O'Leary, 1991. For the Greek case, see Alivizatos, 1993. Moreover, King (1994) classifies Greece and Ireland in the six western European states with the most 'influential' heads of government.

11 See Articles 30–50 of the Greek constitution.

12 See Articles 12–14 of the Irish constitution.

13 See Articles 15–27 of the Irish constitution.

14 See Articles 51–80 of the Greek constitution.

15 Considering the limited role and power of the Seanad in Irish politics, the focus of our analysis is on Dail (see Gallagher, 1999).

16 For the Greek case, see Alivizatos, 1993: 70. For the Irish case, see Gallagher, 1999: 179; Sinnott, 1999: 116–117.

17 It should however be mentioned here that the decline in the ability of parliaments to control the executive is a common characteristic of most EC/EU states since 1950s (see Raunio and Hix, 2001).

18 It must also be noted here that the prime ministers in both systems are both head of their governments and their parties.

19 It is also in her/his responsibilities to appoint the Attorney-General who, in the Irish case, also has a seat in the cabinet (Elgie, 1999: 238).

20 This view is also held by Peter Cassells (personal interview, 27 June 2002). Peter Cassells is Chairman of Forfás (National Policy and Advisory Board for Enterprise, Trade, Science, Technology and Innovation), Executive Chairperson of the National Centre for Partnership and Performance, and former General Secretary of the ICTU (1987–99). He was personally involved in all of the negotiations for partnership agreements since 1987.

21 Mavrogordatos (1988, 1993) and Lavdas (1997) adopt different

approaches in the definition of the Greek interest intermediation system. Mavrogordatos argues that the Greek system is a characteristic case of 'state corporatism'. Lavdas, adopting a more qualified approach, argues that although state corporatist elements have historically been present at various sectoral levels of the economy, the institutional character of the Greek interest intermediation system as a whole is closer to what could be termed 'disjointed corporatism'. For a literature review on this issue, see Featherstone, 2008.

22 For a study of socio-political change in modern Ireland through a *dependency* theoretical prism, see Jacobsen, 1994.

23 It is interesting that, when studying the 'collaborative production' in Ireland, many scholars distinguish between 'unionised' and 'non-unionised workplaces' (see, for instance, Roche and Geary, 2000). For the issue of flexibility in the Irish labour market, see Gunnigle and Brosnan, 2001. Moreover, for the effect and practices of US firms in the Irish workplace, see: Gunnigle *et al.*, 1997; Geary, 1999; Gunnigle and McGuire, 2001. Gunnigle and McGuire (ibid: 59) have two very interesting extracts from interviews conducted with two vice presidents of US multinationals: 'Any country that requires union recognition is immediately stricken off our list of possible locations', and 'We don't deal with unions. We don't have a union in the US. It does not fit with our culture'.

24 For the case of Greece, see Tsoukalas, 1993; for the case of Ireland, see Tovey, 2001.

25 In this context Tsoukalas (1993: 334) notes of the Greek case: '... before the issue of the "degree" of State autonomy can be raised, one should investigate to what extent the development of social and economic forces, and the building of State machinery are processes "external" to each other'. For the issue of 'state autonomy', see the contributions in Evans *et al.*, 1985, and for a Marxist critique see Cammack's (1989) review article.

26 See also the interesting discussion on the emergence and stabilisation of Irish democracy in Kissane, 1995. Kissane argues that in order to understand the emergence of the modern Irish polity, traditional postcolonial explanatory frameworks should be combined with modernisation approaches.

27 For an analysis of this culture in the Greek case, see Diamandouros, 1994.

28 As many Irish grandparents keep saying.

29 The most common Greek version.

30 A caveat should be inserted here. I do not mean to make a value judgement about the aforementioned underdog culture, nor do I subscribe to (simplistic) analyses which equate 'tradition' with 'backwardness'. Indeed, part of the discourse of the 'modernising camps' in both countries has often been based on a simplistic 'binary logic' in which '[t]radition, suitably packaged, homogenised and essentialised, becomes a mere caricature' which is reconstructed and scapegoated as the 'enemy of progress' (Doak 1998: 26). What I do argue is that the changed material and psychological landscape led to the problematisation of historically

well-rooted notions of dependency and insecurity; and furthermore that this changed landscape led to a reflexive and self-confident attitude about the capacity of the two countries to decide for and formulate their own future, and therefore take responsibility for it.

31 Irish neutrality has traditionally been more about not being allied to Britain than about unilateralism per se. In the case of the Nice referendum, however, the concept of neutrality moved beyond an 'instrumental definition', and acquired a central position in the Irish public discourse 'as a synonym for national identity and core political value' (Gillespie, 2002). The same also happened with the referendum on the Lisbon Treaty. For the issue of Irish neutrality, see, among others, FitzGerald, 1998.

32 For the role of church in Greece, see Stavrakakis, 2002; Konidaris, 2003; Ware, 1983; and in Ireland, see Inglis, 1998; Kissane, 2003.

33 In particular, according to the 1991 census, the religious composition in the Republic was Roman Catholic: 91.6%; Church of Ireland (Anglican): 2.5%; Presbyterians: 0.4%; other, or no information or specific religious beliefs: 5.6%. The respective composition in Greece is: Greek Orthodox: 98%, Muslim 1.3%, other 0.7%.

34 Population attitudes towards religion, either as an esoteric belief or as a part of a national identity, should not be equated with population attitudes towards the church as an institution. This becomes clearer when one studies the attitudes of the population not towards religion but towards the church, or when the focus of the analysis is on state–church relations.

35 For convenience, in the case of Ireland, the term 'church' is used to refer to the Catholic church. The 'church of Ireland' is the official name for the Anglican Church.

36 Even though the official Orthodox church took a conservative stance towards the Greek fight of independence in the nineteenth century.

37 The 'national church' is a common characteristic of the Christian Orthodox religion. Thus, national Orthodox churches were founded by Bulgarians (1872), Serbians (1879), Romanians (1885), Finish and Estonians (1923), Polish (1924), Albanians (1937), and Czechs and Slovaks (1998).

38 The term was coined by Kevin Gardiner (1994) in a Morgan Stanley *Euro-letter* in 1994.

39 This contrast between the two surveys of *The Economist*, i.e. from the 'poorest of the rich' (1988) to the 'Europe's shining light' (1997), is well cited in the literature about Ireland. See for instance Murphy, 1999 and Walsh, 2000.

40 The *A. T. Kearney/Foreign Policy* 'Globalisation Index' (GI) was used for the first time in 2001. The GI does not include all the countries of the world. However, the 62 countries ranked, account approximately for 95% of the world's GDP and 84% of the world's population (see, *Foreign Policy*, 2004: 58). In terms of research methodology the GI uses 14 variables

grouped in four baskets, in order to measure the degree of openness/globalisation. These are as follows: (a) economic integration: trade, FDI, portfolio capital flows, investment income; (b) personal income: international travel and tourism, international telephone traffic, remittances and personal transfers; (c) technological connectivity: Internet users, Internet hosts, secure servers; (d) political engagement: memberships in international organisations, personnel and financial contributions to UN Security Council missions, international treaties ratified, governmental transfers (ibid.). Notwithstanding its potential flaws, the variety of variables used in the GI makes it a good general indicator of state openness and global engagement. For criticisms of the GI, see Kudrle, 2004 and Lockwood, 2004. Another index with a growing visibility in the globalisation literature is that of the Centre for the Study of Globalisation and Regionalisation (CSGR) of the University of Warwick (at: http://www2.warwick.ac.uk/fac/soc/csgr/index). In this index, Ireland was the most globalised country in economic terms (economic ranking), and the second most globalised country in economic, social and political terms (overall marking), throughout the period 1998–2001 (see Lockwood and Redoano, 2005).

41 Greece joined the eurozone two years later (1 January 2001).

42 Giddens (1990: 38, 1991, 1995) argues that in late-modern societies 'social practices are constantly examined in the light of incoming information about those very practices, thus constitutively altering their character'.

43 For the concept of 'collective intentionality', see Searle, 1995: 24–26. In particular Searle argues: 'The crucial element in collective intentionality is a sense of doing (wanting, believing, etc.) something together, and the individual intentionality that each person has is derived from the collective intentionality that they share' (ibid.: 24–25).

44 For this point, see the contributions in Goetz and Hix, 2001. In their introduction the editors note: 'In the main theories of integration, domestic politics is a central explanatory factor of the integration process ... Much less effort has gone into thinking about the reverse effect: European integration as an explanatory factor in domestic political continuity or change' (2001a: 1).

45 In this context Professor Tsoukalis argues that 'there is no doubt that EU membership is perceived by many Greeks as a means of strengthening their national security' (2001: 125). For a discussion of the effect of Europeanisation in Greece, see Ioakimidis, 1996, 2001; Featherstone, 1998, 1998a, 2005; Lavdas, 1997; Kazakos, 1999, 2004; Mitsos and Mossialos, 2000: parts III and IV; and Pagoulatos, 2001, 2003. More general studies on the Greece–EU relationship include: Kazakos and Ioakimidis, 1994; Dimitrakopoulos and Passas, 2003; Featherstone, 2005.

46 The nineteenth-century famine in Ireland has been one of the most formative experiences in the development of the modern Irish identity. The failure of the potato crop for successive years, in a population almost

dependent for its diet on the potato, led to a major famine which lasted from 1845 to 1851. According to estimations, in a total population of 6 to 8 million, 1 million people died of starvation and 1.5 million emigrated abroad, mainly to Britain and the USA. The Irish considered Britain as partly responsible for the famine (Collins and Cradden, 2001: 2–3; Finnegan and McCarron, 2000: 31–41).

47 For the poor historical record regarding Ireland's economic performance before the 1990s, see Barry, 1999, 2003.

48 See O'Connor, 2001. For the relationship between FDIs and the economic boom, see Walsh, 2000: 118–120. For the argument that the economic boom was merely due to a huge flow of US investments, see Allen, 2000: 21–29.

49 For the reflexive rearticulation of Irish identity, see also Tonra, 2000. Tonra links changes in Irish foreign policy to changing conceptions of Irish identity.

50 See for instance, IMF, 1999.

51 See, among others, Petrakos and Totev, 2000; Wallden, 2000; Kamaras, 2001.

52 In the same context Diamandouros (2001: 72) notes: 'Greek society has until very recently thought of itself as a country of emigrants. It is a society and a country whose literature, whose poetry, whose folklore resonates with the notion of nostalgia, of emigration, of the desire to return. Objectively speaking, all of these things are, in fact, things of the past'.

53 Some analysts put the turning point at 1994. See Murphy, 1999.

54 Kazakos (1992a) argues that elements of the new paradigm were already in place after the second half of the 1980s. On the same issue, Ioakimidis (1996: 41) notes: 'Only in the years 1992–93, under the ND government, did privatisation (apokratikopiisi) policy appear to be pursued as a clear political preference'.

55 For these coalition governments, see Pridham and Verney, 1991. The new ND government was based on a coalition of ND with an independently elected MP.

56 The period after the collapse of the colonels' regime in Greece and up to the PASOK's rise to power, that is 1974–81, is characterised by an intensive and remarkably successful democratisation and modernisation process. Nevertheless this process had also its 'darker side', the main characteristics of which were the 'anticommunist' and socially exclusive state strategies, which had created deep cleavages in the Greek political scene (Diamandouros, 1997). It was these ideological cleavages and hatreds that the coalition governments of 1989/90 put at rest.

57 Pappas (2001) argues that the reason for the decline of the polarisation in Greek politics is to be found in the 'new party system' which emerged after the 1981 elections.

58 Progressive Democrats 'had initially resulted from a division within Fianna Fáil over its policies in relation to Northern Ireland, but quickly

won support from elements in both major parties [Fianna Fáil and Fine Gael] on the basis of its essentially conservative economic policies and liberal stance on "moral" issues' (Mair, 1999: 141).

59 Both 1997 and 2002 elections led to a coalition government between Fianna Fáil and the Progressive Democrats. Marsh and O'Malley (1999: 425) referring to the 1997 elections note: 'In fact, Fianna Fáil lost one seat to the Labour party. It did not manage to convince the electorate that there would be advantage in making government less dependent on independents for parliamentary majority'. This trend was enhanced in the 2002 elections, one characteristic of which was the considerable increase in the power of small parties (Green Party and Sinn Fein). Finally, the 2007 elections led to a coalition government between Fianna Fáil, the Green Party and the Progressive Democrats (which lost most of its electoral power).

Part II

Institutional reproduction and social transformation: the hegemonic discourse of globalisation in action (1995–2001)

The literature on the emergence of globalisation discourse in specific countries is not as developed as one would expect. Significant contributions in this regard include the works by Hay (2001) and Kjaer and Pedersen (2001) on the diffusion/translation of neoliberal norms in the UK and Denmark respectively. The analysis of the deployment of the discourse of globalisation by New Labour in Britain, by Hay and Watson (1999), has also been an important contribution. Hay and Watson argued that the impact of globalisation on the British political economy 'may be more rhetorical than substantive, *but no less real for this*' (ibid.: emphasis in the original; see also Rosamond, 1999, 1999a). Pushing this line of inquiry further, Hay and Rosamond (2002) attempted one of the first mappings of the different ways in which the phenomenon of globalisation has been conceptualised and treated in different European countries, using as case studies Britain, France, Germany and Italy (see also Antoniades, 2007). They concluded that in all these cases globalisation was strategically deployed to legitimate specific social and economic reforms. They also found that the mode and characteristics of that deployment remained 'strikingly different' in different national settings (Hay and

Rosamond, 2002: 22). Two volumes on regional and national perspectives on globalisation, edited by Paul Bowles *et al.* (2007, 2007a), have enriched this literature on globalisation, although their focus is only partly on globalisation discourse. Nicola Smith (2005) was one of the first authors that attempted an in-depth country-specific study on the impact of globalisation discourse, focusing on the Irish case. Confirming the analysis of Hay and Watson (1999) she claimed that '[i]n acting as if globalisation were a material reality, Irish policy makers may actually be creating the very outcomes they attribute to globalisation itself'. This research was then pushed forward by Hay and Smith (2005, 2008), through a comparison of the UK and Ireland.

In the aforementioned literature much of the emphasis is on attitudes, narratives and strategic deployment. Here in contrast the main emphasis is on the (re)production of actors and domestic realms. Within this framework Part II examines the materialisation of the globalisation discourse in Greece and Ireland. The focus is on domestic institutional actors. What are their main issues of concern and how do they relate to globalisation (if they do so)? How is globalisation discourse implicated in their positions, policies and discourses? How do the various institutional discourses on globalisation 'speak' to and 'lie' on each other, and how are they locked in, and evolved, at a national level? What is the changing balance of power between the various institutional actors and what are the main drivers of it? In so doing, the aim is to examine how the hegemonic is internalised and biopolitically transforms national settings, public discourses and their agents. In this way we also aspire to shed light on the power conditions that underlie the way in which the *hegemonic* is materialised at a national level.

Hence, this analysis has two aspects. At a first-order level it is exemplified that the practices that are generated by the globalisation discourse produce clear 'winners' and 'losers'. They both benefit and damage, empower and weaken social actors in the same social setting. Therefore the analysis of the 'politics' of globalisation discourse, in terms of its impact on the organised, vested and mediated interests and interest structures, is put forward with a double purpose: first to examine how the hegemonic discourse influences the existing institutional configuration at the national level (i.e. which actors are empowered and which are weakened or marginalised); second to examine how the existing institutional configuration influences the way in which the 'politics' of the hegemonic discourse is produced and negotiated at the national level.

On a second-order level, however, the proposed research aims to illustrate that while the politics of a hegemonic discourse is negotiated, this discourse has a deeper biopolitical effect on the subjects of the public discourses and through them on the public discourses themselves. Thus, while social actors are negotiating how the 'new conditions' (e.g. 'globalisation') should be dealt with, in fact they materialise these 'new conditions', and thus also experience their consequences.

We start our investigation with the case of Greece, and we turn to Ireland in chapter 4. We then summarise and compare our findings in chapter 5.

3

Globalisation discourse in Greece

The study of the materialisation of globalisation discourse in Greece aims to examine the effect that this discourse had in the reproduction of the Greek public discourse and politico-economic system. Some broader contextualisation might be helpful here. It was argued in chapter 2 that 1990 could be considered a turning point for Greek politics. In the same framework it can also be argued that 1996 signified both the consolidation of this turning point and a new significant shift in Greek public discourse. In particular in 1996 Andreas Papandreou, the historical leader of PASOK, who had returned to power with the elections of 1993, died. This event symbolically brought to an end the period of charismatic leaders in Greek politics. The other side of this development was that Costas Simitis, against all odds, replaced Papandreou as the leader of the PASOK government, and within a few months was also elected president of the party. Simitis was part of the 'modernisation wing' of PASOK that was always a minority within the party (see Featherstone, 2005a). This wing was defined in opposition to Papandreou's populist style of governing, and had only little influence, if any, in the bureaucratic party machine. It is indicative that Simitis had resigned from the position of minister of national economy in 1987, during a Papandreou government, accusing the latter of violating the agreed governmental programme of economic stabilisation. It should also be mentioned here that this political stance of Simitis and PASOK's modernisers, made them, if not popular, sympathetic to many voters of both the New Democracy (right-to-centre) and Synaspismos (left).

These developments constituted the peak of the shift that had taken place in 1989–90. The Greek political system seemed to leave behind the increased polarisation and the 'Koskotas scandal', and an old political project, that of 'modernisation', seemed to form a new and dynamic historical block, creating a new public discourse which challenged the traditional party division lines. Based on these trends, it can be argued that 1996 signified the emergence of a new public discourse. The purpose here is to study how this changing public discourse in Greece interacted with the emerging, in the same period, globalisation discourse; how the hegemonic discourse was implicated in the public discourse formation, and how, conversely, the emerging public discourse was created and expressed in the terms of the globalisation discourse. The institutional actors examined for this purpose are the main political parties (PASOK, ND, the Communist Party of Greece (KKE), Synaspismos) and their leaders (respectively C. Simitis, K. Karamanlis, A. Papariga, N. Constantopoulos), the main social partners, (the Greek General Confederation of Labour (GSEE), the Federation of Greek Industries (SEV), the Economic and Social Council of Greece (OKE)) the church and a press sample (the Sunday edition of the newspaper *To VIMA*). It should be mentioned here that there may be slight differences in the period of examination of each institutional actor. Thus although the overall span of our research is from 1995 to 2001, in the case of political parties for instance, I take as a point of departure the electoral year 1996. Whenever such variations in the examination period do apply, a detailed reasoning is offered. The analysis of the institutional actors takes place as follows: first, where necessary, the identity of the actors/institutions is presented; second, the rationale of the analysed documents is discussed. Finally, the nature of engagement with the globalisation discourse is analysed. All translations of the official documents in this chapter are mine, unless otherwise stated.

The main political parties and their leaders

The criterion for the selection of the political parties to be studied was a double one: first, their 'representativeness', as expressed by votes in the national elections; and second their continuity in the political scene. In this regard the following parties were examined: (a) the Πανελλήνιο Σοσιαλιστικό Κίνημα/Panhellenic Socialist Movement (PASOK), which during the 1990s won the 1993, 1996 and 2000 elections. PASOK is a centre/left-to-centre party. (b) The Νέα Δημοκρατία/New Democracy (ND), which during the same period won the 1991 elections. ND is a right-to-centre party. (c) The Κομμουνιστικό Κόμμα Ελλάδας /Communist Party of Greece (KKE), which was the third biggest party in Greek politics, and has steadily been represented in parliament since its foundation in 1974. KKE is a traditional communist party. (d) The Συνασπισμός της Αριστεράς και της Προόδου/Coalition of the Left and Progress (Synaspismos), which was the fourth biggest Greek party in the 1990s. Synaspismos is a 'progressive' left party. It was founded in 1989, and with the exception of the 1993 elections, it was the only small party which had a constant presence in the Greek parliament during the period 1990–2001 (for the Greek party system, see Pappas, 2003; Lyrintzis, 2005; Nicolacopoulos, 2005).

In order to study the engagement of the above parties with the globalisation discourse, their electoral manifestos and the speeches and interviews of their leaders were analysed for the period 1996–2000. The analysis of the party electoral manifestos[1] was based on a 'double reading' methodology. First, I examined how the manifestos mobilised the concept of globalisation (παγκοσμιοποίηση), along with its derivatives such as globalised, globalising and global. Here the focus of the analysis was on content and context of these references, as well as how the different references within each manifesto related to each other. Second, I examined what were the dominant concepts and themes in these manifestos irrespective of the concept of globalisation. Finally, for each party separately, the manifesto of 1996 was compared with that of 2000 in order to trace changes and continuities in discourse, stance and strategy. For the collection of the speeches and interviews of party leaders I used the official party on-line archives that contained the public pronouncements of their leaders since approximately the beginning of 1997.[2] These pronouncements include: (a) speeches delivered in parliament and at events organised by a wide variety of social organisations and associations; (b) short statements made in a variety of occasions (e.g. new year messages, comments on the air strikes in Kosovo, comments on industrial actions, etc.); and (c) interviews in the press or on TV. In this regard, the on-line party archives constitute a great source for the study of party leaders' discourses. The rationale was that even if this material did not include all the public interventions of the political leaders during 1997–2000, it included a critical mass, able to give us an accurate picture of the discourses of political leaders. With regard to methodology, a 'key-word-in-context' and a 'word-count' methodology were combined.[3] The keyword given was 'globalisation' (παγκοσμιοποίηση). Wherever it was judged necessary, more key keywords were examined (e.g. globality/παγκοσμιότητα).

Panhellenic Socialist Movement (PASOK)

Electoral manifestos 1996, 2000
PASOK published electoral manifestos for both the 1996 and 2000 elections. The 1996 manifesto (PASOK, 1996) was characterised by an internal tension. At the level of the broader ideological platform of the party, as this was set out in the introductory section of the manifesto, and with regard to economic globalisation, references to the danger of a 'new barbarism' (6),[4] as well as to 'the domination of a narrow economic logic which has profit as its absolute criterion' (ibid.), 'social injustice' and 'exploitation' (ibid.) were dominant. Therefore a rather negative stance towards economic globalisation was adopted. Yet at the various sectoral, policy specific sections of the manifesto (e.g. on the economy and education), globalisation and economic globalisation were recognised as a given historical condition, as a/the new international structure. Consequently, the urgent need for adjustment to the new conditions was repeatedly underlined. The following extract is indicative in this regard: 'We live in a period of unrelenting competition among countries, in which the main stake is who will succeed in adjusting more, faster and more effectively in the new models of production and competition that have emerged. It's not enough to keep going. We must go faster than the others' (35). Along similar lines, while the manifesto criticised the ND for demanding 'less state and privatisations' (37), it itself propagated the need for a more flexible state and flexibility in industrial relations. In conclusion it can be argued that when the *new reality* and its requirements were under discussion in the various sectoral sections of the manifesto, the ideological stance of the party was neutralised or just ignored.

As in 1996, the 2000 manifesto (PASOK, 2000) gave primacy to the concept of globalisation, but this time in a positive way. In the opening statement of the manifesto, globalisation was conceptualised as a phenomenon that created 'new relations, new problems, new political questions and challenges which need to be met' (8; see also 9). This introductory statement included also a subsection, entitled 'the security of our society in conditions of globalisation' (10), where it was stated that: '[w]e consider that market liberalisation, globalisation, the restructuring of the production and technological change constitute the driving forces for development' (10). The concept of globalisation was also prominent in the various sectoral/policy sections, where globalisation was presented as a 'new reality', a new set of conditions which required particular actions at the domestic level. Furthermore, the manifesto was full of references to a 'new economy' (for instance 6, 58, 59), a 'new age' (1, 58, 59, 130, 131) or as already mentioned to a 'new reality' (16). Thus, there is indeed a clear shift in PASOK's position towards globalisation between 1996 and 2000. Abandoning the negative stance adopted in 1996, the 2000 manifesto attempted to present globalisation as a new reality and a positive challenge for economic development. These trends were conducive to the emerging international debate between social democratic parties and leaders, on the issues of 'the future of social democracy', the 'third way' and 'progressive governance'.

Party leader: Costas Simitis
The concept of globalisation figured prominently in the public pronouncements of Costas Simitis, prime minister and president of PASOK, during the period 1996–2004. In particular, from the 347 documents (including speeches, interviews and other statements) that were available in PASOK's electronic archive for the period 1997–2000, 68 were found to include an explicit reference to globalisation; that is approximately 20% of the total. The evolution of these references was as follows. In 1997, 23.6% of Simitis' public pronouncements included a reference to globalisation, and this figure was 29% in 1998, 6.7% in 1999, and 21.1% in 2000. It is important to underline here that these numbers and percentages should be treated as indicators of tendencies and not as absolute figures. Many of the examined speeches and statements were delivered on occasions when a reference to globalisation would be rather 'out of context' (e.g. short public statements on domestic issues such as presidential elections). Taking this into consideration, the fact that the percentage of public interventions that made a reference to globalisation remained as high as 20% is indeed striking. Therefore, the first general observation to be made is that globalisation constituted a constant theme, an integral part, of the prime minister's discourse. Furthermore, considering the dynamic of references during the years 1997 (23.6% of Simitis' public interventions) and 1998 (39%), it can be argued that globalisation was also implicated in the 'modernisation project' discourse of PASOK, and through it, it became an integral feature of Greek public discourse.

Figure 3.1 classifies the 68 pronouncements that made a reference to globalisation, in different categories, according to the content of these references.

As evident in Figure 3.1 the great bulk of Simitis' references to

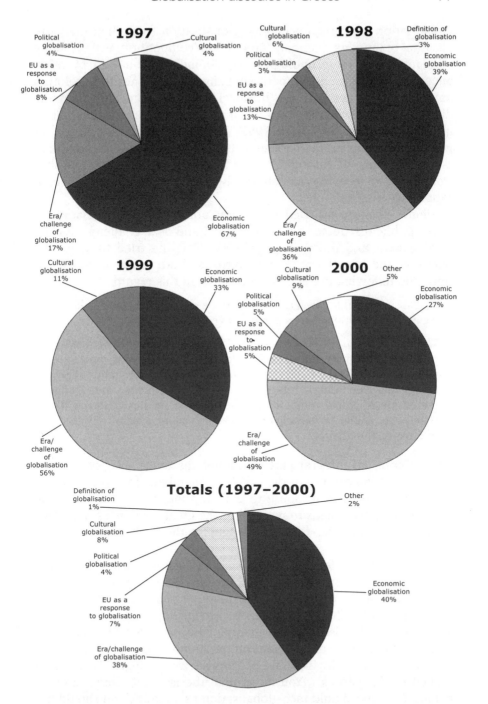

Figure 3.1 Content of Simitis' references to globalisation (1997–2000)

globalisation concerned economic globalisation (including the globalisation of markets/economy/production/competition, usually along
with references to technological developments), followed by references to globalisation as a new 'challenge' or 'era'. Yet the evolution
of these references was not linear. There has been a shift in the
discourse of the prime minister from an emphasis on economic globalisation, during the years 1997–98, to a broader depiction of
globalisation as a new era and as a challenge that had to be faced and
taken advantage of, during the years 1999–2000. This signified a shift
from a *passive* to a *proactive* approach to the phenomenon of globalisation (see also below).

Simitis strenuously tried to present and defend globalisation in
Greek public discourse as a 'new reality', and as a 'challenge' for the
development and prosperity of Greece. Thus he tried to stress the
potential and benefits of taking control and advantage of globalisation. The following extracts are indicative in this regard.

> Globalisation is not only a challenge for the country but also a field that
> we are well-positioned to take advantage of.[5]

> The globalisation of the economy and the development of technology
> create opportunities and capacities to those able to adjust and those
> who have the will and the creativity to take advantage of them ... Tech-
> nology and globalisation integrate the national economies and change
> the nature of global competition. They give to smaller countries like
> Greece the ability to participate further and more dynamically in the
> international markets.[6]

Furthermore, an integral part of Simitis' discourse on globalisation
was also the importance of the Greek EU membership and the importance of the EU as a response to globalisation dynamics. 'European
integration is the means to respond to the great challenges that characterise our era. The first [challenge] is the globalisation of the
economy.'[7]

A decisive factor for the development of Simitis' discourse on globalisation was his confrontation on exactly this issue with the head of
the Greek church, Archbishop Christodoulos. As analysed below, by
1999 the Greek church through its Archbishop had developed an
explicitly hostile discourse towards globalisation. Simitis was asked
on several occasions to comment on the Archbishop's negative stance
and rhetoric. In a high-profile TV interview in 'Mega Channel', he
replied in this context: 'You mentioned the issue of globalisation; I
believe that one should face globalisation as a reality, and should not
fight it. What one should fight for is to adjust the country to

globalisation ...'.[8] In a similar context, responding to a question about the danger of global cultural homogenisation, raised by the Archbishop, he replied that Greece should respond to this danger with increased 'cultural production', rather than closeness.[9] Finally, gradually Simitis used globalisation with reference to an expanding list of issues such as international governance/political globalisation and crime.

New Democracy (ND)

Electoral manifestos 1996,[10] 2000
The economic manifesto for the 1996 national elections (published by ND in 1995) made no explicit reference to the term globalisation. It seems however that instead of this term, the concepts of 'internationalisation' and 'internationalisation of the world economy' were used to signify the same developments. Furthermore, as with globalisation, the concept of internationalisation was used to signify the nature of the new international environment that, according to ND, necessitated a wide range of policy and structural changes in the Greek politico-economic system. The emphasis was on this need for adjustments. The manifesto did not take a stance towards the process of internationalisation. The latter was neither criticised nor applauded. It was just presented as the new international economic order.

As in 1995, the 2000 electoral manifesto (ND, 2000) did not develop a discourse on globalisation per se (the term was only used once). Yet there were many references to a 'new era' and a new 'global reality' (84) in which Greece had to adjust. In this context the manifesto referred positively to the phenomenon of the 'globalised economy', as one of 'the new big challenges' for the development of Greece (53), and included a reference to the concept of globality (παγκοσμιότητα) (32). Thus, avoiding the concept of globalisation, both ND's manifestos put forward the notion of an emerging new global reality that presented a developmental challenge, to which Greece should adjust in order to prosper.

Party leader: Kostas Karamanlis
After its defeat in the 1993 elections, the New Democracy party underwent an identity crisis, trying to delineate its political and ideological space. In this process, prominent neoliberal as well as extreme-right members of the party were marginalised or expelled. Kostas Karamanlis, who took over the presidency of ND from Miltiadis Evert on 22 March 1997, attempted to promote the concept of 'middle

ground' (μεσαίος χώρος) as both the political space of belonging and ideological orientation of the party.

Karamanlis avoided the concept of globalisation throughout the period under examination here. In particular, from the 556 documents (including speeches, interviews and other statements) that were available in ND's electronic archive for the period 1997–2000, only 42 were found to include a reference to globalisation or globality; that is approximately 8% of the total. More specifically the references to these concepts during 1998 and 1999 were negligible (1% and 2.2% of the examined documents respectively), while in 1997 they were 6.8% of the examined documents and only in 2000 rose to 18.3%. The latter increase, however, signified an increase in the use of the term globality that Karamanlis used most of the time, after 1999, instead of the term globalisation. Figure 3.2 offers a clearer picture of the content of Karamanlis' (limited) discourse on globalisation. There are no figures presented for the years 1997 and 1998, as the number of absolute references were low.

For most of the period up to 2000 Karamanlis used the concept of globalisation in a narrow manner to refer to the international economic environment. However, the more the concept of globalisation was ideologically charged – both domestically and internationally – the more Karamanlis adopted a more critical stance towards it or avoided referring to it altogether. This should also explain the lack of references to globalisation in ND's electoral manifestos. At the same time the conceptualisation of the EU as a response to globalisation became an integral part of Karamanlis' discourse.

From the last months of 1999 the leader of the opposition started to make use of the more neutral concept of globality (παγκοσμιότητα). Karamanlis used globality along with technology and knowledge to define the nature of our age. The context of his references to globality was repetitive and served an introductory purpose in his speeches. The following extract is characteristic of these references, and was also found in the 2000 electoral manifesto:

> It is a common belief that the world is at the end of an era and the beginning of another. We are already at the first stage of the post-industrial era. The first stage of the era of globality, technology and knowledge. The developments in all the sectors of human activity have acquired an unprecedented speed.[11]

The concept of globality gave to Karamanlis an ideological-free alternative to the concept of globalisation. Its use could itself be considered as a critique of the concept of globalisation as a 'challenge

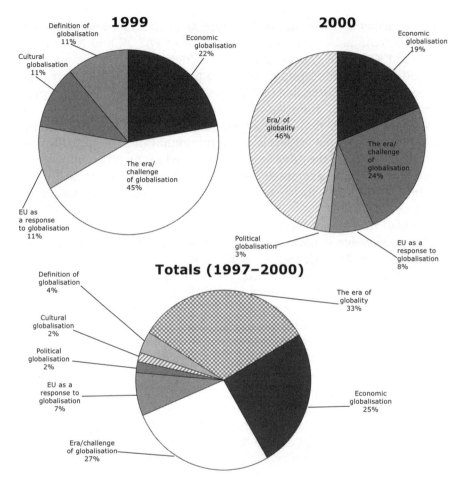

Figure 3.2 Content of Karamanlis' references to globalisation
(1997–2000)

for development' advanced by Simitis. Thus Karamanlis was implicitly taking the Archbishop's side in the 'war' between the latter and the government, on the concept and consequences of globalisation; a move which no matter how genuine it was, was a convenient way to increase his party's popularity.

Communist Party of Greece (KKE)

Electoral manifestos 1996, 2000
The 1996 electoral manifesto of KKE (1996: np) made no reference to the concept of globalisation. This however was due to the fact that

the processes and conditions that were associated with globalisation and internationalisation in the manifestos of PASOK and ND, in the case of KKE, were conceptualised as a 'new imperialist order' that served the interest of 'plutocracy', and posed an immediate threat to Greece. Thus the discourse of KKE remained grounded in a conceptualisation of the international politico-economic order as an imperialist terrain that served particular economic interests. Along these lines the increased levels of internationalisation or globalisation signified, for KKE, the advancement of an old plutocratic and imperialist order that promoted the interests of 'monopolies', the 'industrialists', the European Union and 'imperialist organisations' such as NATO.

Instead of a single electoral manifesto, in the 2000 elections KKE published twelve leaflets, with a sectoral (e.g. for farmers and self-employed) or thematic (e.g. on education and on the pension system) focus. Some of these leaflets did make reference to globalisation. For instance, the leaflet on education (KKE, 2000: np) claimed that, '[s]truggling ... to win the trust of the plutocracy, both PASOK and ND focus on the no-alternative of EMU and "globalisation"'. The KKE's main position in this electoral campaign was that globalisation was used by PASOK and ND as a means for justifying policy reforms that served the interests of 'big monopolies and multinationals corporations' in Greece. In both electoral campaigns KKE remained constant in its conceptualisation of the 'new world order' as an imperialist and plutocratic order, and accused the two big parties of using globalisation (and the EU) as an excuse to advance the changes demanded by plutocracy and its forces (mainly the multinational enterprises (MNEs)).

Party leader: Aleka Papariga[12]
Aleka Papariga, who was the leader of KKE throughout the period under examination here, adopted from the very beginning a highly critical approach to both the phenomenon of globalisation as such and the way in which globalisation was used by the government. The focal point of her discourse on globalisation was that it constituted a development inexorably related to the evolution and expansion of the capitalist system – it was the modern face of imperialism.[13] In this discourse the European Union was part of the 'imperialist problem', rather than part of its solution or a response to it, and both PASOK and ND were accused of using the rhetoric of globalisation to serve the interests of plutocracy in Greece. Thus on several occasions the central committee of KKE declared that, '[t]he one-way of "globalisa-

tion" and the "new order of things" that the government tries to impose, is fake'.[14] 'The workers can choose between two paths. Either they will be subjugated in the inhuman globalisation of EMU ... or they will follow the path of class struggle, adopting as their vision the overturning of the monopolies' domination and power'.[15]

Following this logic the KKE adopted an explicitly supportive stance towards the anti-globalisation movement (including its radical expressions). For instance, after the protests in Goteborg, in 2001, the central committee of KKE criticised Simitis for supporting 'state violence' that had led to 'hundreds of prosecutions and ... one clinically dead protester'.[16] Moreover, according to the central committee, these developments demanded 'an equally strong response to be given to the imperialist barbarism'. The announcement concluded that '[t]he struggle against NATO and EU is of vital importance'.[17]

Thus it can be argued that Papariga and KKE remained faithful to their traditional negative understanding of the European Union as a 'neoliberal project' that serves the interests of the global and local plutocracies. Along the same lines KKE, approached globalisation as a new form of imperialism that had to be resisted through class struggle.

Coalition of the Left and Progress (Synaspismos)

Considering the width of the gap between KKE on the one side, and PASOK and ND on the other, it is indeed interesting to see how Synaspismos positioned itself towards the changing international environment, of the time. Its 1996 electoral manifesto (Synaspismos, 1996: np) did not engage, at least directly, with the concept of globalisation. It propagated the need for a 'modernisation with a human face', and argued that '[t]he proposals of Synaspismos constitute and promote a modernisation which is not neutral, which is not a boring technocratic process'. In this regard it can be argued that Synaspismos was reading the need for modernisation of the Greek politico-economic system, not as something that was externally required, but as something that was a domestic societal need. Thus the manifesto attempted to relate the 'modernisation proposals' of PASOK and ND to bureaucratisation, and argued for a 'progressive' and 'people-driven' modernisation. Yet, since the manifesto was mainly domestically focused with no explicit reference to the 'new international conditions', no firm conclusions can be drawn on its stance towards globalisation.

The manifesto for the 2000 elections (Synaspismos, 2000: np) was much more internationally oriented. It analysed the 'problems and demands that emerged from the new reality that was characterised by the revolution in science and technology, and the globalisation of markets', and concluded that, *'the model of uncontrolled markets, and of the domination of market over society, cannot be the future of the country in the new century'* (emphasis in the original). Furthermore, the section on 'sustainable development' placed globalisation among the factors that damage the quality of human life. More generally, the focus of the manifesto was on the 'post-EMU' era in Greece. It attacked the 'neoliberal orthodoxy' and 'warn[ed] the Greek people that PASOK and ND prepare[d] ... a new round of deregulations and blood-sacking of the weaker social classes, in the name of the adjustment of the Greek economy in the post-euro reality'. Overall, it can be argued that the focal point of criticism in the manifesto was neoliberalism and the process of the domination of economy over society that was associated with the phenomenon of globalisation.

Party leader: Nicos Constantopoulos

Nicos Constantopoulos was Synaspismos's president during the period 1993–2004. From the 81 speeches of his that were examined for the period 1998–2000 only 11 made an explicit reference to the concept of globalisation (14% of the documents).[18] In particular, this figure (i.e. percentage of documents that made a reference to globalisation) was 14% in 1998, 18% in 1999 and 10% in 2000. Figure 3.3 offers some qualitative information on these references. As analysed below, however, this low number of references rather fails to capture the dynamic, continuity and coherence of Constantopoulos's critical discourse on globalisation.

The focal point of Constantopoulos's discourse was that the phenomenon of globalisation is a hegemonic ideology aiming at the subjugation of politics and society by the market. Constantopoulos's discourse was also decisive in the institutionalisation in the Greek public discourse of the critique of globalisation as an excuse used by the government to promote particular (neoliberal) policies and laws. The following extract is indicative in this regard:

> The government constantly uses the gospel of globalisation of market and the commandments of uncontrolled free competition, asking citizens to accept ... their subjugation in the economic, social, cultural and regional inequalities that are generated and getting deeper by the governmental policy itself.[19]

In the same manner, in his last speech before the 2000 elections he called for resistance to globalisation at the European level in order

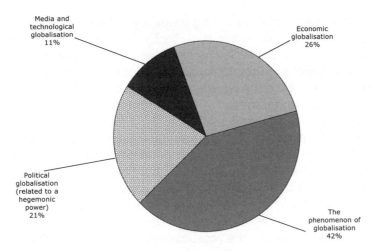

Figure 3.3 Content of Constantopoulos's references to globalisation (1998–2000)

'not to surrender democracy and society to uncontrolled globalisation'.

Finally, Constantopoulos tried to differentiate himself and his criticism from the critical stance towards globalisation taken by Archbishop Christodoulos. Within this framework he condemned critiques of globalisation that had as their reference point 'forces of darkness that aim to take the soul of our faith and destroy our national identity'.[20]

Party discourses: a first reflection on the findings

By studying the discourse of political parties and their leaders, we have examined one of the most fundamental nexuses of ideology production in Greece. During the period under examination, the party in power, PASOK, changed its stance towards globalisation significantly. From warnings against the danger of a 'new barbarism' in 1996, it moved to a relatively positive treatment of the concept of globalisation, as a 'new reality' that demanded domestic changes, and which was the driving force for international development. On the other hand ND had a more neutral approach from the outset. For this party, the internationalisation and globalisation processes signified a 'new global reality'; the ordering principle of a new era to which the country had to adjust. On the left of the political spectrum, the different positions seem to converge during the period under investigation. In 1996 KKE defined the 'new world order' as another plutocratic and imperialistic order, whereas Synaspismos argued for a modernisation with a human face, as an internal, societal necessity. Yet by 2000, both parties accused the PASOK government of using globalisation as an excuse, in order to promote particular neoliberal policies that were against the interests of the weakest social classes. Table 3.1 attempts to summarise these findings.

Moving from a rather static to a more dynamic frame of analysis, it can be argued that we observe the gradual emergence of globalisation as a new zone of contestation, a new political axis in Greek politics. This axis has globalisation as an 'opportunity for development' at one end, and as a 'new imperialism' at the other. Hence, globalisation either as a 'positive thing' and an opportunity for Greece, or as an excuse and a great imperialistic threat, came by the end of the twentieth century to dominate the vocabulary and the conceptual arena of the Greek politico-economic life, at least as the latter was reflected in the party discourses.

Consequently the examination of party discourses revealed a gradual but critical restructuring of Greek public discourse in terms of the hegemonic/globalisation. Thus the discourse of globalisation seems to have emerged as a new zone of contestation, a means through which social interests and conflicts were reordered and expressed anew. Moreover globalisation did not emerge, and was not communicated, as a thematic, issue-specific discourse. It was about the economy and the opportunities for future development, as it was about culture and the danger of homogenisation; it was about the environment and social inequalities, as it was about the role of the state and capitalism. It can thus be argued that the emergence of globalisation discourse in Greece was about the conceptualisation and definition of the conditions and environment the country was in. Put differently, globalisation was all about social becoming and everyday life, its constraints, its opportunities, its conditions of production and reproduction.

Ultimately this process of everyday life reconceptualisation and restructuring is about politics, because it carries with it the *politics of the hegemonic discourse*, in terms of power relationships and 'winners' and 'losers'. But it is not only about politics, at least when the latter is narrowly defined. It is also about biopolitics, i.e. the (re)production of *subjects*, their self-understanding and their social space of existence.

The Greek public discourse however cannot be boiled down to the discourses of the political parties and their leaders. Broader social institutions that underlie or/and interact with the world of political parties, such as the church, organised interests and the media have to

Table 3.1 Political party discourses on globalisation in Greece

Nature	Positive	Neutral	Negative	Negative	Negative
Content	Globalisation as an 'opportunity' for economic development	Globalisation as a 'new reality'/ 'new era'	Globalisation as an 'excuse' for neoliberal economic policy changes	Globalisation as a 'new barbarism'	Globalisation as a 'new imperialism'
Promoted by	PASOK (2000)	ND (1996, 2000) PASOK (1996, 2000)	Synaspismos (2000) KKE (1996, 2000)	PASOK (1996)	KKE (1996, 2000)

be taken into consideration. This is the subject of the following sections.

The Archbishop of Athens and All Greece, Christodoulos and the Greek church (1995–2001)

The church can exert significant influence in the formation of the Greek public discourse, and has the power to mobilise people when it feels that its interests are at stake.[21] In order to study the Greek church, the speeches and public pronouncements of Archbishop Christodoulos were examined. Such a narrowing down of the research cannot be fully representative of the various and diverse positions that existed within the Greek church in the second half of the 1990s. Yet, the Archbishop was the leader of the church and, in terms of public influence, was the single most important personality in it.

Globalisation figured most prominently in the Archbishop's discourse. From the 54 speeches, letters and interviews of his that were available in the on-line archive of the church of Greece (for the period 1995–2001), 12 made a reference to globalisation (i.e. 22%), and most of these references were rather extensive. Furthermore, most of these documents were gathered together in a thematic subdirectory devoted to 'globalisation' (the main directory was 'Europe'). In the English section of the website, 3 out of the 8 speeches made a reference to globalisation (i.e. 40%). Nevertheless, these figures do not really capture the influence that Archbishop Christodoulos exerted on Greek public discourse through his after-Mass talks every Sunday that were reproduced and commented on in the news, or through books and other publications that focused on the phenomenon of globalisation.

For the Archbishop, globalisation represented a great and multilevel threat not only for Greece but for European societies in general. He called for resistance against the 'thailandisation of Europe', arguing that 'development is the opposite trend, namely the elevation of the Thai and other poor populations to the standards of the Europeans' (Christodoulos, 1998). Within this context he stressed 'social solidarity' as a key aspect of the 'European model': 'the European civilization has been the product of a parallel action of two elements: of free economy and social solidarity. And we all Europeans paid very dearly whenever we hazarded to abolish that parallel action' (Christodoulos, 1999; original text in English).

Another key reference point of his globalisation discourse was 'Americanisation':

Is it, indeed, about globalisation? ... Instead, we have the exportation of a model, which belongs to only one country and the imposition of that model on other countries. Hence, whoever does not wish to play with words and the reality these words signify should speak of world Americanisation rather than globalisation – even if he does not a priori oppose Americanisation. (Christodoulos, 1999)

He also criticised the determinism found in the arguments of the proponents of globalisation by saying: 'there are many catastrophes which are inescapable, but this does not mean we are obliged to applaud them; on the contrary, we are obliged to find out ways, which can secure the survival of Man and civilization' (ibid.).

Most of these arguments were being replicated in his everyday speeches and interviews. For instance, in one of his speeches after a Sunday Mass he stressed:

Today the Church tries to protect the people from their entrapment in the new forms of the demonic. Today the implementation of globalisation is dramatic, and appears with the mask of global economic development ... globalisation is the means and not the end; it is the means which leads to the imposition of syncretism. Syncretism is promoted by the same forces which promote globalisation ... A second step in the promotion of syncretism is the cold planned effort for the destruction of Christianity. (Christodoulos, 2000)

Hence, Archbishop Christodoulos conceptualised globalisation as a manipulated process, which was driven by particular interests that aimed at the 'annihilation' of the cultural diversity around the world in general, and the 'Christian discolouring of Europe' and thus of Greece in particular (see also Christodoulos, 2002). The main reference points of his discourse were Americanisation, American cultural imperialism, the danger of cultural homogenisation, secularisation, social estrangement and individualism/egocentrism. It would not be an exaggeration to say that he personified and declared a war on globalisation. Sometimes, the object of this war was concrete, for instance the protection of the European socio-political model. Yet, most of the time more abstract and transcendental categories were employed to describe the 'enemy', such as the 'forces of evil'. Concluding, it can be argued that the Archbishop was very effective in articulating a discourse of globalisation as a real and immediate threat to the Greek national identity and way of life. This anti-globalisation stance of the Archbishop created a wide popular trend against globalisation. His critics have argued that the demonisation of globalisation by the Archbishop, was one way of securing and justifying the active role of church in the Greek socio-political system.

The social partners: employers, workers, and the social and economic council

While studying the social partners, both in Greece and Ireland, it is important to keep in mind the developments at the EU level as a significant backdrop. We refer to these developments below, but it should be mentioned here that since the mid-1990s the dialogue within the European employers' associations (UNICE, European Centre of Employers and Enterprises providing Services (CEEP)) and workers' unions (ETUC) had been enhanced. This interplay between the European and the national levels becomes clear also from the fact that the national employers' associations and workers' unions used UNICE's and ETUC's decisions and positions, in order to promote or justify their ideas, positions and policies within their domestic institutional settings. Yet the dialogue was not only enhanced within but also between the European social partners, especially after the Treaty of Amsterdam in 1997, with which this dialogue was institutionalised (see Berndt and Platzer, 2003; Hoffmann *et al.*, 2000). This led to increased pressures from the EU on its member states to institutionalise domestic tripartite consultation mechanisms. The member states were forced to create (if they did not already have in place) policy mechanisms that institutionalised the participation of social partners in various aspects of their public policy-making, a development that had considerable impact both on domestic public discourses and policy-making processes. Finally, relevant events and developments at the international level, such as the International Labour Organisation (ILO) annual conferences or reports published by the OECD and the International Monetary Fund (IMF), also exerted common influence on the respective social partners' discourses and strategies.

Federation of Greek Industries (SEV)[22]

Considering the widespread penetration of political parties in the structure of interest representation in Greece, it can be argued that SEV is the most enduring and 'party-independent' group of organised interests that has ever existed in the Greek industrial relations system. In order to capture SEV's discourse, the following documents were analysed: (a) the annual activity reports (Απολογισμός, henceforth 'annual report' or 'Report') of SEV for the period 1995–2001; and (b) the speeches of SEV's chairmen, during the annual meetings of SEV's general assembly for the period 1998–2001.[23]

The main conclusion from the analysis of SEV's discourse is that it did not develop, or attempt to develop, a discourse on globalisation as such. Thus the concept of globalisation was not prominent in SEV's official publications nor in the speeches of its chairmen. SEV's discourse and strategy were focused on the need for 'structural changes'. Key themes here were the need for the acceleration of privatisations, the redefinition of the role of state in the economy, the need for greater flexibility in the labour market and the deregulation of the Greek economy. Thus the 'dominant objects' of economic globalisation discourse ('flexibility', 'privatisation', 'deregulation' and the need for a smaller state) were at the heart of SEV's discourse. In this context, it is also interesting that SEV translated the 'race to the bottom' debate[24] as proof of the need for immediate and 'brave' economic reforms. On this basis it criticised PASOK's 'tax reform' (promoted with the law 2753/99) as limited and ineffective (see SEV, 2000: 33–35). Furthermore, it severely criticised PASOK for organising a 'fake' social dialogue that resulted 'in the creation of rigidities in the organisation of labour and in the rise of labour cost' (SEV, 2001: 60–61).

The lack of references to globalisation could be explained by the fact that the 'economic side' of globalisation discourse did not offer something new in the discourse of SEV. The arguments in favour of privatisation, deregulation and competitiveness had always been central to SEV's interventions in the public discourse. As Iason Stratos put it, 'globalisation and the need for adjustment to market forces was not something new for SEV; it was what SEV was fighting for since the late 1980s'.[25] On the other hand, after 1995, globalisation was increasingly charged with a heavy ideological content, and arguably SEV's leadership wanted to avoid associating its policy prescriptions with a concept towards which a large number of Greek people were negatively predisposed.

In order to understand the dynamics at work in the formation of SEV's discourse, one should also turn to the developments at the European level. The 'Essen strategy', that is the 'five action points' agreed in the European Council in Essen in December 1994, constituted an important point of reference that became a focal point in SEV's discourse. The second 'action point' of the Essen strategy referred to flexibility, suggesting that employment and economic growth could increase 'through a flexible organisation of work and working time, moderate wage settlements and new areas of employment'.[26] Another important development in this context was the publication of the 'Concluding Report' of the 'Molitor group',[27] on the simplification and deregulation of European and national legal frameworks; a report which also triggered a UNICE report, published in

October 1995. It is also worth mentioning here that with the Treaty of Amsterdam, competitiveness became a main task for the European Union (see respective reference in SEV, 1998: 122). These European-level developments were instrumental in the formation of SEV's discourse, strategy and policy.

The aforementioned EU pressures on its member states to institutionalise tripartite consultation mechanisms in their public policy was also an important factor in SEV's changing role in Greek public policy setting. SEV's representatives were participating in an ever-longer list of public committees and working groups (SEV, 1998: 22, 92). The following instance is characteristic of these institutional changes. In the European Council in Luxembourg (November 1997), the member states agreed to submit each year a 'national action plan' for employment that the national governments had to prepare in consultation with their social partners. Yet the first plan submitted by the Greek government in 1998 had not followed this consultation process. Following the criticism of the European Commission, the Ministry of Labour was forced to change its policy process, accommodating the requirement for consultation (SEV, 2000: 22). Within this context another important development was the creation by SEV and GSEE in November 1996 of the National Observatory for Industrial Relations.[28]

To conclude, it can be argued that SEV was very active in promoting the economics and politics of globalisation (in terms of the 'needed structural adjustments') and generating a discourse based on the 'dominant objects' of economic globalisation, such as 'anti-statism', 'privatisations', 'deregulation' and 'flexibility'. Its overall strategy and discourse was characterised by a 'new reality' approach to globalisation, even if the term globalisation itself was generally avoided.

Greek General Confederation of Labour (GSEE)[29]

Traditionally, GSEE was dominated by political parties, and thus the potential for the articulation of an independent stance and discourse was extremely limited.[30] Since the beginning of the 1990s, however, GSEE started, if very slowly, to acquire a more independent stance. Two factors have played a significant role in this change. First, was the integration of GSEE in the structures of social partnership at a European level. These structures, as has been argued, demanded an institutionally independent role from GSEE in public policy making (see also the respective SEV section). The intensification of the interaction between GSEE and the workers' unions of other EU member states also had a significant impact on the changing nature of GSEE. These developments led to the creation by GSEE of the Institute of Labour (INE), in December 1990;[31] a think-tank aiming to 'scientifically' support the Greek 'trade union movement'.[32] INE, which is chaired by the chairman of GSEE, has invested GSEE with an epistemic capacity that significantly enhanced its ability to develop an independent role and discourse. Thus INE broke the tradition that wanted 'scientific' research and arguments to come only from the government or SEV (leaving GSEE to manifesto-like interventions). Moreover, the creation of INE, i.e. an independent unit of analysis and a pool of experts, reduced GSEE's dependency on political parties and their experts.

To examine the role of GSEE in the materialisation of the globalisation discourse, I analysed INE's monthly newsletter *Enimerosi* for the period 1995–2000.[33] During 1995–96, the concept of globalisation did not figure significantly in the argumentation and public interventions of GSEE. Instead, the focal point of its discourse and critique was the concept of 'neoliberalism', as well as the issues of 'flexibility' and 'deregulation' (which were also in the front line of SEV's public interventions).

In 1995 the pressure for 'structural adjustments' was translated in Greece into the flexibility in labour market vs. reduction of working-hours debate. Responding to pressures for flexibility in the labour market, exercised by SEV and the government, GSEE focused on the issue of a 35–hour working week, and indeed it succeeded in bringing this issue onto the public agenda, forcing both the government and the employers' associations to take a stance on this subject.[34] A demand for a 35–hour week was also adopted by the 8th Congress of ETUC, in 1995.[35]

This confrontation was carried forward in 1996, and in general remained central throughout the period 1995–2000. In its positions that were publicised in March 1996, GSEE rejected 'the unrestrained "flexibility" that deregulates the social life of employees and increases their insecurity and exploitation'.[36] Yet it remained within the 'game', asking 'for ... the establishment of minimum requirements for the implementation of part time and other flexible practices', rather than rejecting flexibility policies altogether.[37] This modest strategy bore fruits. In a survey on the issue of the 35-hour week conducted by DIMEL on a significant sample of Greek companies, the results were as follows: 40% replied that the unions' demand was right, 25% that it was premature, 29% that it would create problems in the function of companies and 6% did not answer.[38]

During the same year the concepts of internationalisation and 'globalisation of markets and economies'[39] started to gain increasing visibility in GSEE's vocabulary. Internationalisation along with 'new technologies' was conceptualised as the new defining parameter of industrial relations.[40] Neoliberalism, however, remained the main point of reference. In this context, Professor Pierre Bourdieu was invited to give a lecture to GSEE on 16 October 1996. He argued for the need to create an 'anti-trend, against the trend of neoliberalism', and criticised the 'fatalisme néolibéral', i.e. the tendency to approach neoliberalism as a historically inevitable process.[41] Christos Polizo-gopoulos, the chairman of GSEE, in his welcoming remarks for Bourdieu's speech, referred to 'neoliberal policies that diminish the welfare state and workers' rights'.[42]

It was not until 1997 that the concept of 'globalisation' came under GSEE's spotlight, along with the distinction between different models of capitalism. With regard to the latter, GSEE, in its written response to the government's proposal for a 'Social Dialogue', argued:

> The demand for adjustment to the new laws of global competition leads to the transfer of practices and experiences that ... dominate at the 'Atlantic side'. These practices demolish the European social model ... and deregulate the system of labour relations ... developments which do not fit in the traditions and vested rights of the European people.[43]

GSEE's approach was based on the conceptualisation of globalisation as market domination.[44] The way in which *Enimerosi* reacted to an IMF report published in 1997 is also indicative of the position that globalisation had acquired in GSEE's discourse. The report (*World Economic Outlook,* May 1997) had as its main subject the effects of globalisation, and one of its conclusions was that globalisation in the form of competition from low-wage countries 'does not seem to constitute the main factor for the negative developments in employment and income distribution which are observed in many advanced economies' (ibid.). *Enimerosi*'s editorial comment, was that 'what of course the IMF report does not mention is how many rushed and wrong decisions have been taken in the EU during the last five years due to exactly this erroneous dominant belief with regard to globali-sation'.[45]

After 1997 globalisation remained central to GSEE's discourse. It was treated more and more as an excuse used by SEV and the government to promote their (neoliberal) policies. During this period, Dimitris Katsoridas, an economic analyst in INE, published widely on the issue of globalisation in *Enimerosi*. One of his first articles was

'The Globalisation of the Economy: Myth or Reality?', where he argued that 'the concept of "globalisation" is often used with ideological purposes, to bend workers' resistance ... by supporting the 'inevitable' and the 'omnipotence' of the market-without-frontiers'.[46] This conceptualisation of globalisation as an instrument for policy justification dominated INE's discourse. Another article published in 2000 and signed by three of the main economic analysts of INE, N. Grammatikos, D. Katsoridas, G. Kollias, argued:

> In most cases the term 'globalisation' is used as an inaccessible – enforced from the outside – force, to which states have no choice but to adjust. Moreover, it is used as an excuse for the introduction of changes in labour market.[47]

At the same time other aspects of the international anti-globalisation discourse were also acquiring a prominent position in the public interventions of GSEE. For instance, at the 9th Convention of ETUC in Finland, at June 1999, GSEE submitted a proposal 'for the implementation of the TOBIN-Tax'.[48] Moreover, the general council of GSEE, in its decision taken on 10 December 1999 (after the Seattle protests) urged for 'flexibility within socially accepted limits' and stated that: 'The General Council supports the need for *international solidarity* among workers, in order to put a limit to the omnipotence and arrogance of globalised economic power'[49] (emphasis in the original).

To sum up, globalisation acquired a prominent position in the discourse of GSEE, after 1997. Furthermore, maybe for the first time in its history, GSEE was not the social partner which followed a policy of slogans, but the partner which accused the government and SEV of doing so, trying at the same time to scrutinise the phenomenon of globalisation by using 'scientific' evidence and data (see also below).

Beyond the emergence of globalisation discourse, the study of *Enimerosi* for the period 1995–2001 revealed a number of dynamics that were at work in Greek industrial relations and institutions, during the second half of the 1990s. First, is the gradual normalisation of the relationship between workers and employers, and the intensification of the process for the construction of a 'social partnership'. Indicatively, a joint publication by INE and the Federation of Industries of North Greece (published in 1995) was described by C. Protopapas, the chairman of GSEE in 1995, as an innovation for Greece.[50]

Second, one clearly observes the first instances of a more proactive and epistemic stance of the labour movement in Greece. For instance, GSEE managed to put into the public agenda the issue of the 35-hour working week.[51] In order to support this demand, a number of 'scientific' articles were published by the research team of INE from 1995 onwards.[52] The publication, for the first time, of an 'Annual Review of the Greek Economy' by GSEE, in 1999 (along with the traditionally published annual reviews by the Bank of Greece and SEV) was also part of this new dynamic. Such a scientific approach was gradually adopted for many issues that were raised in public agenda and were of interest to GSEE. At the same time, as in the case of SEV, the EU integration process necessitated GSEE's independence, while its representatives were increasingly invited to sit in committees and working groups at various ministries.[53] This rapid trend towards an 'epistemisation' of GSEE (i.e. a more 'scientifically centred' public intervention) triggered internal reactions and accusations over the 'bureaucratisation' of the Greek labour movement. In this context, when GSEE consented to the 'Social Dialogue' proposed by the government in 1997, it also made it explicit that this Dialogue would 'not replace the action of trade unions'.[54] Furthermore, the decision of the Annual Convention of INE/GSEE into 1997 included the following caveat: 'The transformation of INE into either a public relations mechanism or a tool for the bureaucratisation of the syndicalist movement ... must be avoided'.[55]

Third, one can observe an impressive level of interaction and knowledge transfer between the trade unions of the EU countries. In this regard, numerous common projects with other trade unions through the FORCE-NEPTURE, the Association for European Training of Workers on the Impact of New Technology (AFETT) and the LEONARDO DA VINCI programme (on vocational training) were mentioned in *Enimerosi*'s pages. Furthermore, the interaction and knowledge transfer between Greece and the rest of the Balkan countries increased rapidly after 1995 (the PHARE programme was essential in this regard).[56] For instance in 1996 INE/GSEE worked with its counter-part FRATIA in Romania for the development of the Romanian Institute of Labour, co-organised a seminar in Bulgaria on electronic communications and labour unions, and co-organised a training programme on collective bargaining and social pacts in Albania.[57] It is worth mentioning that such an interaction was not entirely centralised, but was also taking place through the various peripheral or sectoral channels and institutes which constitute INE. For instance, the sectoral institute of INE which specialises in banking and securities (INE/OTOE) was very active in developing various joint projects with Albania, Bulgaria, Romania, FYR Macedonia, Serbia and Cyprus through the LEONARDO and PHARE programmes and AFETT.[58]

The Economic and Social Council (OKE)[59]

It should be noted from the outset that OKE's influence in Greek public discourse, since its creation in 1997, has been minimal, if not negligible. Yet its analysis does provide some interesting information on the interaction of social partners on the issue of globalisation.

In July 2000 the European Economic and Social Committee (EESC), of which OKE is a member, discussed in a plenary session a working paper on the issue of globalisation of trade in the framework of the World Trade Organisation (WTO). As a follow-up of this event and in order to contribute to the globalisation debate in Greece, OKE published an 'Opinion' paper, entitled 'The Globalisation of Trade in the Framework of WTO' in October 2000. This document, albeit close to the end of the period under investigation, is important because it is the only single document which was explicitly about globalisation, and was prepared by all social partners (i.e. government, workers, employers). The second section of this document was entitled 'the positions of OKE' and started as follows:

> Greece is a country which has been integrated in the phenomenon of globalisation, thus facing both the prospects and the consequences that are generated by it. Yet the dialogue on this issue in our country has not acquired the publicity that it should, whereas whenever the issue is raised, it is raised in such an ideological and philosophical manner that the substance of the matter is put at risk. OKE considers that globalisation is a development that creates serious threats, but also important potentials for the economic and social conditions of the countries which participate in it. (OKE, 2000)

This paragraph summarises the tensions that existed in Greek public discourse with regard to globalisation. First, is the view of the critics, mainly labour unions and left-wing parties, that globalisation carried threats with it. Second, is the view of the government and the employers that no matter what globalisation was or did, Greece was part of it, and in any case globalisation created also many opportunities. It is also interesting that the 'Opinion' acknowledged that the debate on globalisation in Greece was so ideologically laden that it tended to miss the point. In this regard the equilibrium reached in OKE can be said to be closer to the stance taken by the PASOK government and the employers. Maybe this is why a caveat was put in the introduction of the document, that declared that the 'Opinion' referred to the respective document which was to be discussed by the EESC 'and it does not constitute a general statement on the phenomenon of globalisation' (OKE, 2000).

Up to this point, the discourses of political parties and social partners were examined. Yet any study of public discourse formation and transformation would be incomplete without an analysis of the role of media in these processes. The media is an institutional actor which has the power to give voice or to impose silence, to create events or to sentence events into oblivion. Besides being an *institutional actor*, with its own – diverse and conflicting – agenda, the media is a *mirror* of its society. Indeed, media coverage in a dialectical process both reflects and creates the public agenda. Analysing media coverage allows us to study what was considered to be 'news' and what was at the forefront of public consideration and public agenda at a certain period in time.

Media coverage

The aim of this section is to study in a consistent manner a representative source of media coverage in Greece, throughout the period 1996–2001, in order to examine: (a) the volume and the evolution of the use of the term 'globalisation'; (b) the context of its use; and (c) the composition of the people using this term. Through this investigation we also aim to capture the discourses and activities of groups that have not been studied above, such as think-tanks, academics and anti-globalisation protesters. In the case of Greece, such a representative source of coverage was judged to be the Sunday edition of daily newspapers. It is representative because the Sunday edition of Greek newspapers summarise all the important weekly events and include several special supplements and sections on topical issues, books and journals reviews, cultural events, etc. It is also important to note that in Greece the circulation of Sunday editions is much higher in comparison to daily ones. Moreover, when it comes to Sunday editions, party-preference as a criterion for choosing a newspaper is, if only partly, relaxed. Therefore during the period under examination many readers would buy the newspaper of their political preference along with one of the newspapers that were (at least in the period 1995–2001) in the first ranks of circulation among the Sunday editions i.e. *To Vima*, *Kathimerini* and *Eleftherotypia*.[60] It can thus be argued that these three newspapers have had a considerable effect on the formation and change of Greek public discourse. From these three newspapers the newspaper *To Vima* (henceforth VIMA) was selected as a 'sample source' because its Sunday edition had the highest circulation for most of the period under investigation.[61] According to the Athens Daily Newspaper Publishers' Association (EIHEA) the aggregate percentages of circulations of the main Greek newspapers for the period 1995–2001 were as follows: VIMA 21%, Eleftherotypia 20%,

Ethnos 16%, Kathimerini 13%, Eleftheros Typos 10%, other news-papers 20%.

The discourse of globalisation in the newspaper VIMA (1996–2001)
VIMA has an on-line archive for all its Sunday editions, from 14 July 1996. Using this archive I collected all articles/texts that included a reference to globalisation during the period July 1996–December 2007. This work was based on a 'keyword' and a 'keyword-in-context' method-ology,[62] the 'keyword' being globalisation (παγκοσμιοποίηση). This section analyses the findings for the period 1996–2001, which is the main period under investigation in this project. I return to the find-ings for the period 2002–2007 in chapter 5, where I compare the dynamics at play in Greek and Irish public discourses and politico-economic systems. The main findings for the period 1996–2001 are as follows.

First, the references to globalisation found in VIMA can be classi-fied into three broad categories: (a) references in articles in which globalisation itself was a 'news item' (e.g. the anti-globalisation protests, or a conference or a book on globalisation); (b) references in articles in which the term globalisation was used in the commen-tary of everyday social, political and economic news; (c) references found in press releases, statements, remarks, announcements, etc. made by specific institutional actors (e.g. political parties, workers, the church).

Second, as Figure 3.4 demonstrates significant numbers of refer-ences to globalisation can be found since 1997, i.e. well before the anti-globalisation protests in Seattle in December 1999.

Specifically, the comparison of the second semesters (July–December) of 1996 and 1997 demonstrates a threefold increase in the use of the term globalisation (from 16 in 1996 to 45 references in 1997). Then again the number of references on an annual basis doubled in 1998 (from 80 in 1997 to 156 in 1998) and remained at approximately the same level up to the end of 1999 (142 references). Finally, the Seattle events in December 1999, led to an approximately 50% increase in the references to globalisation in 2000 (230 refer-ences) in comparison to 1999, and approximately the same levels were maintained in 2001 (204 references). After 2001 the references returned to their 1997–98 levels.

It is important to note here that the numbers of references to glob-alisation do not speak for themselves. It is the comparison of the references per year that can demonstrate the dynamics at play during the respective period. As Figure 3.4 shows the emergence of

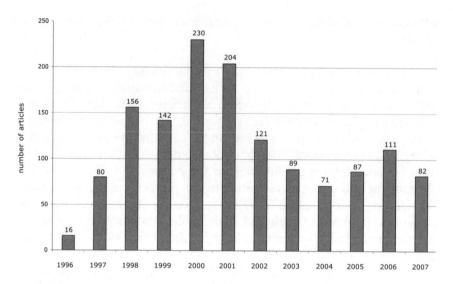

Figure 3.4 References to globalisation in Sunday editions of VIMA

Note: Data collected in January 2008; 1996 covers 14 July to 31 December.

globalisation discourse took place gradually, in a process that started at least in 1997. Furthermore, taking the year 2000 as the 'peak-point' of globalisation discourse in VIMA, it can be argued that globalisation had had a considerable impact on this newspaper's discourse since 1998. In order to better grasp the dynamics that these data signify, one should study the composition of the authors of these references, as well as the distribution of the references in the various sections of the newspaper.

Figure 3.5 offers aggregate data for the distribution of references in the various sections of VIMA for the period 1996–2001, while Figure 3.6 monitors the evolution of this distribution per year.

Based on these data a number of observations can be made. First, the references in the main, political section of the newspaper (section A) remained dominant throughout the period under investigation, even though the evolution of these references was not linear. After a 'peak-point' in 1998, these references started to decline; a trend that was reversed after the anti-globalisation protests in Seattle at the end of 1999. The same event seems to have had an opposite effect for the references in the economic section (section D). In this section the references increased gradually but steadily up to 2000, when a significant decrease in their number took place. This decrease could be explained by the fact that the concept of globalisation, as we saw in

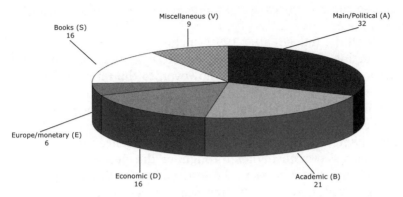

Figure 3.5 References to globalisation by section of publication in Sunday editions of VIMA (1996–2001) (percentage of total references to globalisation)

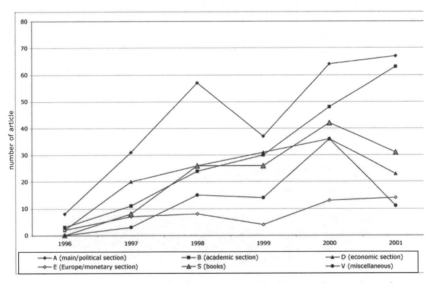

Figure 3.6 Evolution of references to globalisation by section of publication in Sunday editions of VIMA

the discourses of the political parties, the workers and the church, had acquired an ideologically charged, negative connotation in Greek public discourse and therefore its use was avoided in relation to economic policies and related economic issues. The most linear pattern is found in the academic section (section B), in which the references steadily increased throughout the period 1996–2001, surpassing the references of the economic section in 2000, and approaching the references of the political section in 2001. A similar dynamic appears also in the book section (section S), despite the decrease in 2001. Indeed, after 1999 (inclusive) the references in the political section were outnumbered by these in the academic and book sections counted together. If, however, to the references of the political section one adds the references of the economic section in order to juxtapose the references made in the 'politico-economic pages' (sections: A+D) with those made in the, broadly speaking, 'academic pages' (sections: B+S) then the references to the 'non-academic pages' remain higher throughout the period 1996–2000. With regard to the references in the rest sections of the newspaper it can be observed that after a significant increase in 2000, they returned to their pre-Seattle levels in 2001.

Based on these data it can be argued that the implication and the effects of globalisation discourse in Greek public discourse seem to be much deeper and wider than those of an elite-based discourse, limited to academic circles. These findings can be further sharpened if combined with information about the identity of the people who wrote the respective articles. Figure 3.7 presents the percentage of the aggregate number of articles that made references to globalisation,

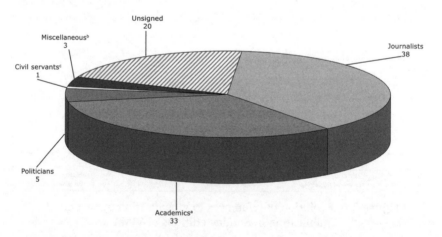

Figure 3.7 References to globalisation by authors' identity in Sunday editions of VIMA (1996–2001) (*percentage of total articles*)

[a] Includes all articles in the book section.
[b] Includes managers, consultants, artists and Archbishop Christodoulos (interview in 1998).
[c] This category refers to the highest ranks of public services, such as the chairman of the Bank of Greece and the vice-chairman of the public employment organisation OAED.

classified according to the identity of their authors. Thus here we see the percentage of articles published by different author categories.

Thus we see that even if all references to the book section are considered references by academics (although only part of the book reviews are written by academics), the articles by journalists remain the majority for the period 1996–2001. Furthermore, if we consider the unsigned articles as articles by journalists (which is true at least for the great majority of them) and add them to those signed by named journalists then the overall percentage of articles by journalists is approximately 58%. The next two figures enrich this picture by focusing on the evolution rather than the aggregate percentage of these categories. In particular Figure 3.8 shows the evolution of the volume of articles published by different author categories, while Figure 3.9 focuses on the evolution of these author categories themselves.

Based on these data it can be observed that during 1998–2000 the number of journalists who used the concept of globalisation in their articles outnumbered that of academics who did so. If the number of articles rather than the number of authors is taken into account, then the journalistic references outnumbered the academic ones for the period 1997–2000.[63] This finding enhances the conclusion reached in the analysis of references according to the newspaper's section of appearance, i.e. that references to globalisation in 'non-academic

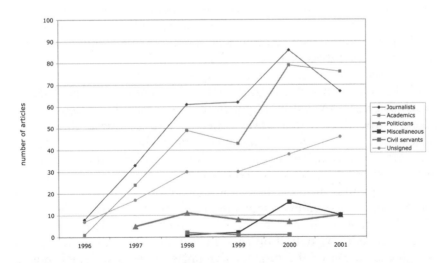

Figure 3.8 Evolution of references to globalisation by authors' identity in Sunday editions of VIMA

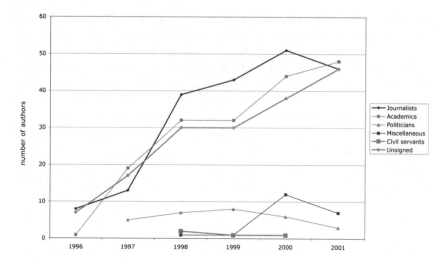

Figure 3.9 Evolution of authors' categories writing on globalisation in Sunday editions of VIMA

pages' remained higher throughout the period 1996–2000. It is also important to note that the 'journalistic engagement' with globalisation discourse was led by journalists who were widely read and had a significant influence on public discourse, such as D. Mitropoulos, R. Someritis, N. Nikolaou and J. Pretenderis. Finally, the coming into the picture of more author categories such as 'miscellaneous', 'politicians' and 'civil servants', can be seen as an indicator of the wider diffusion of globalisation discourse.

The evolution of the number of signed articles with references to globalisation points clearly to the intensification of the globalisation discourse in VIMA and more generally in Greek public discourse (at least to the degree that VIMA reflected and produced this public discourse). The category of unsigned articles, however, adds equally important information to the evolution of globalisation discourse. The constant increase in references in this category can indeed be seen as an indicator of the 'quotidianisation' of the globalisation discourse, i.e. its gradual embeddedness into the realm of the *everyday*, the *conventional* within VIMA and Greek public discourse.

To conclude, by definition the analysis of VIMA can only offer a rough indication of the broader dynamics at work in Greek public discourse. Yet the findings from this analysis support the argument about the gradual transformation of Greek public discourse, in terms of the then newly emerging hegemonic discourse of globalisation.

After 1997 globalisation was implicated in the discourse generated by the newspaper VIMA and it was to be found more than anywhere else in the construction/production of news in its political and economic columns. In this regard, it can be argued that the emergence of globalisation discourse in VIMA, and consequently in Greek public discourse was a long and gradual process rather than a sudden rupture that happened with the Seattle events in 2000.

Conclusion

This chapter investigated the discourses of key institutional actors in Greece, in order to trace changes or continuities in the production of Greek public discourse during the period 1995–2001. Through this investigation we saw that globalisation gradually emerged as a new point of reference, through which the institutional actors rearticulated their interests and goals, renegotiated their identities and redefined their strategies. Thus globalisation was defended as an opportunity for economic development (e.g. PASOK), accused as a new means of imperialist or neoliberal expansion (e.g. KKE, Synaspismos, GSEE), associated with the forces of evil (e.g. the church), taken for granted as a new reality (e.g. SEV) or was just avoided as a concept (e.g. ND, SEV). This analysis brought also to the forefront changes in the power of the different actors, as these were manifested in the evolution of their interaction. For instance, we saw how workers, after a period of resistance, accepted discussion of proposals for flexibility policies in the labour market – a traditional demand of employers. This is also an example of how the (new) politics of globalisation, in terms of 'winners' and 'losers', was materialised at the national level. The sample of press coverage that was examined supported the above analysis. Globalisation after 1998 occupied a considerable position in the discourse of the Sunday newspaper that had the highest circulation during the period in question. This cannot but mirror the increased importance of the concept of globalisation in the discourses of key institutional actors. It also, however, manifested the increase of the importance of globalisation both as an independent news item, and as a way of reading events and changes in the domestic and international realms. Here, VIMA not only mirrored the changing Greek public discourse, but it was also an agent in this change.

A detailed conclusion of this chapter is offered in a comparative perspective with the Irish case in chapter 5. Yet, it is clear that globalisation discourse did not 'arrive' in Greece with the Seattle protests. Rather the opposite was the case. The events in Seattle signified (in Greek public discourse) not the beginning but a 'peak' of a longer hegemonic restructuring process to which these events were a reaction. The increased references to globalisation throughout the period 1998–99 in VIMA should be conceptualised in this context. Such a reading does not aim to undermine the crucial impact of the 'Seattle events' on public discourses around the world, and the new dynamics they created. It rather aims to place these events in the broader social, material, technological and conceptual dynamics of which they constituted an integral part. These included the internationalisation of production through MNCs; the globalisation of financial markets, the increasing power of short-term capital and the financial crises of the 1990s; the spread of new communication and information technologies – most importantly the Internet, which started to bio-politically restructure world politics, economics and everyday life, at least since the late 1970s. The hegemonic discourse of globalisation came out of the dynamics that were unleashed from these new developments, and Greek public discourse was produced and reproduced in interaction within this new environment.

Notes

1 For a short history of the study of electoral manifestos through content analysis, see: Budge and Bara, 2001. For a review of manifesto-based research, see Budge and Bara, 2001a.
2 The KKE's archive contains documents published after 1998.
3 See, Denzin and Lincoln, 2000: 775–777.
4 The term 'barbarism' made an explicit reference to the political philosophy of Cornelious Castoriadis. Castoriadis formed the 'Socialism or Barbarism' group in 1948, and was the founding editor of the journal *Socialism or Barbarism*.
5 Speech in Lamia, 4 July 1998
6 Speech at the event 'youth and democracy', in Pnyka, 22 July 1999.
7 Speech at an international seminar, 14 November 1998.
8 Interview with Stavro Theodoraki, in *Mega Channel*, 2 April 2000.
9 See the press conference during the International Conference on Progressive Governance in Berlin, 2 June 2000.
10 The New Democracy did not publish a single electoral manifesto for the 1996 elections. It issued, however, a detailed programme on economic policy (60 pages long) that along with the sectoral sections on banking, trade, securities and maritime affairs, it covered broader issues, such as the role of the state in economy and society, the social and political cohesion of Greece, and the definition of the new international environment. It is this economic manifesto (ND, 1995), that was used here as a substi-

tute for a general electoral manifesto. This was also the suggestion of the ND's 'Electoral Manifestos Section'.

11 Speech at the Annual Assembly of the Federation of Greek Industries, 20 January 2000.

12 For the purposes of the analysis of the KKE leadership's discourse on globalisation we not only examined the Papariga's speeches and interviews that were available in the on-line party archive, but also the available decisions and press reports of the party's central committee, that constituted the greatest part of the KKE's archive. That is why we do not offer a table with the specific context and content of Papariga's discourse on globalisation. The analysis in this section focuses on the period 1998–2000.

13 See Aleka Papariga, 'For the Capitalist Globalisation', *Rizospastis*, 20 May 2001, page 6.

14 Announcement of the Press Office of the Central Committee of the KKE regarding the entrance of Greece in to the EMU, 20 June 2000.

15 Declaration of the Central Committee of the KKE on 1 May 2000. See also the speech of Papariga in the meeting of the European United Left in *Rizospastis*, 12 April 1998.

16 Announcement of the Press Office of the Central Committee of KKE on the protests in Goteborg, 19 June 2001. Available at: www.kke.gr (accessed 6 November 2002).

17 Announcement of the Press Office of the Central Committee, 19 June 2001.

18 The analysis in this section focuses on the period 1998–2000, for which there was a developed on-line archive with Constandopoulos's speeches and interviews.

19 Speech in parliament, on 28 April 1998.

20 Speech at the 3rd Annual Conference of Synaspismos, in 2 July 2000.

21 This became clear during the confrontation between the church and the government of PASOK on whether religious affiliation should be mentioned on identity cards.

22 SEV was founded in 1907 and is the main national association that 'represents and speaks for industry, and for the economy's private sector in general, vis-à-vis state authorities and other societal institutions'. SEV's 'members are individual enterprises or employer organisations, both sectoral and regional'. 'More than 85% of its members are manufacturing enterprises and the corresponding sectoral or regional employer organisations'. See SEV's webpage at: www.fgi.org.gr

23 Iason Stratos was SEV's chairman throughout the period 1995–2000, when he was replaced by Leuteris Antonacopoulos.

24 To face this 'negative' race ECOFIN adopted a code of conduct on 1 December 1997 (SEV, 1998: 98).

25 Personal interview, 30 April 2002.

26 See SEV, 1996: 42–43. For the presidency conclusions of the European Council in Essen see: http://ue.eu.int/ueDocs/cms_Data/docs

/pressdata/en/ec/00300–1.EN4.htm (accessed 11 April 2008). This trend towards more flexibility in the labour market was also exemplified at the agreement signed by the social partners at the EU level on the issue of part-time jobs, facilitating the use of flexible modes of employment (see SEV, 1998: 15, 89).

27 A group of independent experts on legislative and administrative simplification and deregulation, which had been founded by the European Commission.

28 For the SEV's stance towards the role of social partners, see SEV, 2001: 46.

29 GSEE is the main national association which represents workers and employees in the private sector.

30 It is revealing that up to 1995 87.9% of the trade unions' leaders belonged to a political party. See *Enimerosi*, no. 3, May 1995, p. 7.

31 ADEDI, the union for the public sector employees, also participates in INE.

32 Quotations are from the official webpage of the Institute of Labour. See at: www.inegsee.gr/ INE-profile.htm (11 accessed June 2008).

33 *Enimerosi* allows one to trace and monitor all the main issues of concern, positions, pronouncements and activities of INE and GSEE.

34 *Enimerosi*, no. 3, May 1995, p. 2.

35 See *Enimerosi*, no. 3, May 1995, pp. 3, 5.

36 *Enimerosi*, no 12, March 1996, p. 6.

37 In particular GSEE's demands included: (a) the specification of a maximum percentage of part-time workers per company; (b) the specification of a minimum time of employment per day; (c) payment of part-time workers on the basis of their working hours (with an increased ratio) (ibid.). Moreover, in 1996 INE published two studies on flexibility and its affects. See *Enimerosi*, no. 22, February 1997.

38 *Enimerosi*, no. 16, July–August 1996.

39 See for instance ibid., p. 16.

40 See for instance the intervention of S. Laimos, the Vice-General Secretary of GSEE and secretary of social policy, in *Enimerosi*, no. 17, September 1996, pp. 15–16.

41 *Enimerosi*, no. 18, October 1996.

42 Ibid. GSEE tried to maintain its relationship with P. Bourdieu, and a common research project was included in its annual activity plan of 1997. See *Enimerosi*, no. 22, February 1997, p. 2.

43 *Enimerosi*, no. 24, April 1997, p. 5.

44 Indicatively see *Enimerosi*, no. 27, July–August 1997, p. 13.

45 *Enimerosi*, no. 29, October 1997, p. 17.

46 *Enimerosi*, no. 44, 1999. See also D. Katsoridas, '"Globalisation"' or Internationalisation of the Economies', *Enimerosi*, no. 45, 1999.

47 *Enimerosi*, no. 61–62, July–August 2000.

48 *Enimerosi*, no. 54, December 1999.

49 *Enimerosi*, no. 54, December 1999.

50 *Enimerosi*, no. 1, March 1995, p. 6.
51 *Enimerosi*, no. 3, May 1995, p. 2.
52 For instance, see *Enimerosi*, nos 2, 3, 7 (special section), 10, 16.
53 See *Enimerosi*, no. 34, 1998.
54 *Enimerosi*, no. 25, May 1997, p. 17.
55 *Enimerosi*, no. 27, July–August 1997, p.13.
56 The PHARE programme, originally created in 1989, aimed to assist the applicant countries of Central and Eastern Europe in their preparations for joining the European Union (until 2000 the countries of the Western Balkans also participated in PHARE). See the official webpage of the programme at: europa.eu.int/comm/enlargement/pas/phare
57 See *Enimerosi*, no. 11, February 1996, p. 11.
58 See *Enimerosi*, no. 23, March 1997, p. 19.
59 OKE was founded in 1997 as a tripartite, consultative organ, and it is a member of the EESC. It includes representatives from the government, employers, employees and other civil society organisations.
60 The ranking of the daily editions during the same period was different.
61 VIMA was first in circulation throughout the period 1995–99. *Eleftherotypia* surpassed VIMA in 2000–01, but their distance remained within approximately 1% (source: EIHEA).
62 See Denzin and Lincoln, 2000: 775–777.
63 It is important to keep in mind that the above analysis is independent of the sections in which these articles were published. Thus many academics have permanent columns and/or occasionally write in the main political section of the newspaper, and not in the academic one.

4

Globalisation discourse in Ireland

As argued in chapter 2 the decade of the 1990s signified a turning point for the Irish political system. The well-established 'Fianna Fáil versus the rest' political pattern – which had dominated the Irish political life for approximately fifty years (1948–89) – ceased to define Irish politics and gave way to a 'new politics of coalition-making' (Mair, 1999). Moreover, the turn from the 1980s to the 1990s witnessed the significant empowerment of the socio-economic role of the institution of 'social partnership'. Within this context a new public discourse started to emerge, with new points of references and signifiers (e.g. Celtic tiger, Europe's shining light). As in the case of Greece, the purpose is to examine the nature of the relationship between this emerging public discourse and the hegemonic discourse of globalisation.

This chapter replicated the structure and methodology followed in chapter 3. Hence, the discourses of the key institutional actors were analysed in order to examine the following questions. How was the globalisation discourse implicated in the discourses, strategies, policies and identities of these actors? How was the materialisation of globalisation discourse affected by the domestic institutional configuration, and what impact did it have on this configuration? What did these changes mean for Irish public discourse? The institutional actors examined for this purpose are the main political parties (Fianna Fáil, Fine Gael, Labour Party, Progressive Democrats), the main social partners (ICTU, the Irish Business and Employers Confederation (IBEC), NESC), the church and a press sample (the daily newspaper *The Irish Times*).

The main political parties[1]

Two criteria were used for the selection of the political parties. First, their 'representativeness', as expressed by votes in the national elections, and second their 'continuity' in the political scene and/or participation in government. The inclusion of the 'participation in government' criterion was deemed necessary because of the existence of coalition governments since the early 1990s. Based on the above criteria we have studied the following parties: (a) Fianna Fáil: the Republican Party (FF), which got the majority of votes in all the elections since 1989 (i.e. in 1992, 1997, 2002), and formed coalition governments with the Labour Party in 1992 (lasted until 1994), and with the Progressive Democrats in 1989, 1997 and 2002. (b) The Fine Gael (FG), which came second in all the elections in the 1990s, and was in power, in a coalition government with the Labour Party during 1994–97. (c) The Labour Party (LP), which is the third biggest party, and was in power as a partner of FF during 1992–94 and as a partner of FG during 1994–97. (d) The Progressive Democrats (PD), which is the youngest party (founded in 1985). It came fourth in the elections of 1989, 1992, 1997 and 2002, but participated in coalition governments with FF in 1989, 1997 and 2002.

Both Fianna Fáil and Fine Gael are considered to be conservative parties. It is indicative that in the European Parliament, along with New Democracy and British Conservatives, Fine Gael belongs to the European People's Party and European Democrats group that includes Christian Democrats, Conservative and other centre-right political forces. On the other hand Fianna Fáil belongs to the Union for Europe of the Nations group, a Eurosceptic and rather nationalistic group. Regarding the smaller parties, the Labour Party is a rather progressive left party that, along with PASOK and the British Labour Party, is a member of the Party of European Socialists group in the European Parliament. Finally, the Progressive Democrats, which has its origins in Fianna Fáil, is a right-wing party with a strong liberal character both economically and politically.[2]

For the study of Irish political parties we take as our starting point the 1997 elections that signified the end of a long period of short-lived coalition governments (1992–97). Furthermore, it signified the consolidation of the post-'FF versus the rest' political scene, and the crystallisation of a new political dynamic, based on the FF–PD governmental cooperation. The choice of 1997 as a point of departure, forced us to include in our research the year 2002, which is marginally outside the period under examination, but is the year when the next election campaign took place in Ireland. Therefore the analysis of the party discourses is based on the analysis of their 1997 and 2002 electoral manifestos.[3]

Fianna Fáil (FF)

Although in opposition during 1994–97, Fianna Fáil, did not dispute in its 1997 electoral campaign –and it could not meaningfully do so– the fact that Ireland experienced economic growth, success and prosperity. The focal point of its campaign was how this prosperity should be managed and what strategies should be followed from that point onwards. The main line of its manifesto (FF, 1997) was the following:

> [The Irish] now have the opportunity to build on the current wave of success, laying solid foundations for a prosperous Ireland in the 21st century ... Or we can watch helplessly while lawlessness takes over our country, and the gap grows wider between the haves and the have-nots ('Introduction' by B. Ahern, p. 2) ... Irish people [do not] want a society that is at war with itself, because of growing gaps between the 'haves' and 'have nots'. (21)

So, for Fianna Fáil what was at stake in the elections, was not how prosperity should be created, nor about what should be the basic choices of economic policy, but rather how the existing success could work better for all social strata in Ireland. Thus, the wealth-creating mechanisms and policies (for instance corporate tax cuts) of the Irish political economy, being the undeniable reason for the economic success, remained *outside* party competition, at least as the latter was set in the Fianna Fáil's manifesto. Furthermore, even when these mechanisms entered into the electoral game, it was not in order to be disputed. Rather the opposite. Political parties competed with each other which one would protect and extend further the range of these mechanisms and policies. Tax cuts is perhaps the most prominent example. The second chapter of the manifesto 'Economy & Taxation', substantiated Fianna Fáil's 'prudent' profile in economic management, on its past 'ability to reduce the tax burden' (7). It is indicative that 'tax cuts' was the fifth most popular concept in the manifesto.

Along similar lines, the section on the public sector declared that '[Fianna Fáil will take] a practical rather than an ideological approach to State companies ... rejecting ideology in favour of practicality ... It is a time of change in the State Sector, change that is being driven by technology, by EU deregulation and competition' (109, 110). Within this context Fianna Fáil criticised the FG–LP coalition for lacking a 'strong pro-enterprise attitude' and for following a tax policy that put in danger 'Ireland's attraction as a location of inward investments' (p. 6).

This 'apoliticisation' of the followed economic policy should not only be attributed to the positive impact that this policy had on economic growth and living standards. Another equally important factor was the role played by the 'social partnership'. Reading the manifesto one gets a clear picture of how social partnership had been evolving as the new core of Irish politics – the means through which politics was to be delivered. The content of the politics to be delivered seemed rather to be taken for granted. The concept of partnership/social partners was indeed the second most popular concept of the 1997 manifesto, and Fianna Fáil stressed that the 'ground-breaking social partnership' was its own initiative in 1987 (7).

The manifesto made no reference to the concept of globalisation. Yet, the concept of the 'information age' was the most popular concept in the manifesto, while the concept of 'Ireland's attraction' (to foreign investments), and the concept of 'world marketplace' were the third and fourth most popular concepts respectively. Furthermore, the manifesto was scattered with references to a 'new world' (32), 'new era' (69) and 'new age' (69). The way that the information age was conceptualised and used was as follows:

> [The] Information Age offers Ireland a massive opportunity ... The reason is that the new age offers us ... a way around the disadvantages we have always suffered because of our remote position ... In the Information Age, where we are will no longer matter. Ireland will be as well-placed as any country in a truly global market-place ... However ... the dividend from the Information Age will not come automatically. On the contrary: if we do not prepare properly, we will be left behind ... (82)

In sum, it can be argued that economic globalisation, not as a concept but as a set of specific policies and practices, was ever present in the manifesto. Furthermore, it was not contested or discussed, but it was present as a promise to be promoted.

The 2002 electoral manifesto (FF, 2002), does not change much from the above picture. Of course the context was not the same. In 2002 Fianna Fáil was not trying to defeat a government, but to stay in power. In this regard the issue of the growing gap between the 'haves' and the 'have-nots', central in the 1997 manifesto, gave its place to confident statements such as: the 'era of mass unemployment and emigration has been brought to an end' (3, 4); we 'consolidated an economy that is still the envy of the world' (6); '[u]nder Fianna Fáil Ireland has been the world's most dynamic economy' (4, 25).

It is indeed striking that, although this was an electoral competition that took place in 2002, once again the manifesto of the biggest party (FF, 2002) did not make a single reference to the concept of globalisation. Yet the hegemonic discourse of globalisation in terms of specific dominant concepts, policies and practices was ever present.

We are committed to maintaining a favourable business environment,
so that we can continue to attract mobile capital investments and technology. (26)

In order to progress as a society, we will be seeking a maximum propor-
tion of skilled, well-paid and flexible forms of employment, both full
and part-time, for the benefit of everyone seeking paid employment.
(29)

In 2002 Ireland ranked first in the world as the world's top globalised
economy (A.T. Kearney Consultants Survey) ... As one of the most
successfully globalised countries in the world, we will continue *as
labour market conditions require* .... (29–30, emphasis added)

The above approach towards the concepts 'globalised', 'flexibility' and
'mobile capital investments' is instrumental in understanding where
the Fianna Fáil's discourse lay with regard to globalisation discourse.
Policies related to labour market flexibility and mobile capital investments were considered to be prime policy targets and positive
achievements. Thus Fianna Fáil emphatically argued for, and tried to
achieve what the anti-globalisation movement had as its focal points
of criticism (flexibility and mobile capital investments). At the same
time the proposed (economic) policies were considered as manifesta-
tions of a new approach to economic development, the 'Irish
economic model'. 'Our policy is to further develop the Irish economic
model, combining ... our own experience, with the dynamism,
investment and light regulation characteristic of the US economy and
the social solidarity and inclusive participation characteristic of the
European economy' (26). Finally, while the issue of tax reduction,
and the criticism against 'ideological approaches' to economic policy
remained central, the most popular concept within the manifesto was
that of 'social partnership'/'social partners'.

To conclude, two things must be underlined with regard to FF's
discourse. First, the absolute absence of references to the term globalisation in both the 1997 and 2002 manifestos. Second, the fact that
policies strongly associated with the phenomenon of economic globalisation, such as flexibility in labour market, corporate tax cuts and
incentives for mobile capital investments, were conceptualised as
non-ideological and were pursued not in the name of globalisation or
external pressures, but in that of the guaranteed success of the Irish
economic model.

Fine Gael (FG)

In 1997 Fine Gael was trying to stay in power by taking advantage of the unprecedented economic boom that was experienced in Ireland. Its electoral manifesto consisted of four different documents under the title *Securing your Future* (FG, 1997a–d).[4] Addressing the Irish people's worries and FF's accusations about the growing gap between the 'haves' and 'have-nots', the manifesto paid particular attention to how FG would 'share [prosperity] fairly for the benefits of all our citizens' (FG, 1997a: 2). Within this framework the concept of social partnership/social partners was the most popular concept in the manifesto (FG, 1997a–d), and implicitly the strongest evidence put forward by FG that prosperity would be secured and fairly shared.

Fine Gael's aim and electoral pledge was 'to see Ireland attain a permanent place in the top 10 league of international competitiveness' (FG, 1997a: 5). The means to achieve this were flexibility, tax cuts, inwards mobile investments and 'corporatisation'. Along these lines FG promised to continue the 'Fine Gael-inspired initiatives to promote more flexible systems of wage and salary compensation' (ibid.: 4), to reduce further 'the burden of enterprise taxes' (ibid.: 16), and to continue the '"corporatisation" drive among all the Commercial State-Sponsored Bodies (CSSBs)'. The policy of 'corporatisation' required 'all the CSSBs to act "as if" they were corporates in the private sector, by requiring them ... to generate dividends ... and commercial returns' (ibid.: 14). It is also indicative that after social partnership, 'tax reductions' was the second most popular concept in the economic manifesto (see for instance 2–3, 9, 10, 15, 17).

Thus although the concept of globalisation was only used once, the dominant objects, policies and practices of economic globalisation were all dominant in the FG's manifesto. The way in which these policies and practices were treated is equally important. Fine Gael did not support flexibility as a necessary evil but on the contrary tried to persuade the electorate that flexibility policies were FG-inspired. The same goes for mobile capital, which was not approached as the 'curse' of globalisation, but as the 'magic touch' of Irish economic success. The choice of the term 'corporatisation' is also telling, if only on a semantic level, about the dynamics found in Irish public discourse. Removed from the Irish context, 'corporatisation' would sound more like an anti-globalisation slogan.

The document that focused on education and healthcare (FG, 1997b) included however some 'warnings' on the impact of these economic developments on Irish society. It focused on the importance of Irish traditional values such as family and community, and in a manner that resembled a cultural critique of globalisation it proclaimed that '[c]hanges in society such as the growth of individualism and secularisation, urbanisation, technological change, changing work practices and changed gender roles are placing families under pressure . . . (ibid.: 5). In this regard it is indeed interesting that the this document (FG, 1997b) identified as a problem, what the economic document (FG 1997a) promoted as a policy for wealth-generation, i.e. changing work practices.

In the 2002 elections, Fine Gael pushed this kind of identity critique further.[5] There are two key documents in this regard: the general 2002 electoral manifesto, under the indicative title *Towards a Better Quality of Life* (FG, 2002a), and a separate economic manifesto, entitled 'Just Economics' (FG, 2002b). Strikingly, none of these documents made a reference to the concept of globalisation. Yet, Fine Gael brought the issue of quality of life, and the fading values of Irish society to the forefront of its electoral campaign. The issue of 'community spirit vs. selfishness', the importance of family and traditional values, along with a critique of the nature of 'Celtic Tiger' created by FF and PD, were all central to its manifesto (FG, 2002a). Furthermore, the manifesto stressed the widening 'gap between the have and have nots' (ibid.: 2, 22) (a critique which had also been used by FF in 1997). Developing his vision of Ireland in the introduction of the manifesto, Michael Noonan declared (ibid.):

> [Fine Gael vision is an] Ireland built on a sense of community – not one that has room only for individual selfishness. (2; see also 23, 29).

> So the choice is stark: it is a choice between a philosophy that says money is all that counts, and one that puts money in the wider context of quality of life. (3)[6]

> One of the greatest strengths in the Irish tradition has always been . . . family life. Under Fianna Fáil and the PDs, the Celtic Tiger has put this tradition under serious stress. (10)

> [FF and PD's economic policy] has been a policy of survival of the fittest. This policy . . . runs the boilers at full speed and never minds who gets caught in the backwash'. (22)

Beyond the above criticism Fine Gael tried also to develop an outside-in critique. It argued that 'Irish policy positions [in the EU] have become narrow and selfish' and that '[u]nder Fianna Fáil and the PDs, Ireland had become "the bad boy" of Europe' (ibid.: 34). It furthermore promised that under an FG government 'Ireland's new reputation as a selfish, greedy country ... [would] decisively [be] put to rest – forever' (ibid.: 35).

The economic manifesto (FG, 2002b) complements the above picture. In their introductions Jim Mitchell (Deputy Leader) and Michael Noonan stressed that Fine Gael was 'proud of the part it ... played in bridging about this economic miracle' (ibid.: 2). Mitchell declared that 'the end for which we are working is A JUST SOCIETY ... However, to achieve this Ireland must always be at the cutting edge of competitiveness and flexibility' (2; capital in the original). This exemplifies the extent to which concepts and policies such as flexibility were embedded in the Irish public discourse and politico-economic system. The economic manifesto declared also that the 'era of unprecedented growth known as the Celtic Tiger came to an end in 2001' (9), and analysed how the 'Irish Economic Model' could be developed as 'a third way between Boston and Berlin' (12–14).

The above examples make it clear that the electoral strategy of Fine Gael wavered between two opposites: on the one hand, a critique of the FF's and PD's version of Celtic Tiger and its negative socio-cultural effects; on the other hand, an attempt to cash in on the role it had played in bringing about the economic miracle of (the same) Celtic Tiger, and to make clear that it would continue the followed economic policies. Hence, whereas one can find in the Fine Gael's critique of the 'Celtic Tiger model' elements of a cultural critique of globalisation, the economic side of the latter seems to remain beyond any contestation in the policies and ideology promoted by both FG and FF (i.e. the two biggest Irish parties) throughout the period 1997–2002. Indeed, during that period, at issue was only who would promote economic globalisation policies further.

Labour Party (LP)

The aim of the Labour Party in the 1997 elections was to stay in government, while in 2002 to come back as a partner in power. It is important to start our analysis by pointing out how the Labour Party identified itself and its priorities, in its 1997 manifesto (LP, 1997):

> Our object is ... [t]he prioritisation of enterprise and innovation as a key elements in the creation of wealth. (6)

> Labour is the party of work and the party of enterprise. Without enterprise in the public or private sector, there is no wealth and no basis for social progress. Labour is committed to a strong market economy based on competition. (11)

It would be hard to guess that the above extracts were found in the electoral manifesto of a Labour Party (at least in continental Europe). Indeed the 'commitment' to a 'strong market economy', and the self-identification of the Labour Party as the 'party of enterprise' elucidate conceptually where the 'parliamentary left' of the Irish political system drew the line of ideological and political confrontation; the line of what could be considered to be 'practical policies' (1), and what should be considered as 'ideological policies'. This is important because it indicates the area of economics and politics that was conceptualised and treated as non-ideological, and thus as not contestable, by the main Irish political parties and their ideology production mechanisms. Along the same lines, the new anchor of Irish politico-economic life, i.e. the social partners/partnership, was dominant in the Labour Party's discourse, being also the most frequently used concept within its 1997 manifesto (see for instance, LP, 1997: 5–6, 8–10, 16–25, 35, 68).

The manifesto made only one reference to the concept of globalisation. In contrast however to the manifestos of the two big parties, there was some engagement with the globalisation debate that emerged at a European level after the mid-1990s. The following extracts are indicative of the Labour Party's position on this (LP, 1997):

> The global dimension is intruding ever more strongly into national and local economies. The 'Information Society' is upon us. These are the realities. They are challenges to be met with enthusiasm ... [4; see also 11, where the EMU and globalisation are defined as the context of the suggested economic policies] ... [I]t is within our abilities to ensure that this time, the information revolution does not leave us behind. (49)

Therefore, the Labour Party conceptualised globalisation as a 'new reality' that should be met with enthusiasm. Its effort however to combine this approach with a more traditional rhetoric was dominated by serious contradictions. The following extracts are indicative:

> In accepting the market system with private enterprise and private property we recognise that we also have to seek to humanise it where necessary, but without undermining its capacity to perform. (4)

> Labour is opposed to individualism ... Thatcherites and their Irish clones follow an alien creed (4). [Yet, in] the Information Age citizens will find it necessary to think even more for themselves. (50)

The LP's opposition to individualism conflicted with the same party's diagnosis of the nature of the 'information age'. The need to 'humanise' aspects of the market system was overruled by the need to secure that this system will continue to perform. These positions are one more important indication of the 'ideological consensus' found among Irish parties, on what was acceptable/unacceptable in the realm of public policy. Finally, the 1997 manifesto included some discussion on the cultural aspects of globalisation and the Irish-Gaelic identity and language. Yet its approach to the future of Gaelic tradition was more positive and confident than negative or defensive (46–47).

The 2002 manifesto (LP, 2002), signified a shift in the party's discourse, towards the endorsement of a 'classical' left critique of globalisation. Thus the manifesto articulated a discourse on globalisation through repetitive references to 'global capitalism' (1), 'global capital' (2, 32), 'global economic justice' (10), 'global economic development' (16), 'globalising economy (32)', 'global militarisation' (33), 'global community' (34) and the need for 'the introduction of the Tobin tax' (35). Thus although the manifesto made only one reference to the term globalisation, the term 'global' was its most popular term. Interestingly, the mobilisation of the concept of social partnership was very low in comparison to the 1997 manifesto. Furthermore, the emphasis in the self-positioning of the party shifted from the importance of 'enterprise' to the identity of the party as a 'part of the European Social Democratic and Socialist Parties' (32, see also 2, 13). Within this context, the manifesto declared:

> This election is about values ... This Government [i.e. FF and PD] has been guided by a combination of crude Thatcherite ideology ... and the populist complacency of the larger Government Party ... Labour believe that the State has a vital role to play in Irish Society ... As globalisation has driven a new way of economic change and opportunity, it has brought with it uncertainty, and in some cases gross injustice ... Unchecked by democratic control, global capitalism has the potential to do severe damage to the social and economic rights of the individual. (1)

The manifesto furthermore claimed that as a result of the 'simplistic economic individualism' (2) and the 'simplistic right-wing' agenda (indicatively 2, 7) followed by the governmental coalition, a 'deadening cynicism has taken hold in Irish politics' (2).

What about the principle of flexibility, the cornerstone of Irish economic success? The Labour Party did not go so far as to dispute its necessity. Thus, '[r]edundancy payments legislation' had to be upgraded so that employers may 'deliver the flexibility *required* to remain competitive in the new economy' (9, emphasis added). Again, this is very telling about the consensus found in Irish public discourse regarding what was considered to be not ideological or disputable in the realm of economic policy. And this consensus was not affected by the assertions of the Labour Party that it 'believe[d] in the European Social Model' (32). Considering its stance on flexibility, it can therefore be argued that the Labour Party in the 2002 elections did not really dispute the heart of economic policies followed by FF and PD, but rather the 'compensation mechanisms' that accompanied these policies.

Progressive Democrats (PD)

It would not be an exaggeration to say that the Progressive Democrats, although the youngest party, had the greatest impact on Irish politics in the 1990s. As described in chapter 2 it was through the Progressive Democrats that the traditional format of Irish politics, the 'FF vs. the rest' system, was brought to an end. It is also worth mentioning that the Progressive Democrats were the only right-wing party with a clear *ideological* stance in Irish politics, i.e. an open neoliberal agenda.

The Progressive Democrats' electoral strategy for the 1997 elections was similar to that adopted by Fianna Fáil. It attempted to bring to the forefront the issue of social inequalities and the danger of a 'two-tier', 'divided', society (PD, 1997: 1). Mary Harney, the leader of the party, declared in her party's manifesto (ibid.):

> We are in the midst of an unprecedented economic boom. But it has not impacted on the lives of thousands of our people. The more we grow, it seems, the greater of isolation of those on the fringes.

The reasons for this 'unequal' development were not clearly elaborated. Instead the focus of the manifesto was on how to maintain economic growth by 'rewarding work' (PD, 1997: section 1), 'promoting enterprise' (ibid: section 2), 'controlling public spending' (ibid.: section 3) and enhancing the competitiveness of the public sector (ibid.: sections 5, 6). Primacy was given to the issue of 'tax reform' and 'tax reductions' (indicatively 2, 4, 29, 41, 44), along with a set of policies that focused on 'non ideological privatisations' (7) and 'less regulation'/deregulation (3). Along these lines, the manifesto attacked the unemployment benefits system for leading to 'dole' rather than to employment (see section 8: 13, 16). Furthermore, although the importance of the social partnership was stressed and the partnership maintained a significant place in the manifesto, the Progressive Democrats did not hesitate to put this partnership and its consensus under critical scrutiny. Breaking with what was a norm in the public discourse, the manifesto declared that 'Consensus is no bad thing in some regard – but if it props up the status quo, it cannot be productive' (1). Finally, the changes proposed in the manifesto were not related to globalisation or any other 'new reality'. Indeed, any references to globalisation, or to an 'information society', a 'new age', etc. were absent from the manifesto.

The Progressive Democrats kept high in their 2002 manifesto (PD, 2002) the need for an 'inclusive society' (14–19) and in the chapter on agriculture acknowledged that 'some have gained more than others' and thus that the existing 'pattern of growth has been uneven' (55). The dominant concept of the manifesto was that of 'enterprise'. Abundant references made to an 'enterprise economy' (for instance 14, 44, 46), an 'enterprise approach' (for instance with regard to education and curriculum development 70–71, see also 44), and an 'enterprise society' (for instance 70). In particular, a whole chapter of the manifesto was devoted to the issue of 'A Pro-Enterprise and Pro-Consumer Society' (44–47). In its introduction it was declared that:

> Enterprise is at the heart of a vibrant, developing society. An enterprising approach is about taking initiative to make change for the better happen. Enterprise creates wealth, delivers jobs and improves people's lives ... no more so than at local community level where initiative and enterprise bind strong communities together. (44)

It is again striking that the term globalisation was only used twice in the manifesto, in a rather neutral manner. As in 1997, the PD's calls for a pro-enterprise society and for liberalisation, deregulation and tax cuts were not justified in the name of external pressures. Even though many references were made to the need for modernisation in various sectors, such as in education and the economy (see PD, 2002: 6, 22, 48, 61, 79), enterprise and deregulation policies were put forward as a social necessity and precondition for the development of a wealthy and inclusive society. In this regard the most suggestive reference was that relating enterprise to the reproduction of the local communities, by arguing that 'enterprises bind strong communities together' (44). It would not be an exaggeration to say that enterprise was suggested by Progressive Democrats as the new 'core' through which (traditional) social life should be organised and reproduced.

Party discourses: a first reflection on the findings

The study of Irish party discourses for the period 1997–2002 revealed an interesting paradox. The concept of globalisation is virtually almost absent from all the parties' manifestos (with the exception of

LP, 2002), in the most globalised country of the world, in two electoral campaigns that took place at the high period of globalisation
discourse. Taking into consideration the fact that political parties
define one of the most fundamental ideology production mechanisms
in Irish politics, it can be assumed that the concept of globalisation
had not become a central point of reference in Irish public discourse
and life in the period under examination.

But let us return to the basic research question: what do the
discourses of the Irish parties tell us about the emergence and
communication of the hegemonic discourse of globalisation in
Ireland? An easy answer is that the globalisation discourse, contrary
to what happened in Greece, had not become a new zone of contestation through which Irish politics were reordered and redefined. Yet
our findings suggest more than this. It can be argued that our research
revealed a non-ideological, i.e. not contestable, space in Irish politics
and economics. This space consisted of policies and concepts which
have been widely associated with extreme aspects of economic globalisation. Thus economic policies, which had been widely contested
in many European states, which constituted the main target of the
anti-globalisation movement, and which were promoted by most
European governments as a necessary evil due to globalisation and
external pressures, in Ireland constituted the given, the uncontested,
what was to be taken for granted, what needed to be protected and
promoted. They thus constituted an all dominant *policy and cognitive
space* for which Irish parties competed only in terms of safeguarding
or expanding it. Towards the end of the period under examination,
the parties in opposition did raise concerns about the cultural implications of some of these policies. Yet, these concerns did not (aim to)
challenge or contest the followed economic policies.

This is a challenging phenomenon to conceptualise. It can be said
that Irish political and economic life reproduced itself through this
non-ideological space, which, however, was nothing else than the
core of the hegemonic discourse of globalisation. I come back to this
argument in chapter 5. What needs to be stressed here is that as long
as the consensus on the non-ideological space was maintained by the
Irish parties, the hegemonic discourse seemed to be equated with the
Irish model of development (see also Hay and Smith, 2005: 136). It
was thus becoming an integral part of Irish identity production, and
was read as the reason for Irish economic success. In their investigation of the discourse of globalisation in Ireland, Hay and Smith
(2005) seem to arrive at a similar conclusion: ' ... globalisation
[rather than to be presented] as a set of external challenges (still) to

be accommodated, it is introduced more as a means of reflecting posi- tively on the distance already travelled by the Irish economy in its rise to '"tigerdom".' (ibid.: 136).

It is now necessary to examine whether the above conclusion about the non-ideological space applies beyond the party discourses. In this way we will get a more accurate picture of the dynamics under way in the production and reproduction of Irish public discourse. This is the purpose of the following sections.

The social partners: employers, workers, and the social and economic council

Irish Business and Employers Confederation (IBEC)[7]

Being an integral part of the institution of social partnership, IBEC has had a decisive and independent role in the formation and change of Irish political economy. It is worth mentioning here that the increase of its influence that followed the revival of the social part- nership in the late 1980s, was accompanied by a decline in its membership, mainly due to the increasing numbers of multinational corporations that refuse to bargain with trade unions and join employers' associations.[8]

Important factors in the formation of IBEC's discourse have been the developments at the EU level, and the European employers' asso- ciation UNICE. Having referred to the role of these factors in the case of Greece, here the analysis proceeds directly to the examination of IBEC's discourse for the period 1996–2001. For this purpose I analysed the following sources: (a) the annual reviews of the IBEC for the period 1996–2002. The reviews cover all the activities of the IBEC, including its publications. (b) The speeches and interviews of IBEC's executives (i.e. the chairpersons and the directors general), as they were published in the newspapers *The Irish Times* and *Irish Inde- pendent* during the period 1996–2000, as well as all the articles that included both the terms 'IBEC' and 'globalisation' and were published during the same period in these two newspapers. This research was conducted through the electronic database Lexis-Nexis Executive.

The main conclusion from the study of IBEC's discourse for the period 1996–2001, is the same as that reached from the study of SEV's discourse. IBEC did not develop a discourse on globalisation as such. It is indeed suggestive that throughout this period the term globalisation was used only one time in IBEC's annual reviews to refer to the 'growing globalisation of business' (IBEC, 2002: 15). Similarly, throughout the period 1996–2000 there was no article published in

The Irish Times or *Irish Independent* that included the name of an IBEC executive together with the term 'globalisation' (regardless of whether the use of the term was attributed to those executives or not!).[9] Furthermore, a similar research that focused on articles that included the terms 'IBEC' and 'globalisation' for the period 1994–2001, led us only to twenty-one articles. Based on our content analysis, however, none of them offers any indication of IBEC's engagement in the debate about globalisation.[10]

As in the Greek case, the lack of references to globalisation should not be interpreted as an absence of the hegemonic discourse of globalisation. For, dominant 'objects' and 'themes' of economic globalisation, such as tax cuts, reduction of corporate taxes, competitiveness, flexibility, liberalisation, privatisation and enterprise culture, were all dominant in the IBEC's discourse (and as one would expect, this list of dominant themes was complemented by the issue of social partnership). This becomes clear not only from the analysis of IBEC's reviews but also from the analysis of the aforementioned two Irish newspapers. For instance, referring to a speech by John Dunne, the Director General of IBEC, in 1996, *The Irish Times* noted:

> While accepting a need remained for achieving greater social cohesion, [John Dunne said] ... this could not deflect the social partners from 'the primacy of competitiveness'.[11]

Our research revealed also that IBEC changed significantly its rhetoric and stance towards domestic politico-economic developments in 2000. Until that year, its rhetoric was characterised by strong optimism based on the assumption that the economy and the social partnership were moving on the right track for Ireland's international competitiveness. IBEC characterised the year 1996 as a year of *Strong Growth and a New Agreement* (IBEC, 1997: 4). The respective title for 1997 was *A Year of High Growth and Low Inflation* (IBEC, 1998: 2). Furthermore, the notion that the 'economic performance of Ireland ... has been ... the envy of ... [its] ... fellow European members' (IBEC, 2000: 3) was widespread in all the reviews for the period 1996–99. This strongly positive and optimistic rhetoric was qualified to an extent in the analysis of the economic year 2000, which, however, remained a year in which *Growth Exceed[ed] Forecasts* (IBEC, 2001: 4). The optimistic stance changed with regard to 2001, when IBEC claimed that, as 'we predicted in last year's Annual Review the Irish economy slowed down *dramatically* in 2001' (IBEC, 2002: 4; emphasis added).

Regarding this shift in IBEC's discourse it can be said that even though there was a slowdown in the Irish economy (from 9.4% GDP growth in 2000, to 6.1% in 2001 and 6.6% in 2002; source: OECD) the growth rates of the Irish economy remained the highest within the OECD (the OECD average was 3.9%, 1.2% and 1.6% in 2000, 2001 and 2002 respectively) and hardly justified the use of dramatic tones by IBEC. Thus, as analysed below, the repetitive use of the term dramatic by IBEC in 2002 must have been serving a different purpose.

In the beginning of the period under examination IBEC defined as reasons for Ireland's economic success, the successful macroeconomic management, the 'continued consensus approach' and the success in attracting high-quality FDIs (IBEC, 1997: 4). At the same time Anthony Barry, the president of IBEC, was congratulating the government for following an employment policy based on flexibility, 'which largely reflected the policy objectives for which ... IBEC ... had campaigned over the years (ibid.: 3; see also 7). Building on this approach, in the 1998, Barry claimed that 'we now have to look forward to even more radical changes ... to meet the greater changes of an expended marketplace' (IBEC, 1998: 1). Along these lines he called for the reduction of corporate and capital gains tax, and underlined that 'wealth must be generated before it can be redistributed' (ibid.). Along similar lines IBEC claimed that it intensively and successfully lobbied the government, to force it to accept IBEC's recommendations with regard to public–private partnerships (see IBEC, 1999: 9; 2000: 3, 10). Another burning issue on the agenda of Irish industrial relations was that of the recognition of trade unions. On this IBEC forcefully argued for the

> important principles which the Confederation had articulated over the past number of years: that the voluntary system of industrial relations must be underpinned and reinforced; and that no action be taken to impose mandatory trade union recognition on employers. (IBEC, 1999: 4)

In defending its flexibility agenda IBEC did not hesitate to qualify its general pro-European stance. For instance it repeatedly expressed 'grave concerns' with regard to the 1999 EU Working Time Directive (IBEC, 2000: 9, 11). Furthermore, with regard to the Irish proposal for tax cuts it noted: 'The EU Commission ... had a different view and its very public disagreement with the government on the issue did nothing to improve the image of the EU among Irish citizens' (IBEC, 2001: 5).

It can thus be concluded that IBEC contended that the economic miracle was based on the fact that the government and the other social partners (mainly ICTU), had conceded, subscribed to and followed the 'policy objectives for which ... IBEC had campaigned over the years' (IBEC, 1997: 3). Taking into account the economic policies that dominated in the Republic after the end of the 1980s, IBEC's claim seems to be a valid one, i.e. it is rather clear that it was IBEC that set the parameters within which the social partnership strategy was moving and changing. It must, however, be pointed out that even though these parameters triggered industrial action, mainly in the public sector (see for instance IBEC, 1998: 4; 1999: 4–5), they generated such an unprecedented wealth that any trade union opposition to them became unsubstantiated, if not irrelevant.

This 'successful recipe' was challenged in 2000. Above all it seemed that the parameters set by IBEC were no longer to be taken for granted even if they bore the partnership's imprint. To face this situation IBEC tried to maximise the pressure on its partners through warnings such as the following:

> the failure of trade unions to deliver their commitments under PPF [the 2000 social pact *Programme for Prosperity and Fairness*] was a major source of unease, calling into question the very validity of such agreements in the future. (IBEC, 2001: 15)

In addition, in its message in the 2002 review, William Burgess, the then new president of IBEC, noted:

> The Confederation has been seriously concerned for some time that business is the only social partner which remembers that the prosperity of the nation depends on our ability to sell our goods and services at the right price in the global market. (IBEC, 2002: 1)

It was within the above context that by 2002 IBEC talked about a 'dramatic slowdown', 'weakening confidence' and 'eroded' competitiveness with regard to the Irish economy (see for instance IBEC, 2002: 4, 5; see also Hardiman, 2005).

Last but not least, it should be noted that the analysis of the articles that were published in *The Irish Times* and *Irish Independent* during the period 1994–2001 and included both the terms 'IBEC' and 'globalisation' (see above) led us to an interesting finding. The IBEC's economic globalisation discourse and agenda were not the most radical of their kind on the Irish politico-economic scene. The *Irish Independent*, i.e. the biggest in circulation Irish newspaper, throughout the second half of the 1990s, criticised IBEC (and the social partnership as a whole) as a 'dinosaur', 'the voice of the big banks and the semi-states', and 'the old economy',[12] as opposed to 'the tigers', i.e. the multinational companies, and the 'new economy'. Thus, throughout the 1990s, one of the two most important newspapers in Irish public discourse, and that owned by the so-called 'baron' of the Irish media, Tony O'Reilly,[13] was strongly pushing and arguing for the extension of the non-ideological space of Irish politico-economic scene, accusing the official body of business representatives of being a 'dinosaur', suffering from a 'semi-state mindset',[14] and not serving the needs and interests of the Irish economy. This criticism went so far as ironically to suggest that IBEC 'should apply for membership of ICTU'.[15] Thus, a major part of the mainstream press criticised IBEC's economic discourse and agenda, not for demanding too fast, too much of economic globalisation but for not demanding enough.

To sum up, the lack of any references to globalisation in IBEC's discourse was compensated for by an omnipresent economic globalisation agenda, in the name of which IBEC did not hesitate to confront and criticise the European Commission, or even to dispute the validity of the social pacts, so central to the Irish economic miracle. Thus, it could be argued that the non-ideological space that was traced in the manifestos of the political parties, found its source and generating dynamic in the discourse of IBEC.

Irish Congress of Trade Unions (ICTU)[16]

As we saw in chapter 2 the role of ICTU in Irish economy and society changed fundamentally in the end of the 1980s. A key factor for this change was the agreement *Programme for National Recovery* that was reached by the social partners in 1987. This agreement met its aims and led to a new one for the period 1990–93, entitled *Programme for Economic and Social Progress*. As Peter Cassells, the General Secretary of ICTU for the period 1987–99, has commented, this second agreement 'worked better than expected thus creating a new and unprecedented dynamic in Irish politico-economic life; a dynamic which found at its core the institution of social partnership'.[17]

We analysed above how IBEC seemed to set the parameters for this dynamic, and how it *did not* speak about globalisation. We also demonstrated the emergence of a non-ideological space in Irish politico-economic life; a space which would be defined by most globalisation critics and anti-globalisation protesters as a paragon of globalisation. Within this context it is important to study how Irish workers read these developments and (re)articulated their identity, role, aims and strategy. The importance of the EU level in these developments should always be kept in the background of our analysis (see the relevant section in the Greek case).

In order to study the discourse of ICTU we examined two of its periodical official publications for the period 1995–2001: (a) the biennial Report of the Executive Council (REC) that cover in a comprehensive manner all the annual activities of ICTU. (b) The Reports of Proceedings (RP) of the Biennial Delegate Conferences of ICTU. The 'Delegate Conferences' were established in 1993 and aim to set the 'strategic orientation' for the ICTU's Executive Council. They bring together a large number of delegates from most, if not all, the Irish trade unions, along with invited speakers.

Unlike the IBEC, ICTU did develop a discourse on globalisation. For instance, Peter Cassells used the term globalisation in his introduction for both the 1997 and 1999 Reports of the Executive Council. In particular, in the 1997 report (for the years 1995–97) he noted: 'We also worked closely with the International Confederation of Free Trade Unions in highlighting the implications of globalisation for workers in the developing world' (ICTU, 1997: 5). This issue was then explored further in the section on the international activities of ICTU (ibid.: 61).

Yet the concept of globalisation was more prominent in the 1999 report. In his introduction to the latter, Peter Cassells noted that the changes under way in the Irish politico-economic system were 'occurring in a world seeking to cope with the impact of globalisation' (ICTU, 1999: 4). Furthermore, the section on the Irish economic situation concluded that the 'sustained pattern of growth reflects the resilience of the Irish economy to increasing globalisation' (ibid.: 12); whereas the section on the social partnership argued that there 'is still the challenge of securing the European social model in the face of globalisation which seeks to build a competitive edge on low wages and low standards' (ibid.: 16). Furthermore, the report included a small subsection entitled, 'Responding to Globalisation'. There, one reads:

> Globalisation can be described as the increased integration of national economies into the world economy which significantly reduces the scope for independent national economic policy-making and increases the inter-dependence between nations and regions of the global economy. Ireland as a small open economy is one of the most global economies ... Around 45% of the workshop in manufacturing industry are employed in foreign owned companies. In the face of the challenges presented by globalisation Congress has consistently advocated the need to adopt a 'high road' strategy to economic development. (ibid.: 92)

According to Cassells such a 'high road' strategy should be based on investments in technology and on social partnership, in contrast to a 'low road' strategy that would be based on 'deregulation, unfettered competition, low wages' (ibid.).

Thus after 1998 the issue of globalisation acquired a more central position to the discourse and agenda of ICTU. This is also exemplified by the fact that in the Biennial Delegate Conference, in 1999, the third motion carried (out of seventy-seven) was exclusively devoted to globalisation. The motion was put forward by Inez McCormack who was representing UNISON. It was entitled *Globalisation: Social Ground Rules,* and its first paragraph reads as follows:

> Conference recognises that in order to tackle the effects of globalisation it is essential to lay social ground rules to enable all to claim their fair share of wealth ... and to ensure that social progress goes hand in hand with economic progress. Conference therefore commits itself to vigorously campaign for such a global ethic. (ICTU, 1999a: 11)

Similar positions were taken in the 2001 report, that declared:

> Globalisation refers to major shifts towards the elimination of controls on markets both through the reduction of barriers to international trade and investment and the deregulation and privatisation of national industries that has occurred during the past twenty years ... Congress and the international labour movement are not against globalisation: indeed we would agree that globalisation can be a big part of the answer to the problems of the world's poor. But it is also a big part of the problem ... Unfortunately this move towards free trade has not been balanced by the development of a social dimension. (ICTU, 2001a: 61; part of a special section on globalisation entitled *Globalisation: the Need for International Standards*)

Within this context, ICTU was eager to manifest its commitment to the 'European model of development' (ICTU 2001: 9–10). For instance, a motion carried in the Delegate Conference, in Bundoran, in 2001, was entitled *Economic Strategy: Nearer to Brussels than Boston,* and declared that 'globalisation should be underpinned by social ground rules and a commitment to the redistribution of wealth' (ibid.: 9–10). Following this line, ICTU maintained that it would keep working towards a more equitable sharing of 'the profits of globalisation' between companies and workers (ICTU, 2001a: 62).

What have been the factors that determined the formation and evolution of the ICTU's strategy and discourse, and its engagement with the hegemonic discourse of globalisation? There are three crucial contextual factors that delineate also three different but interacting phases in ICTU's discourse on globalisation. The first factor had to do with the impact of the 'Irish miracle' itself. This miracle was based on 'economic globalisation policies', such as corporate tax reductions, non-mandatory recognition of trade unions and flexibility in the labour market. These were policies that brought to Ireland significant investments from big pharmaceutical and IT companies, and generated for more than a decade the highest growth rates within the OECD countries. They also generated full employment, reversing a historic trend towards emigration. They thus elevated Irish society from deprivation and misery to economic success, delivering for the first time in Irish history the promise of a wealthy and prosperous society. This could not but lead to the emergence of a set of policies and practices that were beyond contestation – what we have defined here as the non-ideological space of the Irish politico-economic system. Within this context, at least for the first years of the second half of the 1990s, the discourse of ICTU on (economic) globalisation could not be negative, as happened with many trade unions in many countries around the world. Yet, ICTU was not insulated either from these foreign unions or from the debates within the left and the international labour movement. Arguably that is why in the beginning globalisation was conceptualised and presented by ICTU as a phenomenon with implications for developing countries, disassociated from everyday life in Ireland. In short, it can be said that the problematisation by ICTU of the parameters of Irish economic development was not a logical option at the time, because these parameters and the respective policies were delivering unprecedented wealth in the Irish society.

The second factor that conditioned the workers' discourse was the issue of social partnership. The view that IBEC set the broader parameters of policy agenda is not indeed an accurate picture of the Irish politico-economic scene of the second half of the 1990s. It seems to be the case that a *genuine* social partnership had been developed between IBEC and ICTU (or, in any case, ICTU and the majority of the trade unions were thinking so). Thus, in the years up to 1997–98, not only did ICTU not develop a 'mainstream' European trade union discourse on globalisation, but to a large extent it endorsed many aspects of the European employers associations' discourse. For instance: (a) the priority that was given by ICTU to the concept of competitiveness, in the name of the improvement of living standards (see for instance ICTU, 1997: 10; the 'Partnership 2000' was crucial in this regard). (b) The adoption of flexibility in the labour market as something given. For instance, the 1995 Delegate Conference 'calls on the Executive Council to campaign to ensure that ... flexible working practices are jointly agreed by employers and trade unions' (carried motion 33, see: ICTU, 1995: 70; see also ICTU, 1997: 7, 25; 1999: 51, 57). (c) The soft stance that was adopted towards 'the necessity for restructuring', the need to increase the 'atypical and part-time employment' and the 'reform of the public sector'; which were conceptualised as rather natural and inevitable effects of the 'changing economic and commercial environment' (see for instance ICTU, 1997: 28–30). (d) The emphasis that was paid on the 'necessity for modernisation'. For instance, the motion Economic Progress Through Partnership in 1997 acknowledged that 'much more needs to be done to modernise our economy and our workplaces for the challenges of the new millennium' (ICTU, 1997a: 41; see also relevant references in ICTU, 1999: 2, 12, 44, 60, 67). The need for modernisation was also stressed in the first motion carried out in both the 1999 and 2001 Conferences (see respectively ICTU, 1999a: 9; 2001a: 10). (e) The adoption of the concept of, and necessity for efficiency (see for instance ICTU, 1999: 4, 12, 45).

The adoption, however, of employers' views and their lexicon did not stop the Congress from bringing to the heart of its discourse the issue of the unfair and unequal distribution of the benefits from the economic miracle. But for ICTU a genuine partnership was the best place for addressing and solving this problem. Within the above context, the strategic objective of ICTU was to avoid reducing the bargaining with IBEC to a plain 'pay negotiation' issue, as this would destroy the genuine character of their partnership. This strategy seemed to work well up to the end of the 1990s. Furthermore developments such as the 'Profit Sharing' and 'Employee Share Ownership Plans' were reassuring the workers' representatives for the genuine character of the partnership.[18] Thus, the ICTU's approach to economic globalisation policies remained rather neutral, even if increasingly alarming.

The last factor that influenced and arguably moved the Congress's discourse closer to those of its European counterparts, had to do with what can be described as the identity crisis of the social partnership and of the labour movement. Three interwoven developments were instrumental here. First, was the growing dissatisfaction on the part of labour with the social partnership's failing promise of a more fair and equal society. Thus although all strata of Irish society had moved upwards in terms of economic benefits, both the discourse and the reality of the gap between the 'haves' and the 'have-nots' acquired a central place in the Irish polity after the end of the 1999. Second, this dissatisfaction was enhanced by the fact that some of the social partnership's parameters that were pushed by the unions throughout the

1990s proved to be much less flexible than what a concept of a genuine partnership would imply. For instance, the issue of the mandatory recognition of trade unions, central to the discourse and expectations of the Congress, had reached a stalemate by 1999. Third, and maybe more importantly, a feeling started to be generated among labour unions that although the 'Partnership has ... helped to produce a great number of jobs, ... it has been less effective in ensuing that those jobs are rewarding, less stressful, more secure and compatible with rich family life'; thus the 'work–life balance' had been changed for the worse.[19] As a result the ICTU seemed to abandon in 1999 the prioritisation of competitiveness as a condition for a better future. As Cassells claimed:

> if this country's vision does not reach beyond the goal of economic growth and competitiveness, we could slide into a shallow, selfish, highly divided society where poverty, exploitation and discrimination become permanent features. (ICTU, 2001a: 45)

Thus, the ICTU's discourse and strategy changed significantly after 1999. The need for a 'social dimension' dominated the Congress's discourse (replacing the prioritisation of competitiveness). The negative effects of globalisation were not to be discussed only with regard to developing countries. And the European model of development was promoted by ICTU as a response to globalisation.

National Economic and Social Council (NESC)[20]

The NESC played a significant role in the revival of the social partnership in Ireland in the late 1980s. The personality of Professor Rory O'Donnell, the Director of NESC, was crucial in this regard. Indeed O'Donnell is considered to be one of the main architects of the modern social partnership (i.e. post mid-1980s). NESC was the place where the social partners (including representatives from the government, employers, workers, farmers, the community and voluntary sector, key government departments and independent experts) met and exchanged ideas about a wide range of economic and social issues. The Council's secretariat (led by the director) had a crucial role in this process, for it was up to the secretariat to synthesise and guide the various and often opposing opinions expressed. The published reports and recommendations that constituted the end product of these processes, aimed at delineating, or defining the common ground among the various participants and offering strategic guidance for governmental policies.

After IBEC and ICTU, NESC remains the last piece of the puzzle of social partners' engagement with the hegemonic discourse of global-isation. The analysis of the NESC's discourse was based on the following documents: (a) the press releases of NESC for the period 1993–2001. Through the press releases one can monitor all the activities of NESC. They also included comprehensive summaries of all its publications. (b) The full text of the NESC's reports for the period 1999–2001. Some of these reports focused on general topics, such as the future opportunities and challenges for Irish economy, while others had a more thematic focus, such as the issues of poverty or profit-sharing.

The picture that emerges from the study of the press releases is the following. Up to 1997/98 three issues dominated NESC's discourse: the necessity and primacy of competitiveness,[21] the issue of unemployment (which for the first time since 1990 decreased into a single figure in 1998) and the social partnership as the 'most effective mechanism for developing Irish competitiveness and social cohesion in the ... global context'.[22] While the issues of competitiveness and of social partnership maintained their primacy in the NESC's discourse, after 1998 the emphasis on unemployment was replaced by an emphasis on social cohesion and inclusiveness.[23] Globalisation came to the fore of the NESC's discourse with the report entitled *Opportunities, Challenges and Capacities for Choice* that was published in December 1999 (NESC, 1999). There NESC developed its vision for Ireland for the first decade of the twenty-first century, and explicated the economic and social strategy that had to be followed in order that this vision to be met. Along with plenty of scattered references, the report included a whole section on globalisation (NESC, 1999: 92–109). NESC saw globalisation as one of the three fundamental integration processes that posed a challenge for the development of Irish economy (along with the European and the Republic–Northern Ireland economic integrations). The section started with the acknowledgement that globalisation 'is a term that has become part of everyday life in the 1990s' (ibid.: 92) and defined three factors as the 'main driving forces of globalisation: technology, trade liberalisation and increased capital/financial flows' (ibid.: 95). Based on a detailed reading of the report, it can be argued that NESC attempted to free the concept of globalisation from its negative connotations, and to present globalisation as a given context that necessitated particular policies. Thus NESC adopted a 'new reality' approach to globalisation.

It can therefore be argued that the NESC discourse on globalisation was determined by the attempt of its leadership to define and protect the consensus among the social partners on what were, and what was

demanded by, the prevailing economic conditions. Hence, the engagement of NESC's secretariat with the globalisation debate served,
intentionally or unintentionally, a strategic purpose: to neutralise pre-
emptively any potential attempt by any of the social partners to use
the concept of globalisation as a vehicle to politicise the non-
ideological space that dominated the Irish politico-economic system.

The Archbishop of Dublin and Primate of Ireland, Cardinal Desmond Connell, and the church in Ireland[24]

The church is an important actor in Irish society and therefore its
impact cannot be excluded from the study of Irish public discourse. It
is also worth pointing out that the active stance adopted by Cardinal
Connell in public affairs, did make a difference, reviving in some
respects the role of the church in Irish public life. Of course within the
church one finds different voices and views. Yet the focus of this
section on Cardinal Connell is entirely legitimate as the latter was not
only the head of the Catholic church in the Republic during the period
under examination, but also a religious leader who adopted a very
active stance and exerted significant influence in Irish public
discourse.

Our analysis of the Cardinal Connell's discourse was mostly based
on the press coverage of the Cardinal's speeches, interviews and
public interventions. In particular, the newspaper *The Irish Times* was
selected as the most credible source of references in the Irish press,
and through the electronic database *Nexis UK* (formerly *Lexis-Nexis
Executive*) we collected all the articles that were published in this
newspaper and made a reference to 'Desmond Connell', during the
period 1996–2001. We then used this material as an electronic pool
of articles from which we kept all the articles that included one of the
following keywords: global, globalisation, identity, flexibility and
Celtic Tiger. In addition, articles that included the keywords 'modern'
or 'Europe' were also kept, when the content of the articles was
judged relevant to our investigation. This selection process left us
with forty articles, the great majority of which had direct quotations
from Cardinal Connell, and approximately one-quarter of which were
interviews and articles or speeches of his. This material was then
supplemented by Cardinal Connell's speeches and statements that
were available in the on-line archive of Dublin Diocese for the period
1999–2001.

It is striking, once again, that in *none* of the above articles,
speeches or statements did Cardinal Connell use the term globalisa-

tion or any of its derivatives. Yet, if one accounts for the fact that the concept of globalisation represented no stakes and served no significant function within Irish public discourse, then at least some room for an explanation is made. The Cardinal's discourse could not but exist in a dialectical relationship with the discourses of the other national institutional actors, and as long as the latter did not engage with the concept of globalisation, the Cardinal had no apparent reason to do so either. Nevertheless, Cardinal Connell attacked, with the same ferocity and publicity that Archbishop Christodoulos fought globalisation in Greece, the most important expression and achievement of the Irish non-ideological space: the Celtic Tiger.[25] Furthermore, his critique, having as focal points the issues of secularism,[26] individualism, identity and tradition, had many things in common with Archbishop Christodoulos's critique of globalisation.

In 1998 the Cardinal declared that the 'technological world ... reduces ... [children] to the indignity of products and derives its meaning from power rather than from gift. This becomes all more acute when they find that the brave new world of prosperity leaves them without hope of participation'.[27] In the same year, speaking to Accord (the Catholic Marriage Counselling Service) he characterised the dominant economic system as 'unchecked capitalism', and called for 'a radical re-examination of the whole economic system under which we are living', concluding that 'we are so full of the Celtic tiger that anything else seems unthinkable'.[28] A year later, in 1999, he maintained:

> Co-existing with the prosperity and gain of the Celtic Tiger is the sad spectacle of poverty and exclusion ... The forthcoming budget represents an ideal opportunity for the Government to build further on its commitment to tackling poverty ... it must also take note of what is being referred to as the 'New Poor' in our contemporary society: those who, while gainfully employed, struggle to survive economically. (Desmond Connell, 1999)

Thus the Cardinal articulated a discourse that had as its focal points most of the themes that dominated in critiques of globalisation, e.g. 'unchecked capitalism', 'poverty', 'exclusion', 'consumerism',[29] 'depersonalisation'.[30] He did not however use the concept of globalisation as a means of bringing together and conceptualising these diverse developments. Nor did the Cardinal engage with the all-dominant contemporary debate on globalisation. It seems that rather than using globalisation to attack the Celtic Tiger, he generated a critique of Celtic Tiger 'from within'. In this regard Cardinal Connell's discourse can be considered as the only domestic discourse that aimed from the outset to problematise the non-ideological space of Irish politics and economics.

Media coverage

Focusing on a representative source of media coverage, throughout the period 1996–2001, this section aims at examining: (a) the volume and the evolution of the use of the term globalisation; (b) the context of its use; and (c) the composition of the people using this term. Through this analysis we also aim to capture the discourses and activities of groups that have not been studied above, such as think-tanks, academics, civil servants, artists and anti-globalisation protesters. In the case of Ireland, such a representative source was judged to be the newspaper *The Irish Times*. Although *The Irish Times* was second in circulation among daily morning newspapers during the period under investigation,[31] most Irish scholars agree that it is a more credible source both as an 'archive' of social actors' discourses, and as an indicator of the political debates that dominate in Irish polity. The choice of a daily newspaper in the case of Ireland (six papers per week – not published on Sunday) creates indeed some comparability problems with our findings from the Greek newspaper VIMA, which is a Sunday edition (one paper per week). The problems generated by the comparison of a 'Sunday' with a 'daily' edition should not be downsized or disregarded. Yet our primary aim in the respective sections was to find a representative press sample within the two different national contexts; and the Sunday VIMA and the daily *The Irish Times* serve well this purpose. Of course when the two sources are compared, their difference is taken into consideration.

The discourse of globalisation in The Irish Times *(1996–2001)*
To analyse the emergence of globalisation discourse in *The Irish Times*, we used the *Nexis UK* database (formerly *Lexis-Nexis Executive*) to collect all the articles that were published in *The Irish Times* during the period 1996–2007 and included one or more references to the term globalisation. As in the Greek case, the analysis in this section focuses on the period 1996–2001. The main findings are as follows. Figure 4.1 registers the volume of the articles that included references to the term globalisation during the period 1996–2001.

The first observation to be made is that the number of articles found in the Greek newspaper VIMA exceed, sometimes by far, for

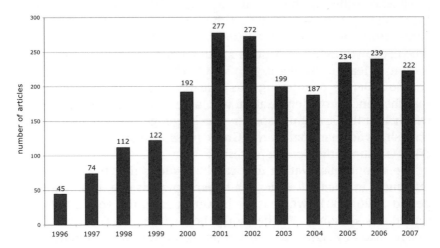

Figure 4.1 References to globalisation in *The Irish Times*

Note: data collected in January 2008.

most of the period 1996–2001 (except 2001), the articles found in *The Irish Times*, despite the fact that in quantitative terms the absolute number of *The Irish Times* papers searched was sixfold (being a daily edition) those of VIMA (being a Sunday edition). Figure 4.2 is suggestive in this regard.

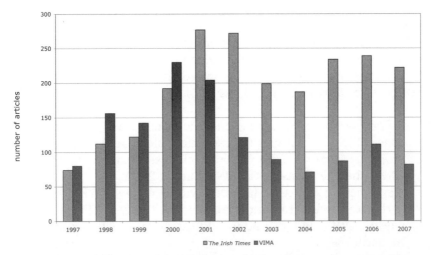

Figure 4.2 References to globalisation in *The Irish Times* and Sunday editions of VIMA

Note: the year 1996 was omitted because of incomplete data in VIMA.

Thus, considering the absolute number of the articles found in *The Irish Times*, it can be argued that the first and most important observation from the study of *The Irish Times* for the period 1997–2001 is the very low number of articles making reference to the term globalisation, at least in comparison to VIMA. This represents an interesting paradox. Before conducting this research our main hypothesis was that the concept of globalisation would be abundant in the Irish press which literally speaking 'speaks' the language of globalisation (i.e. English), and marginal in the Greek press at least up to the end of 1999 (i.e. until the Seattle protests).

The second observation that can be made is that the evolution of references in *The Irish Times* is a linear/upwards one, throughout the period 1996–2001 (whereas in the Greek case, the year 2000 represented a peak point). Furthermore, the 'Seattle effect' does not seem to have had any significant impact on the evolution of references. The 57% increase in references from 1999 to 2000, is lower than that seen from 1996 to 1997 (64%), and close to the change seen from 1997 to 1998 (51%) or from 2000 to 2001 (44%).

Yet, to grasp the nature of the emergence of globalisation discourse in *The Irish Times*, we need to move beyond the aggregate number of published articles, and examine the section of the newspaper in which these articles were published and the identity of their authors. First, we examine their thematic distribution, according to section of publication. The aim here is to elucidate the different aspects of the globalisation discourse (economic, political, cultural, etc.) and their relative gravity within *The Irish Times*.

The articles that included a reference to the term globalisation were found under thirty different section headings and supplements. To facilitate our analysis, we organised these different sections into five generic categories, as follows:

1 *Political sections (PS)* that includes: home news (HN); editorial; front page (FP); news features (NF); opinion; elections 1997; features.
2 *Economic sections (ES)*[32] that includes: business and finance (B&F); business this week (BW); budget 2001.
3 *World news (WN)* that includes: world review (WR); European Parliament news (EPN); the Amsterdam Treaty (TAT); developing world (DW); France; attack on America (AA); Scotland and Ireland (S&I).
4 *Education, Art, Life and Sport (EALS)* that includes: art; media scope (MS); education and living (E&L); style; culture; sport; weekend.

5 *Other* that includes: sound and vision (S&V); computimes; commercial property (CP); obituaries (Obit.); other.

Figure 4.3 offers aggregate data for the distribution of references in the various sections for the period 1996–2001, while Figure 4.4 monitors the evolution of this distribution during the same period.

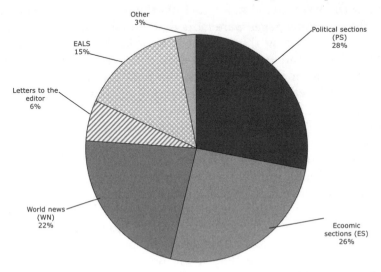

Figure 4.3 References to globalisation by section of publication in *The Irish Times* (1996–2001) (percentage of total articles)

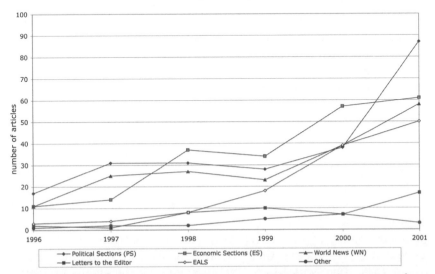

Figure 4.4 Evolution of the references to globalisation by section of publication in *The Irish Times*

On the basis of the above data, a number of observations can be made: First, there appears to be two turning points in the globalisation discourse as this emerged in *The Irish Times*. The first was in 1998, when the economic pages superseded the political pages as the main source of references to globalisation. Thus although a discourse on globalisation emerged first in the political pages and the pages dealing with international news, in 1998 the references to globalisation in the economic pages were more than doubled in comparison to 1997, thus superseding the references both in the PS and the WN sections. The second turning point was in 2001when there was a significant boom in the references in the political pages. Hence the political sections came at the top in terms of references to globalisation, increasing significantly their distance with all other sections. Therefore after a period in which globalisation seemed to be treated as an 'economic issue' (1998–2000), globalisation (re-)entered the political agenda of *The Irish Times*. It should also be noted here that this 'political agenda' did not include the 'world news' (which in 2001 approached the economic pages in terms of references to globalisation). To exemplify further this point, Figure 4.5 breaks down the 'political pages' to its constituent elements, demonstrating that most references to globalisation, throughout the period under examination, were made in the section 'home news'. This dynamic is also depicted in the increase in the 'letters to the editor' (see Figure 4.4). There, although a considerable number of letters discussed globalisation as part of issues of international concern (e.g. world trade, international economy, etc.), the majority of these articles were about domestic issues concerning Ireland, and a significant number of them were dealing with the issue of (Irish) culture.

The second important observation on Figure 4.4 concerns the significant increase of references in the EALS pages. The number of references to globalisation in these pages reached those of the political pages and the world news in 2000, and continued to increase in 2001. This points to a gradual diffusion of the globalisation discourse in the discourse generated by *The Irish Times*. Last but not least, it should be noted that the intensification of the use of the concept of globalisation after 2000, at least in the political pages, seems to be on a much higher scale in *The Irish Times* than that found in VIMA. It is indicative that in VIMA the references in section A (which is the main political section of the newspaper) increased only by 4% between 2000 and 2001, whereas the respective increase in the political pages of *The Irish Times* was 130%. Therefore, even if the events in Seattle were behind the reversal of the downward trend in references in 1999

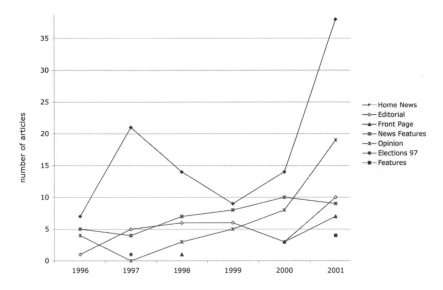

Figure 4.5 References to globalisation in the political sections of
The Irish Times

(in PS, ES, WN pages), these events do not seem capable of accounting for the increase in references between 2000 and 2001. Hence, another dynamic must have been driving the 2001 increase in references.

To address this issue and get a more complete picture of the globalisation discourse in *The Irish Times*, we need to consider not only the section where articles referring to globalisation were published, but also the identities of the authors of these articles. Figures 4.6 and 4.7 do exactly this. The first presents aggregate numbers for the period 1996–2001, whereas the second demonstrates the dynamic of the references in the different author categories.

Based on the above data we can observe the following: first, the above-mentioned boom in references in 2001 was led primarily by journalists and was strongly supported by 'unsigned articles' and 'readers' (i.e. letters to the editor). The increase of references by 'readers' in 2001, indicates that globalisation had started to acquire some gravity in Irish public discourse. This trend seems also to be confirmed by the increase in the 'unsigned articles'. As has already been argued this category can be treated as an indicator of the degree of 'quotidianisation' of a hegemonic discourse, i.e. as an indicator of the transformation of globalisation from an event 'out there', to an integral part of everyday life and everyday news. This conclusion is enhanced also by the increase in references by politicians and

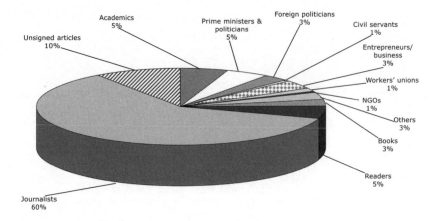

Figure 4.6 References to globalisation by authors' identity in *The Irish Times* (1996–2001) (percentage of total articles)

Note: 'Others' includes: governmental documents, international organisations (e.g. ILO, United Nations, World Trade Organisation), foreign academics, the church, employers' representatives and artists. 'NGOs' includes both Irish–based and overseas organisations. 'Books' includes only book reviews written by journalists. Book reviews written by academics were included in the 'academics' category.

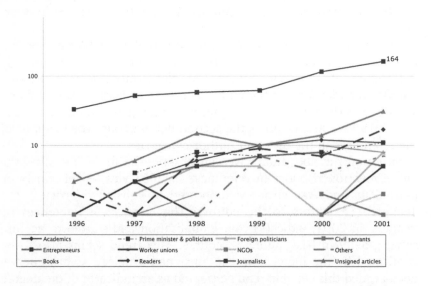

Figure 4.7 Evolution of references to globalisation by authors' identity in *The Irish Times*[33]

Note: The space between the numbers in the vertical axis has been algorithmically adjusted.

academics in 2001. Yet it must be kept in mind that both the dynamics depicted in Figure 4.7 and the aggregate numbers of Figure 4.6 are based on a very low absolute number of articles/references.

With regard to the category 'journalists', some further observations may give us a clearer picture of globalisation discourse in *The Irish Times*. First, it should be noted that the globalisation discourse produced by *Irish Times* journalists was rather dispersed, i.e. it was not produced only by a few *Irish Times* editors or correspondents. In fact the majority of relevant articles were written by a wider pool of journalists. For the period 1996–2001, 33% of the articles were written by other *Irish Times* journalists, 11% by the foreign affairs and development editors/correspondents, 8% by the economics and finance editors/correspondents, 8% by the different media editors/correspondents, 3% by the environment editor/correspondent, 7% by the Europe and Washington correspondent, 8% by the Europe correspondent, 2% by the Washington correspondent, 7% by the Paris correspondent, 5% by the Rome correspondent, and 8% were editorials. Second, after other *Irish Times* journalists, the second dominant category is the European editors and correspondents. If we count the latter together (i.e. Europe, Paris, Rome and half of the references of Europe and Washington correspondents), they amount approximately to 23% of the written articles. Some further analysis is interesting here. The European editors/correspondents covered throughout 1996–2001 the way in which globalisation was conceptualised in Ireland's major European partners. This coverage is interesting because it helps us to understand how globalisation was conceptualised within Irish public discourse. For instance, commenting on the 1997 French general elections, Lara Marlowe (Paris correspondent) noted: 'If globalisation is an almost mystical force, buffering France from afar, le libéralisme is the creed of those who collaborate with it';[34] and, similarly, in 1998:

> France's fitful mood seems rooted in misgivings over globalisation and economic liberalism. A subliminal fear of losing their identity and secure existence.[35]

To better understand these comments we should place them in the context of the confrontation that Ireland had with most of its European partners on the issue of corporate taxation. On this, Patrick Smyth (European correspondent) noted in 1998:

> Socialist EU finance ministers are unlikely to be sympathetic to Charlie McCreevy's [Minister for Finance] ideological case for maintaining our

low corporate tax regime ... In truth, however the argument [against low corporate tax] is somewhat old-fashioned. It may have been a different matter 20 years ago, but we now live in the age of globalisation and extraordinary capital mobility.[36]

In 1999 the focus gradually shifted from this controversy onto the discourse of 'progressive governance' and the respective dynamic that had been created by the meetings of centre-to-left leaders (Bill Clinton, Tony Blair, Gerhard Schroder and Massimo d'Alema).[37] It was within this context that Paul Gillespie (foreign editor) wrote the article 'The Answer to Globalisation is Europeanisation',[38] maybe the only intervention on globalisation that was debated both within and beyond the pages of *The Irish Times*. Furthermore, as became evident during the debate on the 1998 referendum on the EU Amsterdam Treaty, the issue of the relationship between Europeanisation and globalisation came to dominate in the pro-European circles of Irish political life. Finally, *The Irish Times* covered also the more cautious or even sceptical approach to globalisation that was formulated by the Pope John Paul II.[39] Yet this latter approach did not seem to have had any broader impact on Irish public discourse.

To conclude, it can be argued that there are two main findings from the study of *The Irish Times*' globalisation discourse. The first is that, in comparison to VIMA, this discourse seems to have been of very low 'intensity' until 2000, i.e. for most of the period under examination here. Thus, to the extent that the Irish public discourse was reflected in the pages of *The Irish Times*, it can be argued that up to the late 1999 to mid-2000 period, the globalisation discourse was (comparatively to Greece) absent, from Ireland, i.e. the country that internationally was at the heart of the globalisation debate. The second finding is that after the second half of 2000 there was a boom in the use of the concept of globalisation. This boom cannot be unconnected to the 'Seattle effect' and the anti-globalisation protests that followed it. Yet the dynamics it had acquired in 2001, and the evolution of the references in terms both of section of publication and authors, suggest that there must have been a deeper, domestic reason for this development. It might be the case that it was only in 2001 that the rigidity of the social partnership's parameters came to be felt and challenged; or, in broader terms, it might be the case that after a period of unprecedented growth and prosperity, it was only in 2000–01 that notions of 'winners' and 'losers' started to be felt in the population, and thus globalisation discourse, as the latter dominated in Europe, started to make sense and be mobilised as an 'instrument of politicisation' in Ireland. It can also be the case that it was in this period that Irish public discourse started to embrace the way Ireland was conceptualised by its EU partners. We return to this point in the next chapter. Here it is important to point out that the study of *The Irish Times* demonstrated that after a period of absence, from 2000 onwards the globalisation discourse started to be implicated and have a more central role in the reproduction of Irish public discourse. This finding comes to confirm the findings from the study of the evolution of the discourses of the other institutional actors.

Conclusion

The analysis in this chapter revealed an interesting paradox. The concept of globalisation was relatively absent from Irish public discourse during the period 1996–2001. Furthermore, this absence was complemented by the existence of an all-powerful economic globalisation agenda that was both taken for granted, and was celebrated as the reason for the Irish economic miracle by all the political forces, including the employers and – for a long period of time – the workers. Within this context the evolving at the same period of time international debate about the potential negative effects of economic globalisation did not seem to resonate in Irish public discourse. This is not only evident in the discourses of the institutional actors examined, but also in the press sample that was analysed. What we did see emerging from 1996 to 2001 was a Celtic Tiger discourse (see also Smith, 2005: ch. 2; Phelan 2007). The latter had a twofold character. On the one hand, it celebrated the economic success of Ireland. Within this framework, the economic policies that were linked to this success were invested with a non-negotiable, non-disputable quality. On the other hand, however, it brought to the forefront of Irish public discourse a critique of the cultural consequences generated by these economic policies. This cultural critique was led by the church and was later adopted by Fine Gael. In addition, after 1998, there was a clear shift in the discourse and positions of the workers, and (later on also) the Labour Party. Through this shift globalisation became an object of critique, as it was already the case in many other European left-wing parties and workers' unions.

Notes

1 In the case of Ireland it proved difficult to collect in a consistent manner the speeches and interviews of all the party leaders. Thus, unlike in the Greek case, this chapter does not offer a separate section on the discourses of the party leaders.

2 For a short overview of the history of Irish parties, see Collins and Cradden, 2001: 16–31. For a well-documented research on Irish parties and elections, see Sinnott, 1995.

3 For the methodology followed in the analysis of the manifestos, see the respective section in chapter 3 of this book.

4 The four different documents were focused on the economy (FG, 1997a), education and healthcare (FG, 1997b), environment (FG, 1997c) and crime (FG, 1997d).

5 Michael Noonan replaced John Bruton as leader of FG in 2001.

6 A similar reference is made in the economic manifesto: '. . . our people are *living to work rather than working to live*' (FG, 2002b: 9, emphasis in the original).

7 IBEC is the main national association that represents Irish business and employers. It came into being in 1993, as a result of the merger between the Confederation of Irish Industry (founded in 1934) and the Federation of Irish Employers (founded in 1942). See IBEC's official website at: http://www.ibec.ie

8 See the official webpage of the European Foundation for the Improvement of Living and Working Conditions, a 'tripartite European Union body', at: www.eurofound.eu.int/emire/Ireland/employersassociation-ir.html (accessed 12 May 2008).

9 The research was focused on the following IBEC executives: Tony Barry (President, 1996–98), Richard Burrows (President, 1998–2000), John Dunne (Director General, 1992–2000).

10 The organisation of a conference on the impact of globalisation on the food and drink industry in 1998 seems rather to be an exception. See 'Dilger in Call for Big Companies', *Irish Independent*, 21 November 1998.

11 Extract from a speech at the conference Framework for a New Partnership in Dublin. The conference aimed at negotiating the basis for a new social pact among the social partners. 'Director of IBEC Says 10% Pay Rises "out of the Question"', *The Irish Times*, 24 October 1996, p. 10.

12 The quotations are from: 'Tigers Eat up the Dinosaurs', *The Sunday Independent*, 12 December 1999. Among others see also: 'Troops in: Bust AIB's Top Brass', 'Tigers vs Dinosaurs' and 'Did the Unions Dictate the Budget?' in *The Sunday Independent*, 2 April, 16 April and 10 December 2000, respectively.

13 Tony O'Reilly is the Chief Executive Officer and major shareholder of the firm 'Independent News and Media (INM), which is the dominant actor in the Irish newspaper industry. The degree of the concentration of the latter is exemplified 'in that around 80 per cent of Irish newspapers sold in Ireland in 2006 were sold by companies which are fully or partially' owned by INM. See the Irish country report of the European Journalism Centre available at: www.ejc.net/media_landscape/article/ireland/ (accessed 12 September 2008).

14 'Troops in: Bust AIB's Top Brass'; see note 12.

15 'Top of the Agenda the PPF is as Dead as a Dodo', *The Sunday Independent*, 3 December 2000.
16 ICTU was formed in 1959 and is the single umbrella organisation for all trade unions in Ireland. Of Irish trade union members 95% are in unions affiliated to ICTU. ICTU is a thirty-two-county body (including both the Republic and Northern Ireland). See the official website of ICTU at: www.ictu.ie
17 Personal interview, 27 June 2002.
18 See for instance ICTU, 1997: 27; 1999: 6, 44, 69, 82; 2001a: 11, 31.
19 The quotations are from the introduction of Peter Cassells in the 2001 report (see ICTU, 2001a: 3).
20 The NESC was founded in 1973 with as its main task to advise the Taoiseach on the development of the national economy, the achievement of social justice and the development of a strategic framework for the conduct of negotiations between the social partners. See NESC's official website at: www.nesc.ie
21 For the prevalence of this concept in Irish public discourse, see also Smith, 2004.
22 Press release for the Conclusions and Recommendations of the report *NESC Strategy into the 21st Century* (published on 8 October 1996). Available on-line at: www.nesc.ie/press (accessed 22 September 2008).
23 See the press releases for both the 'Overview' and the full text of the report *Opportunities, Challenges and Capacities for Choice*, published in November and December 1999, respectively. Available on-line at: www.nesc.ie/press (accessed 22 September 2008).
24 Cardinal Desmond Connell was appointed as Archbishop of Dublin in 1988 and served in this post until April 2004. He was elevated to the Sacred College of Cardinals in 2001.
25 An editorial of *The Irish Times* claimed in this regard that Dr Connell 'has been among the most insightful critics of the Celtic Tiger' (*The Irish Times*, 2 April 1999, p. 17).
26 For this criticism see for instance his article 'Church Cannot Accept the People Can Do no Wrong', *The Irish Times*, 14 October 1997, p. 16, where he connected the Holocaust and the Nazi and communist regimes, with the ideology of a secular modernity. This article triggered a lot of criticism. See for instance, Fintan O'Toole, 'Time to Move away from Moral Monopoly', *The Irish Times*, 17 October, 1997, p. 12.
27 Extract from a speech to the Life Society, at St Patrick's College. The full text of the speech was published in *The Irish Times*, 8 March 1999, p. 6. With a similar content, see also his article 'Risk in Judging Church with Hindsight', *The Irish Times*, 24 November 1998, p. 16, and his speech 'Science and Technology Bring Benefits but Risk of Depersonalisation', delivered on 10 April 2001.
28 The quotations are from Patsy McGarry, 'House Prices Put Family Life at Risk – Dr Connell', *The Irish Times*, 14 February 1998, p. 3. Patsy McGarry was the religious affairs correspondent of *The Irish Times*.

29 Ibid.
30 Desmond Connell, 'Science and Technology Bring Benefits But Risk of Depersonalisation', see note 27.
31 First in circulation was the *Irish Independent*. For circulation figures, see the database of the National Newspapers of Ireland, available at: www.nni.ie
32 The section of the daily editions of *The Irish Times* that deals with economic issues is headed 'business and finance'. 'Business this week' is a separate economic supplement that is published with *The Irish Times* every Thursday.
33 Some articles, although they explicitly attributed the use of the term globalisation to certain politicians, businesspersons, etc., were not articles written by them, but articles that were focusing on these persons' actions or speeches. I have credited these articles to these persons' categories and not to the journalists that signed the articles. This refers to the 4% of examined articles, and concerns almost exclusively the categories of 'academics', 'foreign politicians' and 'entrepreneurs/business'.
34 'Political Catchphrases that Possess the Elan of a Moose', *The Irish Times*, 29 May 1997, p. 13.
35 'French Jobless Develop a Taste for Strike Action', *The Irish Times*, 31 December 1998, p. 52.
36 'Corporation Tax Deal Could Lose Us EU Goodwill', *The Irish Times*, 30 November 1998, p. 16.
37 See for instance: P. Smyth, 'Transatlantic Alliances Strengthened . . . ', *The Irish Times*, 22 November 1999, p. 11; P. Smyth, 'New Dawn for Socialism but What Does it Mean Anymore?', *The Irish Times*, 31 December 1998, p. 51; P. Gillespie, 'For Europe a Decisive Time', *The Irish Times*, 21 June 2000, p. 60; D. Staunton, 'Fischer Denies German Vision of a Federal Europe is a Form of Imperialism', *The Irish Times*, 22 June 2000, p. 13; P. Gillespie, 'Process of Equalisation Between Europe . . . ', *The Irish Times*, 11 August 2001, p. 11.
38 *The Irish Times*, 30 December, 1997, p. 50.
39 See for instance, P. Agnew, 'Pope's Choices Map out Path to his Successor' *The Irish Times*, 22 February 2001, p. 16.

Part III

Conclusions

5

Facets of globalisation discourse

The aim of this chapter is twofold. First it offers a comparison of the communication of globalisation discourse in Greece and Ireland. Thus it summarises, juxtaposes and compares the main findings of chapters 3 and 4. Second, it analyses how the differences between Greece and Ireland can be explained, and draws some general conclusions on the materialisation of globalisation discourse.

Globalisation discourse in Greece and Ireland: a comparison

The main political parties

Our research revealed two very different modes of materialisation of globalisation discourse. In Greece the discourse of globalisation emerged as a new zone of contestation, as a new point of reference through which political parties came to reconceptualise what was at stake in economic, political and social terms. Thus, globalisation, conceptualised either as a dangerous dynamic that could lead to 'a new barbarism' (PASOK, 1996), or as a new form of imperialism (KKE, 1996), 'the domination of market over society' (PASOK, 1996; Synaspismos, 2000), a 'policy justification instrument' (KKE, 2000; Synaspismos, 2000), or, on the other hand, as a 'new reality' (ND, 1995, 2000) or even as a significant opportunity for the development of Greece (PASOK, 2000: 10), came to dominate and redefine the terms of antagonism between the Greek political parties.

Interestingly, there were changes in the positions of the political parties during the period under examination. For instance, the party in government, PASOK, shifted between the two national elections from a negative conceptualisation of globalisation to a proactively positive approach in which globalisation was conceptualised as a 'driving forces for development' (PASOK, 2000: 10). Moreover, even when the term globalisation was avoided in the party realm, this seemed to be a statement on globalisation itself. For instance, New

Democracy, after 2000 began to use the more 'neutral' concept of globality (παγκοσμιότητα), thus implicitly taking a (rather negative) position towards the concept of globalisation.

In Ireland, on the other hand, the discourse of globalisation emerged as a new zone of consensus, the constituent meanings and practices of which remained beyond public deliberation, ideological contestation or party antagonism (see also Phelan, 2007). It is indicative that the concept of globalisation itself was rather absent from the party political scene. On the other hand, the main 'objects' of economic globalisation (e.g. deregulation, privatisation, tax cuts) were ever present in Irish politics. Yet, these objects did not define a new zone of contestation, but rather a set of taken-for-granted policies and practices. Thus, the Irish political parties redefined their identities, visions, strategies, critiques and policy suggestions, not through a new zone of contestation, but rather through a new zone of a somewhat subliminal consensus that defined what was *not* to be discussed or disputed. In this process, the role and influence of the institution of social partnership was all powerful.

Along these lines, Fianna Fáil, Fine Gael and the Progressive Democrats set as their main governmental objective to do whatever was required in order for Ireland to remain attractive to 'mobile capital investments' (see FG, 1997a: 4; FF, 2002: 26, 29–30; PD, 1997, 2002), while the Labour Party has as its objective, at least in 1997, '[t]he prioritisation of enterprise' (LP, 1997: 6). Yet, as in Greece, some parties gradually changed their stance. For instance, the Labour Party adopted by 2002 a more traditional European left-wing stance that treated globalisation as a 'gross injustice' and as a threat to 'the social and economic rights of the individual' (LP, 2002: 1). In addition, after 1997, FG developed a critique of the phenomenon of the 'Celtic Tiger' that had many things in common with cultural critiques of globalisation. This critique however left 'untouched' the economic policies followed.

The social partners
The second key group of institutional actors that was examined in the two countries was the social partners.

Employers
The pattern of engagement of employers with globalisation discourse in the two countries was similar. On the one hand, they did not use the term or develop a discourse on globalisation as such. On the other hand, as one would expect, both IBEC and SEV promoted eagerly an

'economic globalisation' agenda. Thus, the dominant objects of economic globalisation (e.g. flexibility, liberalisation, deregulation, privatisation, corporate tax cuts) were at the core of their public pronouncements and policy suggestions. Moreover, the leaders of both IBEC and SEV agreed that economic globalisation policies were not something new for their organisations – these were policies for which their organisations had been lobbying since the mid to late 1980s.

There are, however, two interesting differences in the broader social context in which IBEC's and SEV's strategies and policies were developed. In the Greek political scene the concept of globalisation was ideologically charged. Thus, one could assume that SEV avoided this concept in order to avoid associating its proposals with an increasingly negatively charged concept. This was not the case in Ireland. On the contrary, considering the language factor (i.e. English), and Ireland's proximity to the UK and USA (through business and the diaspora) one would expect a wide dissemination of the concept of globalisation. This however did not happen. Another interesting difference between SEV and IBEC with regard to their social context is the following. In Greece, SEV was leading the domestic pro-economic globalisation agenda. In Ireland, IBEC was criticised throughout the period under examination by the bestselling Irish broadsheet, the *Irish Independent*, for not being active enough in the promotion of economic globalisation policies.

Workers

The concept of globalisation came, if in slightly different time frames, to reorder and dominate the discourses of workers. In the case of GSEE this happened in 1997, whereas in the case of ICTU it took place a year later. Furthermore, a significant point of convergence in workers' discourses was the emphasis they paid to the importance of the 'social dimension' of the European model of capitalism.

The first question to be raised then is what was there before these discursive shifts. What was it that globalisation changed or continued in the discourses of the two unions? In the case of GSEE, the central point of reference and object of critique during the period 1995–97 was 'neoliberalism'. Globalisation acquired a considerable position in GSEE's vocabulary in 1996, but it was only in 1997 that it became the new defining conceptual framework through which GSEE read its environment and produced its strategies, policies and vision. In this process globalisation came to be conceptualised as a 'justification instrument' used by the government and employers to promote policies against the vested interests and living conditions of the workers.

In the case of ICTU globalisation did not seem to have replaced any other dominant concept or point of reference. What did seem to happen is that ICTU itself changed the way it engaged with the discourse of globalisation. Thus, globalisation was present in ICTU's discourse since 1995. Yet, this early understanding and mobilisation of the concept of globalisation was associated with developing countries and broader issues of international development. It is in this regard that 1998 seems to signify a shift. From being an 'out there' developmental issue, globalisation began to be treated as an 'in here', first-order, domestic issue. This new type of engagement contested openly, if not the results, the direction of the Celtic Tiger's development.

The church

The study of the church was based on the analysis of the discourse of the head of the church in the two countries. In Greece, Archbishop Christodoulos launched a ferocious attack against globalisation. He portrayed it as a major and immediate threat to European societies in general and Greece in particular, and as a development that was associated with economic exploitation, identity and cultural annihilation, the 'forces of evil' and 'the destruction of Christianity' (Christodoulos, 2000). Cardinal Connell, on the other hand, did not make globalisation a key point of reference in his discourse. Instead he launched a ferocious attack on the concept and nature of the 'Celtic Tiger', relating it to a 'sad spectacle of poverty and exclusion' (Connell, 1999). He also described the contemporary economic system as 'unchecked capitalism'.

Although the referent objects of the two religious leaders were different, it can be said that the content of their discourses was almost the same. They both had as their focal points the issues of national identity, tradition, cultural homogenisation, secularism, social estrangement, depersonalisation, individualism, consumerism, poverty and exclusion. Thus, although their targets were different (i.e. globalisation vs. the Celtic Tiger), they addressed the same issues, pointed to the same problems, and sensed similarly the nature and consequences of the changes under way.

There is, however, one important difference in the nature of the two discourses.[1] The discourse of the Greek church was based on an *outside-in* logic. External forces and interests had penetrated and attempted culturally to annihilate European societies and Greece. Thus, no matter how it was promoted or expressed at the national level, the source of the threat, according to the Greek church, was both external and externally driven. In contrast the church discourse in Ireland, albeit stressing the same 'symptoms', was an *inside-out* discourse. Its principal object of critique was the Celtic Tiger, the most impressive manifestation of the Irish economic miracle, and not external forces driven by globalisation or otherwise. It is interesting that this remained the case despite the concern of Pope John Paul II with globalisation. Thus, to address the same problems the church in Ireland focused on the celtic Tiger, whereas the church in Greece turned to globalisation.

The press sample

The comparison of a press sample in Greece and Ireland came to confirm the picture created by the discourses of the institutional actors examined above. In comparison to the Greek newspaper the VIMA (Sunday edition), the references to globalisation in the daily edition of *The Irish Times* are rather negligible. This dynamic is only reversed in 2001, when the references in *The Irish Times* exceeded those found in VIMA, and continued to do so throughout the period 2001–07.

The high number of references to globalisation in VIMA manifested the centrality of globalisation both as an object and as a prism of analysis; both as news and as a way of reading the news. Furthermore, the gradual increase of the references during the period under examination reflected the gradual domination of globalisation in the discourses of key institutional actors. The opposite conclusions can be drawn in the case of Ireland. Globalisation was not present in the public discourse, as this was reflected in *The Irish Times*, either as a news item, or as a way of reading the news. Moreover, the concept of globalisation was not implicated in the discourses of institutional actors, as these were reflected and reconstructed in the press (at least during 1996–2000).

Conclusions

The first observation to make refers to the *use of the term/concept* 'globalisation' in the two countries. In Greece it emerged as a new referent point that dominated the vocabulary of the key institutional actors. On the contrary, the concept of globalisation was relatively absent from Irish public discourse, especially up to the year 2000.

Yet, the hegemonic discourse of globalisation consists of a productive set of practices and meanings that is not reducible to any single word or exclusive ideational aspect. On this basis, there are three important conclusions to draw from the above findings. First, the reproduction of the Greek and Irish politico-economic systems during the period under investigation was dominated to a significant extent by the same meanings, practices and points of reference. This does not mean that one finds the same practices (e.g. flexibility in labour market) to have been implemented to the same extent in the two countries. It just means that, either as taken-for-granted assumptions or as highly politicised and contested policy concepts and strategies, these meanings and practices functioned as focal points that defined the terms of public discourse reproduction, and the stakes, identities, strategies and power relationships of the actors involved. In this regard globalisation discourse, as a delineation either of the socially given, or of the socially contested, seems to have supplied the common ordering principle/force (based on a specific stock of objects, meanings, practices and policies) on the basis of which both the Greek and the Irish politico-economic systems were being restructured.

The second conclusion to be drawn is that, although the stock of meanings and practices that was present in the two countries was, with few exceptions (e.g. the term globalisation) the same, the way in which this stock was present in the two cases was fundamentally different. In Greece the hegemonic/globalisation was communicated, and thus materialised, as a multilevel struggle over a new *political*. Most social, political, economic and cultural stakes had to be thought through, redefined and fought for anew within Greek society. In Ireland the hegemonic/globalisation was communicated, and thus materialised, as a set of practices and meanings that stood outside the *political*; beyond politics and ideology. It delineated not a zone of contestation, but a zone of fundamental consensus; the underlying *givens* of Irish politics and economics. The critique of Celtic Tiger by Cardinal Connell remains a seeming exception in this regard. Yet, even if this criticism contributed to the development of a cultural critique of Celtic Tiger, it did not lead to a broader politicisation of the main economic policies that produced and sustained the Celtic Tiger. Thus, the findings of our research point to two different facets of the hegemonic discourse of globalisation. In Greece it emerged/materialised as a new *political*, whereas in Ireland it emerged/materialised as a new *apolitical*.

It should be noted here that by referring to the materialisation process in Ireland as 'apolitical' we do not mean to strip it from its political nature. In this sense both the aforementioned 'political' and the 'apolitical' facets of globalisation discourse are highly political, in the sense that they affect the way people organise their communities and live their lives. The political/apolitical metaphor that is employed here aims to underline the contested/uncontested nature of certain aspects of socio-political life. For this reason the 'apolitical' aspects of our socio-political life, those aspects that have escaped the sphere of the conscious, the sphere of the question 'why?' are more *political* in nature in comparison to the openly contested aspects, because they have a much deeper influence and impact on the way we live our lives.

The last conclusion is a more tentative one and refers to the dynamics of the materialisation of globalisation discourse in the two countries. Thus, while during the first part of the period under investigation (i.e. 1995–99) the different facets of the hegemonic seemed to grow stronger and stronger, during the last part of the period under investigation (i.e. 2000–02), these opposing dynamics seem to change, and divergence seems to have given its place to convergence. Thus, in Ireland after 2000 a trend gradually developed towards the politicisation of the 'apolitical space' of the Celtic Tiger. This new dynamic was manifested in the change of ICTU's understanding and treatment of globalisation, in the new discourse on globalisation developed by the Labour Party, and in the adoption of the cultural critique of the Celtic Tiger by Fine Gael. The increased number of references to globalisation in *The Irish Times* after 2001 seems to confirm this new dynamic. The latter had at least two sources: (a) there was a domestic dynamic towards politicisation that was led by the disillusionment and discontent that was generated by the failure –real or perceived– of the 'apolitical' and its underlying institutional apparatus (mainly the social partnership) to fulfil certain promises (e.g. reduction of social disparities, recognition of unionism). (b) There was also a dynamic that was produced by the communication within Ireland of Ireland's (neoliberal) image abroad, and in particular within the EU.

On the other hand, a similar but reverse trend can be traced in Greece. Thus, some highly politicised issues, such as part-time employment, through their *quotidianisation* seemed to be treated as less political within the Greek public discourse. For instance, the labour movement's position and struggle against flexibility was gradually transformed into a new bargain on what the (inevitable) promotion of flexibility should be exchanged with.

Finally, as has already been argued, the EU had a significant role in this convergence process, acting as a powerful generator of economic globalisation objects, policies and practices (see Antoniades 2007, 2008).

To conclude, our research revealed two different facets of the hege-monic discourse of globalisation. In Greece it emerged as a new zone of contestation, while in Ireland it emerged as a new zone of consen-sus, a set of underlying givens. Until this point we analysed the nature of these facets, and the domestic institutional dynamics that underlie their evolution. An important question remains unanswered. What accounts for these different facets? How are the differences in the materialisation of globalisation discourse in Greece and Ireland to be explained? The next chapter deals with these questions.

Note

1 Another difference was Archbishop Christodoulos' critique of 'Americani-sation' and 'American cultural imperialism' (see for instance Christodoulos, 1999).

6

Explaining facets of the hegemonic: political economy, domestic institutions and beyond

The explanations for the different facets of the hegemonic discourse of globalisation can be grouped together into three broad categories: explanations that focus on the nature of domestic economy; explanations that focus more broadly on domestic structures, and especially on the domestic structures of interest representation and state–society relations; and, finally, explanations that try to combine these two factors, i.e. nature of domestic economy and domestic structures. These three different explanations can be translated into the following research questions.

1. Is the nature of political economy sufficient to account for the materialisation process of globalisation discourse? Here, the focus is on the 'goodness-of-fit' hypothesis (among others, see Knill and Lehmkuhl, 1999; Börzel and Risse, 2000; Caporaso *et al.*, 2001). For the purposes of this study, this hypothesis reads as follows: the degree and intensity of the adaptational pressures at the national level depend on the degree of the 'fit' or 'misfit' (i.e. the compatibility) of the national institutions and practices with those promoted by the hegemonic discourse of globalisation.
2. Is the nature of domestic structures sufficient to account for the materialisation process of globalisation discourse? Here, the focus shifts from the analysis of the nature of political economy to the broader structures of societal interest organisation and state–society relations (Cawson, 1978; Lehmbruch, 1979; Schmitter, 1979). These structures are important because they define the ways in which societies negotiate domestically social change and continuity (see also Schmidt, 2002).
3. Can the combination of the above two factors (i.e. the nature of political economy and the nature of interest representation) account for the materialisation process of globalisation discourse?

It should be stressed here that the above questions are not treated in this study as formal hypotheses, the validity of which will be tested against specific empirical evidence. Our purpose is not to use our empirical findings in order to test formally these hypotheses, but to elucidate what had really happened in these two countries, and on this basis to reflect on the explanatory capacity of the factors involved in the above questions. In this manner our case study findings aspire to play not a hypothesis-testing, but a hypothesis-generating role (see Lijphart, 1971: 691–693).

Is the nature of political economy enough to account for the materialisation process of hegemonic discourses?

The nature of political economy is one of the first factors to be considered in the explanation of the observed different facets of the hegemonic. The main hypothesis here would be that there must be a certain degree of 'genealogical compatibility' between the conditions in which a hegemonic discourse originates, and the conditions that a hegemonic discourse in turn generates. Thus in our case, one could assume that the practices and meanings that were generated by the hegemonic discourse of globalisation (e.g. liberalisation, flexibility, deregulation, privatisation, corporate tax cuts) would be more or less taken for granted, or smoothly absorbed in political economies that were based on institutional arrangements that were conducive with the globalisation discourse (i.e. political economies that had a small state control domain and low degree of regulation in the economy), whereas they would generate controversy, tension and clashes in political economies that were based on different, non-compatible arrangements (for instance the Continental/Mediterranean political economies).

Yet, the above analysis is characterised by significant conceptual and practical limitations. It is based on a conceptualisation of globalisation discourse as a predetermined phenomenon, independent of state policies and actions, and it portrays states as static structures, stripped of agency and strategic capacity. Two specific examples may help to clarify this point. The percentage of part-time employment in a country is usually treated as an indicator of the degree of labour market flexibility (the higher the percentage of part-time workers, the higher the degree of flexibility). In 1992 the percentage of part-time employment in Greece was 4.5% of the total employment, in Portugal 7.2%, in Ireland 9.1%, in Germany 14.5% and in the UK 22.9%. By 2002 part-time employment had remained unchanged in Greece at

4.5%, whereas it had increased by 57% in Portugal (classified in the Mediterranean model of political economy with Greece), by 81% in Ireland, by 43.4% in Germany (the main representative of the Continental model) and by 9.2% in the UK (source: Eurostat, European Commission). There are two points to make here. First, it is demonstrated that it is wrong to conceptualise globalisation as something that was taken for granted by genealogically compatible political economies. Ireland, i.e. a 'genealogically' compatible political economy, was not the EU15 member state that made the fewest changes (less adaptation) but, in contrast, the one that adopted the most proactive stance and experienced the most significant change in its labour market. Second, we see that to cope with the same policy issue, similar economies, such as Greece and Portugal, adopted different strategies. This points to the significance of state agency, rather than the importance of the nature of political economy. The same picture emerges if one takes the example of corporate tax cuts. Ireland adopted in the second half of the 1990s the most proactive stance among the EU15 member states, reducing its corporate tax between 1995 and 2003 by 69% (from 40% in 1995, to 12.5% in 2003). In the same period the UK reduced its corporate tax only by 3% (from 33% to 30%), whereas in Spain the corporate tax remained unchanged at 35%, in Greece it was reduced by 12.5% (from 40 to 35%) and in Germany it was reduced by 30.3% (from 56.8 to 39.6%) (source: European Commission).[1] Again, here the most significant 'adaptation' takes place in a genealogically compatible economy (Ireland), while the second most significant change takes place in a non-compatible economy (Germany). On the other hand, the UK (a compatible economy) and Greece (a non-compatible economy) adopted modest changes, and there was no change in Spain (a non-compatible economy). As above, the nature of political economy does not seem able to offer a persuasive answer for the observed variations; nor does the conceptualisation of globalisation as a predetermined phenomenon help us to understand the nature of, and the dynamics at play in, the above changes.

This analysis strengthens the significance of conceptualising globalisation as a hegemonic discourse, for such a conceptualisation suggests an independent and significant reordering effect even on political economies that are 'genealogically compatible' with the hegemonic discourse. Moreover, the outcome of the hegemonic restructuring at the domestic level is far from being predetermined, because the hegemonic discourse itself is not predetermined, and because the materialisation of the hegemonic discourse depends on

the actions and perceptions of domestic social actors. Hence, a hegemonic discourse exerts influence on the conditions in which agency
takes place, it does not replace this agency or neutralise its capacity
for change. It is this agency-centred and undetermined effect of the
hegemonic discourse that breaks down the circular, self-proved
explanation of the goodness-of-fit approach.

Another significant problem of the goodness-of-fit hypothesis is
that it is based on a fixed conceptualisation of models of political
economy. An uncritical endorsement of these models, however, runs
the risk of reducing the factor of political economy to an ahistorical
construct, incapable of strategic adaptation, evolution or learning,
that is beyond change and social agency (see also Crouch, 2005).
Yet, for instance, in Britain in the 1980s, Margaret Thatcher was
functioning within an Anglo-Saxon political economy but, at the
same time, was changing the nature of this political economy by
reversing the long-established tradition of Keynesianism, putting an
end to the powers of the trade unions, and minimising welfare
state provisions. Along the same lines, the rise of the social partnership in Ireland after 1987, although it took place within specific
politico-economic arrangements, in fact transformed Irish political
economy. Thus, a new hybrid politico-economic model emerged that
combined a deregulated Anglo-Saxon political economy with a
centralised, *consociational* mechanism of interest representation –
what in the Irish public discourse started to be referred to as the
'Irish model of political economy'. Therefore, the political economy
factor should always be examined in dynamic terms and not as an
end product.

It is also important to note here that the specific nature of Irish
political economy makes it even more difficult to determine the role
of political economy in the communication of globalisation discourse
(Ireland should be treated here as a representative case of a wider
group of states). For Irish political economy is based on a rather dual-
istic structure. A liberal, highly flexible and foreign-owned sector
(product of the huge increase in inwards FDIs in the 1990s), coexists
with an indigenous, more traditional and regulated, manufacturing
sector (Enterprise Strategy Group, 2004; Hardiman, 2002). Therefore, the assumptions about the 'compatibility' between the Irish
political economy and globalisation, and the role that this compatibility has played in the materialisation of globalisation discourse are
further problematised, for, even if they were true, they would not
really capture the whole of the Irish economy.

Finally, even when the direction of changes generated by a hegemonic discourse is more conducive to the tradition of a certain political economy, one would expect that social groups that are on the losing side of the changes under way would protest and try to block the respective governmental policies. To put this differently, the fact that the contemporary Irish political economy has Anglo-Saxon characteristics (in terms of the degree of regulation and state control domain), does not mean that the changes in the domestic environment and the domestic distribution of power, produced by the hegemonic discourse of globalisation would escape, if not public protest, at least public deliberation. In this regard one must not conflate the (non-) power of an actor with its willingness to dispute or deliberate on existing or changing practices. For instance, the fact that the ICTU and its leaders and members have been socialised within a rather unregulated economic environment, does not mean that when ICTU's suggestions and preferences are marginalised in the policy process, ICTU will not protest, or will not, however unsuccessfully, try to block governmental policies that are disadvantageous for its members (e.g. an 81% increase in part-time employment). The same goes for the ICTU's preferences. The fact that the Irish labour market is flexible in comparison to most of its European counterparts, does not mean that the Irish labour force has a fixed preference in favour of flexibility practices.

Based on these observations it can be argued that the nature of political economy cannot fully account for the materialisation of globalisation discourse. Thus, although the importance of the nature of political economy in the hegemonic discourse materialisation process is undisputable, a clear correlation between the nature of the political economy and the nature of the materialisation of a hegemonic discourse cannot be established.

Is the nature of domestic structures enough to account for the materialisation process of hegemonic discourses?

To get a picture that can better account for the different facets of the hegemonic discourse of globalisation, one could qualify the role of the nature of political economy with a study of the case and time-specific (domestic) conditions that affected the capacity and willingness of the various domestic actors to dispute or deliberate on the practices and policies that were generated by globalisation discourse.

In this regard, the existence of a highly institutionalised, well-functioning, and ever-inclusive social partnership, cannot but be considered instrumental in the explanation of the communication of globalisation discourse in Ireland. Thus, although Irish political economy is usually classified in the Anglo-Saxon group of economies, it was characterised throughout the period under investigation, as mentioned above, by a strong and expanding consociational institutional base – a defining characteristic of Continental political economies (see Hardiman, 2002; Murphy, 1999; O'Donnell and O'Reardon, 2000). It seems certain that this distinctive characteristic of Irish political economy played a crucial role in the way in which the hegemonic discourse of globalisation was materialised. Within this framework it could be argued that the effects that were generated by the production of new winners and losers, inherent in any hegemonic discourse materialisation process, were mediated, negotiated and resolved at the level of this consociational mechanism, ever dominant in the Irish politico-economic life. Along these lines it could also be argued that the fact that many heads or representatives of public institutions in Ireland, have grown up together or have personal/family relationships, because of the small size of Irish society, must have facilitated the above dynamics.

Within the same framework, it could also be argued that, in the case of Greece, it was the confrontational, fragmented and particularistic structure-of-interest representation that gave rise to the 'zone of confrontation' that we observed. In this way, the lack of 'coordinative'[2] and consociational institutional arrangements exacerbated the negative effects of globalisation discourse (in terms of winners and losers) in the public realm.

Does this mean that the structure-of-interest representation can account for the hegemonic discourse communication process? Based on our evidence, the answer is no. While the structure-of-interest representation tells us important things about the forces that underlie the production of a public discourse, it tells us little about actors' preferences and understandings. To put this more clearly, although the study of the structure-of-interest representation tells us much about where and with whom the actors speak, it tells us little about what they say. Thus, it seems that the problem mentioned with regard to the nature of political economy as an explanatory factor, also applies to the structure-of-interest representation. The fact that a political economy is based on consociational institutional arrangements does not mean that the social actors that are negatively affected by the hegemonic discourse will not react; it just means that their reactions will be brought into and negotiated within the framework of these institutional arrangements. Yet in the case of Ireland no such negotiation was found. It was not that the social partners were negotiating economic globalisation policies among themselves, but rather that the promotion of these policies was taken as a given; that is, it was beyond discussion and public or intra policy group deliberation.

I do not mean here to ignore or downgrade the important role of social partnership in fostering consensus around economic globalisation policies. For sure, the 'coordinative' role (see Schmidt, 2002: 232–234) of the social partnership was crucial. But, the important issue here is not how this consensus was fostered but what allowed this consensus to emerge in the first place. Greece for instance did not only lack a social partnership to foster consensus around economic globalisation policies, but most importantly it lacked such a consensus in the first place. Of course, the lack of a 'coordinative' forum exacerbated the controversy over these policies in the public realm at the 'communication stage' of discourse (see Schmidt: 234–239). Thus the key piece of the puzzle still seems to be missing.

Nature of political economy plus structure-of-interest representation: is a combined explanation enough?

It could be argued that it was on the one hand the genealogical compatibility between the globalisation discourse and the Irish political economy, and on the other hand the strong consociational base of the Irish political economy that led to the apolitical facet of globalisation discourse, observed in the Irish case. Respectively, it could be argued that the effects from the incompatibility between the hegemonic discourse of globalisation and the Greek political economy, were exacerbated by the overly fragmented and particularistic structure-of-interest representation that characterises Greek politico-economic life. Thus, it may be the case that the solution to our puzzle is based on the combination of the two factors examined above, i.e. the nature of political economy and the nature of the structure-of-interest representation.

The combination of a nature-of-political-economy perspective with a case-specific, domestic institutional arrangements analysis appears to improve significantly the understanding of the nature of hegemonic discourse materialisation. It takes into consideration, not only factors concerning the degree of genealogical compatibility between hegemonic discourses and national political economies, but also factors concerning the way in which different societies negotiate social change domestically, i.e. whether there is a strong or weak intermediation structure-of-interest representation, and whether this structure promotes consensus building, or rather enhances the reproduction of social divisions and antagonisms. Yet, still this combined explanation does not seem sufficient to account for why there was no public *or* intra-group deliberation/negotiation in the case of Ireland.

Accordingly, the Irish case seems to suggest that the nature of political economy and the structure-of-interest representation cannot on their own account for all facets of the hegemonic; they cannot offer a conclusive explanation for the materialisation of globalisation discourse. To address this problem, some scholars have suggested that we need to take into consideration the different political cultures that exist in different countries. In Ireland this would include the 'non-ideological' and 'consensus-driven' public life, whereas in Greece it would point towards the 'high degree of abstraction and polarisation' that traditionally characterises public debates (see also Antoniades, 2010).

Yet, the factor political culture seems to obscure rather than elucidate the communication of globalisation discourse. In the case of Ireland, for instance, it seems to ignore the turbulent industrial relations that have defined most contemporary Irish economic history. It also fails to provide us with a convincing answer as to why this consensus did not take place earlier (or later), especially since the infrastructure of the social partnership was in place since the early 1970s.

It seems that in order to grasp the apolitical facet observed in the Irish case, one needs to dig deeper into the reasons that affected social actors' understandings, and their capacity and willingness to dispute or deliberate on the meanings and practices of globalisation discourse. Following such a deep, case-specific, analytically bottom-up route it becomes apparent that the social technology (i.e. the hegemonic – globalisation discourse) that in the Greek case came at a certain historical period to be communicated and materialised as a new zone of contestation and confrontation concerning the redistribution of wealth and power; in the Irish case it was communicated and materialised as a historically unique economic miracle, a social technology of prosperity and wealth generation (for the Irish 'economic miracle' see Walsh, 2000; for a critique, see Allen, 2000).

Indeed, as it has been well documented, during the 1990s and up to the first half of the 2000s Ireland was the fastest growing economy in the OECD (see various *Economic Surveys* on Ireland published by the OECD). It evolved from a 'cohesion fund' poor country, to a most prosperous economy. Its gross domestic product (GDP) per capita as a percentage of the EU average increased from 69.7% in 1990 to 135.1% in 2002 – a 93.8% increase within almost a decade! In addition to growth rates, the development of a number of macro-economic factors was also impressive. Unemployment fell from 13.4% in 1990 to 4.3% in 2002. Industrial production (excluding construction) grew with an average of 13.5% during 1992–2000, whereas the EU15 average was 1.7%. The general government gross debt reduced from 94.2% of GDP in 1990 to 32.7% in 2002 (source: European Commission). Thus, from the 'poorest of the rich' in 1988 (*The Economist*, 1988), Ireland became 'Europe's shining light' (*Economist's survey*, 1997) in the 1990s.

For sure, the above numbers tell us nothing about social and income inequalities, and indeed few analysts would dispute the fact that the economic miracle maintained, if not exacerbated, such inequalities (see Allen, 2003; Kirby, 2002). Yet, one can hardly down-grade the positive impact that the rapid economic growth had on Irish population, in absolute terms. Along these lines, Whelan and Layte (2004: 39) note with regard to social mobility:

> Throughout the course of the economic boom Ireland has remained a highly unequal society in terms of the distribution of income and there is no evidence of a movement towards a more meritocratic society ... However ... economic growth and, in particular, the economic boom of recent years has been associated with substantial social mobility and with increased equality of opportunity. (see also Smith, 2005: ch. 2)

The positive impact that the economic miracle had on the living conditions of the great majority of the Irish population is also reflected in the shift in the mood of public opinion captured in Euro-barometer surveys at the end of the 1980s. In particular, during the period 1980–87, to the question whether the next year would be better or worse in comparison to the current one, the Irish were among the most pessimistic Europeans (the percentage of negative replies varied between 45% and 55%). Yet, after this period a radical change in attitude, from pessimism to optimism, is observed. Thus, after 1987 the Irish were constantly among the most optimistic Europeans (and had the highest percentage of positive replies in 1988, 1990 and 1994, and the second lowest percentage of negative replies in 1994 and 1996). This significant shift of attitude cannot but be related to positive personal experiences and absolute gains in living conditions.

Following this reasoning, it can be argued that it was this economic miracle experience that defined what was conceivable and what was

non-conceivable, what was part of politics and what was beyond politics, what in general could be spoken of and how, within the Irish
public discourse of the time. Additionally it can be argued that this
prosperity was so deeply and widely felt in Ireland, that it marginalised or made (temporarily) irrelevant any social clash as to who
gets what. That is, the great majority of the population was experiencing such an absolute gain in the conditions of its everyday life,
that until the end of the 1990s, relative-gains considerations
remained beyond public deliberation.

The explanation proposed here goes beyond the nature of political
economy, and differs from explanations focused on structure-of- interest representation. It is an explanation grounded on changes in the
material environment, but the emphasis is on how and why real
people experience specific changes in specific ways. In this regard, in
the case of Ireland some further historical contextualisation adds
important information to the nature of the materialisation of globalisation discourse. It can thus be argued that the economic miracle was
translated in Ireland into a *positive social shock* that *disrupted* the
continuity of a generations-long collective memory and social self-
portrayal that was driven by the potato famine of the nineteenth
century. Hence, it was this positive social shock that 'placed' the practices, mechanisms and policies of the economic miracle beyond the
sphere of the socially contested and negotiable, beyond the sphere of
the political. Gradually, however, and despite the fact that wealth was
still generated at an unprecedented historical pace, the effect of this
positive shock started to fade away and give way to relative-gains and
wealth disparity considerations. The counterfactual bottom line here
is that if the specific historical experiences were not there, the positive shock would not have had the impact it did. On this basis, it can
also be argued that one cannot easily generalise the findings from the
Irish case, as it should not be taken for granted that the 'economic
miracle' factor will have exactly the same effect on each and every
national context.

Notes

1 All percentages refer to the 'basic' top statutory tax rates on corporate
  income.
2 See Schmidt, 2002: 232–234.

Epilogue

A gap in the ideas literature in international relations/international political economy led us to the concept of hegemonic discourses. The challenge to capture and analyse hegemonic discourses led us to a finer elaboration of the relationship between the *public* and the *hegemonic*; an elaboration through which the hegemonic came to be conceptualised as the social technology of the public's (re)production. In turn, this led us to domestic mechanisms of ideology and politics production.

This conceptual move proved very productive as it assertively pieced together the various elements of this project (texts, policies, practices, actors, institutions, institutional arrangements, policy discourses), creating a framework through which they could be studied and understood in their dynamic interplay. What was at issue in this framework was the *hegemonic* itself. By focusing on the reproduction of two politico-economic systems we tried to capture what globalisation discourse was on the ground, when and how it emerged and dominated, and how it influenced the (re)production of politics, economics and in general social life at least in the two states under examination. The overall purpose of this research was to get an 'anatomy' of the *hegemonic* and its function, in order to start forming an understanding of how human societies become what they are in each historical period. The comparative nature of this project allowed us to dig deeper into the qualities and properties of the hegemonic, thus exemplifying the multiple and often contradictory ways of its materialisation. An exploration of the reasons for these different facets was the last stop of our research endeavour.

Finally, the research strategy and methodology that were adopted attempted to transcend the dichotomy between understanding and explaining in social sciences. It placed the emphasis on understanding the conditions of change in the *international*, in order to explain these conditions, in order to offer a standpoint, a way of influencing the direction of this change. We found no evidence to deny the claim that explaining is a way of changing things on the basis of a given understanding.

Ending remarks

This project attempted a contribution to the existing literature on globalisation through a detailed examination of two case studies. In the case of Ireland, it offered an independent validation of the important research already conducted by Nicola Smith (2005). In this regard, Smith's main position on the all-powerful discourse of competitiveness in the Irish politico-economic life is reaffirmed. Yet, according to our findings, Smith has overemphasised the role and importance of the concept of globalisation in the Irish public discourse. The analysis of the Greek case was rather the first attempt to map how globalisation discourse emerged in this country in the 1990s. The analysis of these two case studies led us to two different facets, two different forms of materialisation of globalisation discourse. At the same time we saw how on the one hand a highly politicised materialisation process led to the reification of specific contested policies and practices (Greece), and how on the other hand a highly apolitical process, was gradually politicised (Ireland).

Then, we examined the role of political economy and domestic institutions in the materialisation of globalisation discourse. The conclusion here is that although these two factors play an important role in hegemonic discourse materialisation process, they cannot account on their own, combined or separately, for the materialisation of globalisation discourse. Along these lines it was argued that a complete reading and understanding of the different facets of the hegemonic and its materialisation cannot but finally rest upon historical and case-specific factors and characteristics. In this regard, state agency, changes in the material environment, and specific historical experiences that influence the way in which these changes impact on specific societies are crucial elements. Furthermore, one cannot exclude or underestimate historical contingency, without underestimating the dynamic and unpredictable nature of the social realities under examination.

The countries examined and the findings presented here point to the significant limitations of the models-of-political-economy approach to IPE. These models not only fail to capture the nature of the states under examination but also obscure significantly the social dynamics that govern social change in world politics and economics.

In this regard, our findings seem to raise a broader issue. Singular factors, such as types of political economy or types of domestic structures, may be of minor analytical value or even meaningless if examined as separate variables, independent of the socio-historical systems in which they are embedded. Thus, the failure of political economy and domestic structures to account for the materialisation of globalisation discourse, observed in this project, should not be interpreted as a call to include more factors in our analysis but rather as a call for new ways of thinking. From our viewpoint, we see it as a call for new theoretical and analytical perspectives that shift the emphasis from singular factors to the broader social systems that define the existence and govern the co-existence of these factors. The purpose here would not be, for instance, to examine which factor matters most in the communication of hegemonic discourses but rather to scrutinise the system that governs the co-existence of the different factors and thus to elucidate the rules that define the social formation/transformation of different societies.

It must be clear by now that the issue in question in this project has not been the causal force of ideational factors in world politics and economics. Rather our main concern was with the role and function of domestic factors in the materialisation of hegemonic discourses, as well as with the nature of this materialisation process itself. Consequently this has not been a study on ideas. The purpose was to examine social change and continuity in two domestic national settings, in order to understand the process through which globalisation emerged as a new dominant 'reality' in world politics and economics. On this basis, in the evolving interdisciplinary debate among the various strands of institutional analysis (see Campbell and Pedersen, 2001), this author joins with those approaches that underline the fundamental role of 'translation' that takes place at the national level. Yet, to our point of view, this translation is, and must be construed and studied as a constitutive part of the writing of the 'original text'. Put differently, the 'original text' *consists of* its multiple 'translations' – there is no 'original text' existing beyond the latter.

By conceptualising globalisation through the prism of hegemonic discourses as a human technology the approach proposed here aspires to open an avenue for reflecting on the human condition as a condition of our own making, rather than as a condition externally given or otherwise externally determined. Such a hegemonic discourse approach aims to bring human agency and its importance to the forefront of theorising and practising world politics and economics. It favours a bottom-up, agent-centric understanding of the becoming of the *international*. Thus, it is not that Greece and Ireland were forced to implement an external, already well-defined set of practices and meanings called globalisation. Instead, globalisation is what these countries were proactively producing through their actions. The aim of such an approach is not to deny historically and agent-specific constraints and limitations. The aim is to avoid a bland, deterministic understanding of what is 'out there' and what this 'out there' does.

In this manner, a hegemonic discourse approach offers a tool for demystifying the 'unchangeable' or the 'universal' of what are in fact historically specific social structures or practices. In the policy process one very often comes across the argument that 'this or that must be done due to external pressures'. It is exactly these 'pressures' and their relationship to the suggested course of action, that are under problematisation in a hegemonic discourse approach. Thus, this approach aims at questioning a narrow deterministic logic to policy-making; it denies a policy-making that is deprived of *politics*. Furthermore, a hegemonic discourse approach aims at opening, rather than closing, the question of what is possible in a specific historical period and what a state can do within a certain historical context. There may indeed be more space for agency, change and imagination in human history. To this end, one must not underestimate the emancipatory potential of reflecting.

Never-ending remarks

Have we been 'trapped' in our own history, as Michel Foucault (1982: 210) argued? And what does this mean? What is the stuff of which our social universe is made and how we are to understand and study the phenomenon of social change? These were the broader questions that led and informed this project. And that is why this project is in essence an attempt to break into and learn to read the socio-historical spiral of social reproduction (if only an infinitesimal moment of it), trying to understand the conditions of this (re)production and thus the conditions of social change. A number of important questions, however, were left unanswered. Here we should at least mention two of them.

Hegemon, hegemony and the in-between:
Q: Tea or coffee? A: Yes, please

In chapter 1 we outlined a political and a biopolitical approach to politics, and argued that in order to capture the conditions of existence and change of our (international) social universe, both these traditions need to be taken into consideration. We need to examine power both as bombs and economic coercion (power without), and as a technology of the self (power within). In order to capture the impact of the hegemonic restructuring process at issue in this project we focused on the domestic mechanisms of ideology and politics production. Furthermore we assumed that these mechanisms, and the actors involved in them, are not passive receivers but active producers of each hegemonic order. The following question is in order. By studying the *hegemonic* as a diffused and decentred phenomenon do we not obfuscate the power relations that dominate in the international system? Do we not lose sight of the role and function of the hegemon? No, or rather yes. Yes, we must not lose sight of the hegemon and its role in the international system. Thus yes, not focusing on the hegemon does obfuscate dominant power relations. But this is only half of the story of life in the international, and to present this half as the whole story is equally misleading with neglecting the role of the hegemon.

It seems that for a long period of time the focus on the hegemon and the 'power without' has consciously or unconsciously acted as an alibi, that helped to obfuscate both the conditions of existence and the conditions of change of life in the international. Indeed, to accuse a hegemon has always been an easy and convenient answer in world politics and economics. The contention here is that it is time to move beyond the idea of the hegemon in order to understand change and continuity in the *international*. Within this framework, decentring the hegemonic and bringing social agency and the subject back in does not manifest a fear of politics, but rather the generalisation/universalisation of politics. Such an understanding does not allow hegemony to lie comfortably 'out there' with a hegemon (be that the MNEs, the USA, financial capital, etc.); it does not allow an externalisation of the international system and thus an externalisation of the responsibility for this system.

Subject, subjectivity and the hegemonic

The conceptualisation of the subject and its place and role in the social universe is central to any inquiry on the production, reproduction and change of politics. This is too big an issue to touch upon in any comprehensible way here. It should be mentioned however that our understanding of hegemonic discourses as phenomena with independent causal power that gradually evolve to internalised technologies of self, does not refute or reject an understanding of the subject as sovereign. What is ultimately at stake in hegemonic discourses is indeed the production of subjects. Yet the 'produced subjects' are always capable of reflecting on and changing the nature of the process that produced them in the first place. This is what makes the subject *sovereign*: its tragic –in an ancient Greek under-standing of the term– freedom to reflect and act (or not) upon the conditions of its existence.

Radical political theorists have thoughtfully suggested that globa-lisation should be conceived as an empty signifier (see Laclau, 1996), i.e. as a particularity that in a certain historical period assumed the representation of an universality (ibid.), thus occupying the 'ahistori-cal', 'empty' and 'ineradicable' space of the social; the space which each historical hegemony comes to occupy, to fill in (see Butler's analysis on Laclau, in Butler, 2000: 31). The hegemonic discourse approach employed here attempts to push this analysis further. It is claimed that one needs to bring this ahistorical, empty and ineradi-cable space of the social, from 'up' and 'out there', 'down' and 'in' the subject. In this way we get a radical different understanding of social change and continuity (see Antoniades, 2008a). The social universe is transformed into an open milieu that is complex, dynamic and productive. It is this understanding of the relationship between the 'subject' and the 'hegemonic' that informed the way we conceptu-alised and approached the role of the social actors, institutions and discourses we examined in this project. Social repetition and every-day life are the strategic fields of social life's production and change.

References

Agamben, Giorgio (1998) *Homo Sacer: Sovereign Power and Bare Life*, Stanford: Stanford University Press.

Alivizatos, Nicos (1993) 'The Presidency, Parliament and the Courts in the 1980s', in: Clogg, Richard (ed.), *Greece in the 1980s*, New York: St. Martin's Press, pp. 65–77.

Allen, Kieran (2003) 'Neither Boston nor Berlin: Class Polarisation and Neo-liberalism in the Irish Republic', in: Coulter, Colin and Coleman, Steve (eds), *The End of History? Critical Reflections on the Celtic Tiger*, Manchester: Manchester University Press.

Allen, Kieran (2000) *The Celtic Tiger: The Myth of Social Partnership in Ireland*, Manchester: Manchester University Press.

Alogoskoufis, George (1995) 'The Two Faces of Janus: Institutions, Policy Regimes and Macroeconomic Performance in Greece', *Economic Policy: A European Forum*, no. 20, April, pp. 148–192.

Antonacopoulos, Leuteris (2000) Address to the Annual Convention by the President of the Federation of Greek Industries (afternoon session). Athens, 24 May. Available at: www.fgi.org.gr (accessed 13 November 2002).

Antoniades, Andreas (2010), 'Readings, Misreadings and Politics: The Irish Model in Greek Public Discourse and Reality', in: Miller, Rory and O'Sullivan, Michael (eds), *What Did we Do Right? Global Views on Ireland* (forthcoming).

Antoniades, Andreas (2008), 'Social Europe and/or Global Europe? Globalisation and Flexicurity as Debates on the Future of Europe', *Cambridge Review of International Affairs*, 21 (3), 2008, pp. 327–346.

Antoniades, Andreas (2008a), 'Cave! Hic Everyday Life: Repetition, Hegemony and the Social', *British Journal of Politics and International Relations*, 10 (3), 2008, 412–428.

Antoniades, Andreas (2007), 'Negotiating the Limits of the Possible: A West European Perspective on Globalisation', in: Bowles, P. *et al.*

(eds), *Regional Perspectives on Globalization: A Critical Reader*, Basingstoke: Palgrave, pp. 54–69.

Barry, Frank (2003) 'Irish Economic Development over Three Decades of EU Membership', *Finance A Uver*, vol. 53 (9–10): 394–412 (available at: www.ucd.ie/economic/staff/barry/ papers/FinanceUver.pdf

Barry, Frank (ed.) (1999) *Understanding Irish Economic Growth*, London: Macmillan.

Beck, Ulrick (2001) 'Redefining Power in a Global Economy'. Unpublished lecture delivered at LSE, on 22 February 2001. Available at: http://old.lse.ac.uk/collections/globalDimensions/globalisation /redefiningPowerInAGlobalEconomy/Default.htm (accessed 3 March 2008).

Berndt, Keller and Platzer, Hans-Wolfgang (eds) (2003) *Industrial Relations and European* Integration, Aldershot: Ashgate.

Biersteker, Thomas and Hall, Rodney (eds) (2002) *The Emergence of Private Authority in Global Governance*, Cambridge: Cambridge University Press.

Blyth, Mark (2002) *Great Transformations: Economic Ideas and Institutional Change in the Twentieth Century*, Cambridge: Cambridge University Press.

Blyth, Mark (1997) 'Any More Bright Ideas? The Ideational Turn of Comparative Political Economy', *Comparative Politics*, 29 (2): 229–250.

Börzel, Tanja, and Risse, Thomas (2000) 'When Europe Hits Home: Europeanization and Domestic Change', *European Integration Online Papers* (EIoP) vol. 4 (15).

Bowles, Paul, Veltmeyer, Henry, Cornelissen, Scarlett, Invernizzi, Noela and Kwong-leung, Tang (eds) (2007) *Regional Perspectives on Globalization*, Basingstoke: Palgrave.

Bowles, Paul, Veltmeyer, Henry, Cornelissen, Scarlett, Invernizzi, Noela and Kwong-leung, Tang (eds) (2007a) *National Perspectives on Globalization*, Basingstoke: Palgrave.

Budge, Ian and Bara, Judith (2001) 'Introduction: Content Analysis and Political Texts', in: Budge, Ian, Klingemann, Hans-Dieter, Volkens, Andrea, Bara, Judith and Tanebaum, Eric (eds) (2001) *Mapping Policy Preferences*, Oxford: Oxford University Press, pp. 1–16.

Budge, Ian and Bara, Judith (2001a) 'Manifesto-based Research: A Critical Review' in: Budge, Ian, Klingemann, Hans-Dieter, Volkens, Andrea, Bara, Judith and Tanebaum, Eric (eds) (2001) *Mapping Policy Preferences*. Oxford: Oxford University Press, pp. 51–73.

Butler, Judith (2000) 'Restaging the Universal: Hegemony and the limits of Formalism', in: Butler, Judith, Laclau, Ernesto and Žižek, Slavoy, *Contingency, Hegemony, Universality: Contemporary Dialogues on the Left*, London: Verso.

Butler, Judith (1997) *The Psychic Life of Power*, Stanford: Stanford University Press.

Butler, Judith, Ernesto, Laclau and Žižek, Slovoj (2000) 'Introduction', in: Butler, Judith, Laclau, Ernesto and Žižek, Slavoy (eds), *Contingency, Hegemony, Universality*, London: Verso, pp. 1–4.

Cammack, Paul (1989) 'Bringing the State Back In?', *British Journal of Political Science*, 19 (2): 261–290.

Campbell, David (1998) *Writing Security*, revised edition, Minneapolis: University of Minnesota Press.

Campbell, John (1998a) 'Institutional Analysis and the Role of Ideas in Political Economy', *Theory and Society*, 27 (3): 377–409.

Campbell, John and Pedersen, Ove (eds) (2001) *The Rise of Neoliberalism and Institutional Analysis*, Princeton: Princeton University Press.

Caporaso, James, Green Cowles, Maria and Risse, Thomas (2001) 'Europeanization and Domestic Change', in: Caporaso *et al.* (eds), *Transforming Europe: Europeanization and Domestic Change*, Ithaca: Cornell University Press, pp. 1–20.

Casper, Steve and Hancke, Bob (1999) 'Global Quality Norms Within National Production Regimes', *Organisational Studies*, 20 (6): 962–985.

Castoriadis, Cornelius (1998) *Political and Social Writings* vol. 2: *1955–1960. From the Workers' Struggle Against Bureaucracy to Revolution in the Age of Modern Capitalism*, Minneapolis: University of Minnesota Press.

Cawson, Alan (1978) 'Pluralism, Corporatism and the Role of the State', *Government and Opposition*, vol. 13.

Central Statistics Office (2001) *Population and Migration Estimates 2001*, Dublin: Central Statistics Office.

Certeau, Michel de (1984) *The Practice of Everyday Life*, Berkeley: University of California Press.

Checkel, Jeffrey (1997) *Ideas and International Political Change: Soviet/Russian Behavior and the End of the Cold War*, New Haven: Yale University Press.

Cholezas, Ioannis and Tsakloglou, Panos (2008) The Economic Impact of Immigration in Greece, *IZA Discussion Paper*, No. 3754, October, Bonn: IZA.

Christodoulos (Archbishop) (2002) 'The Society of People in the Time of Post-Neoterism, of Holisticity and of Globalisation', available at:

www.ecclesia.gr/English/EnArchbishop/EnSpeeches/ the_society _of_people.html (original text in English).

Christodoulos (Archbishop) (2000) Synodic Mass in the Church of St Dionysios in Athens, 19 March.

Christodoulos (Archbishop) (1999) Opening greeting at the 'Athens Meeting 1999' (original text in English).

Christodoulos (Archbishop) (1998) Opening greeting at the 'Athens Meeting 1998' (original text in English).

CKID (2001) *Globalisation and Orthodoxy*, working paper 11, March (in Greek).

Clogg, Richard (ed.) (1983) *Greece in the 1980s,* New York: St Martin's Press, pp. 65–77.

Clogg, Richard (ed.) (2003) *Minorities in Greece*, London: C. Hurst & Co.

Coackley, John (1999b) 'Society and Political Culture', in: Coackley, John and Gallagher, Michael (eds) (1999) *Politics in the Republic of Ireland*, 3rd edn, London: Routledge, pp. 32–70.

Coackley, John and Gallagher, Michael (eds) (1999) *Politics in the Republic of Ireland*, 3rd edn, London: Routledge.

Collins, Neil and Terry, Cradden (2001) *Irish Politics Today*, 4th edn, Manchester: Manchester University Press.

Connell, Desmond (Cardinal) (1999) 'Human Face of Poverty Reflected in Homeless Statistics', mimeo (available from the Dublin Diocese).

Connolly, Eileen and O'Halpin, Eunan (1999) 'The Government and the Governmental System', in: Coackley, John and Gallagher, Michael (eds) *Politics in the Republic of Ireland*, 3rd edn, London: Routledge, pp. 249–270.

Crouch, Colin (2005) 'Models of Capitalism', *New Political Economy*, 10(4): 439–456.

Czarniawska, Barbara and Joerges, Bernward (1996) 'Travels of Ideas', in: Czarniawska, Barbara and Sevón, Guje (eds), *Translating Organizational Change*, Berlin: de Gruyter, pp. 13–48.

Dashwood, Alan (1983) 'Hastening Slowly: The Community Path Towards Harmonisation', in: Wallace, Helen, Wallace, W. and Webb, C. (eds), *Policy-Making in the European Community*, Chichester: Wiley.

Dean, Mitchell (1999) *Governmentality: Power and Rule in Modern Society*, London: SAGE.

Deleuze, Gilles (1988) *Foucault*, London: Athlone Press.

Deleuze, Gilles, and Guattari, Felix (1987) *A Thousand Plateaus: Capitalism and Schizophrenia,* Minneapolis: University of Minnesota Press.

Denzin, Norman and Yvonna, Lincoln (eds) (2000) *Handbook of Qualitative Research*, 2nd edn, London: SAGE.

Diamandouros, Nikiforos (2001) 'Greek Identity in the Context of Globalisation', in: Tsoukalis, Loukas (ed.), *Globalisation and Regionalism: A Double Challenge for Greece*, Athens: ELIAMEP and Hellenic Observatory, LSE, pp. 69–73.

Diamandouros, Nikiforos (1997) 'Greek Politics and Society in the 1990s', in: Allison, Graham and Nikolaidis, Kalypso (eds) (1997) *The Greek Paradox*, Cambridge: MIT Press, pp. 23–37.

Diamandouros, Nikiforos (1994) 'Cultural Dualism and Political Change in Post-Authoritarian Greece', Estudio/working paper 1994/50 (available at: www.march.es/nevo).

Dillon, Michael and Reid, Julian (2001) 'Global Liberal Governance: Biopolitics, Security and War', *Millennium*, 30 (1): 41–66.

Dimitrakopoulos, Dionyssis and Passas, Argyris (eds) (2003) *Greece in the European Union*, London: Routledge.

Doak, Richard (1998) '(De)constructing Irishness in the 1990s – The Gaelic Athletic Association and Cultural Nationalist Discourse Reconsidered', *Irish Journal of Sociology*, 8: 25–48.

Economist, The (1988) *Survey on Ireland*.

Edkins, Jenny (2000) 'Sovereign Power, Zones of Indistinction and the Camp', *Alternatives*, 25: 3–25.

Edkins, Jenny, Pin-Fat, Véronique and Shapiro, Michael, J. (eds) (2004) *Sovereign Lives: Power in Global Politics*, New York: Routledge.

Elgie, Robert (1999) 'The President and the Taoiseach', in: Coackley, John and Gallagher, Michael (eds) (1999) *Politics in the Republic of Ireland*, 3rd edn, London: Routledge, pp. 232–248.

Enterprise Strategy Group (2004) *Ahead of the Curve*, Dublin: Forfás.

Esping-Andersen, Gosta (1990) *The Three Worlds of Welfare Capitalism*, Cambridge: Polity Press.

Evangelista, Matthew (1995) 'The Paradox of State Strength', *International Organization*, 49 (1): 1–38.

Evangelista, Matthew (1988) *Innovation and the Arms Race*, Ithaca: Cornell University Press.

Evans, Peter, Rueschemeyer, Dietrich and Skocpol, Theda (eds) (1985) *Bringing the State Back In*, Cambridge: Cambridge University Press.

Fajertag, Giuseppe and Pochet, Philippe (eds) (2000) *Social Pacts in Europe*, Brussels: European Trade Union Institute.

Featherstone, Kevin (2008) '"Varieties of Capitalism" and the Greek Case: Explaining the Constraints on Domestic Reform?', *GreeSE Paper No. 11*, Hellenic Observatory, LSE.

Featherstone, Kevin (ed.) (2005) *Politics and Policy in Greece: The Challenge of Modernisation*, London: Routledge.

Featherstone, Kevin (2005a), 'The Challenge of Modernisation: Politics and Policy in Greece', *Western European Politics*, 28 (2): 223–241.

Featherstone, Kevin (1998) '"Europeanisation" and the Centre-periphery: The Case of Greece in the 1990s', *South European Society and Politics*, 3 (1): 23–39.

Featherstone, Kevin (1998a) 'Greece and the EU in the 1990s', *Byzantine and Modern Greek Studies*, 22: 121–135.

Featherstone, Kevin and Ifantis, Kostas (eds) (1996) *Greece in a Changing Europe*, Manchester: Manchester University Press.

Featherstone, Kevin and Kazamias, George (eds) (2001) *Europeanisation and the Southern Periphery*, London: Frank Cass.

Ferrera, Maurizio (1996) 'The "Southern Model" of Welfare in Social Europe', *Journal of European Social Policy*, 6 (1): 17–37.

Ferrera, Maurizio (1998) 'The Four "Social Europes": Between Universalism and Selectivity', in: Rhodes, Martin and Mény, Yves (eds), *The Future of European Welfare: A New Social Contract?* Hampshire: Macmillan Press.

Fianna Fáil (2002) *A Lot Done. More to Do*, Dublin: Fianna Fáil.

Fianna Fáil (1997) *People Before Politics*, Dublin: Fianna Fáil.

Fine Gael (2002a) *Towards a Better Quality of Life*, Dublin: Fine Gael.

Fine Gael (2002b) *Just Economics*, Dublin: Fine Gael.

Fine Gael (1997a) *Securing and Sharing our Prosperity*, Dublin: Fine Gael National Headquarters, May.

Fine Gael (1997b) *Education and Healthcare – The Future*, Dublin: Fine Gael National Headquarters, May.

Fine Gael (1997c) *Securing our Environment for our Children*, Dublin: Fine Gael National Headquarters, May.

Fine Gael (1997d) *Securing a Safer Society*, Dublin: Fine Gael National Headquarters, May.

Finnegan, Richard and McCarron, Edward (2000) *Ireland.* Boulder: Westview Press.

Finnemore, Martha (1996) *National Interests in International Society*, Ithaca: Cornell University Press.

Finnemore, Martha and Sikkink, Kathryn (1998) 'International Norms Dynamics and Political Change', *International Organization*, 52 (4): 887–917.

FitzGerald, Garret (1998) 'The Origins, Development and Present Status of Irish "Neutrality"', *Irish Studies of International Affairs*, 9: 11–19.

Foreign Policy (2002–07) 'Measuring Globalization/Globalization Index', Washington A. T. Kearney Inc and Carnegie Endowment for International Peace.

Foucault, Michel (1998a) 'Technologies of Self', in: Martin, Luther, H., (eds), Huck, Gutman and Hutton, Patrick, *Technologies of the Self*, Amherst: University of Massachusetts Press, pp. 16–49.

Foucault, Michel (1998b) 'The Political Technology of Individuals', in: Huck, Gutman and Hutton, Patrick (eds), *Technologies of the Self*, Amherst: University of Massachusetts Press, pp. 145–162.

Foucault, Michel (1991) 'Governmentality', in: Burchell, Graham, Colin, Gordon and Miller, Peter (eds), *The Foucault Effect: Studies in Governmentality*, Chicago: University of Chicago Press, pp. 87–104.

Foucault, Michel (1982) 'The Subject and Power', in: Dreyfus, Hubert and Rabinow, Paul, *Michel Foucault: Beyond Structuralism and Hermeneutics*, New York: Harvester Wheatsheaf, pp. 208–226.

Foucault, Michel (1980) 'Two Lectures', in: Gordon, Colin (ed.), *Michel Foucault: Power/Knowledge, Selected Interviews and Other Writings 1972–1977*, New York: Harvester Wheatsheaf, pp. 78–108.

Foucault, Michel (1978) *The History of Sexuality*, vol. I, *An Introduction*, translated by Robert Hurley, London: Penguin Books.

Foucault, Michel (1977) *Discipline and Punish: The Birth of the Prison*, London: Penguin Books.

Foucault, Michel (1972) *The Archaeology of Knowledge*, translated by A. M. Sheridan Smith, London: Tavistock Publications.

Freeden, Michael (1996) *Ideologies and Political Theory*, Oxford: Clarendon Press.

Gallagher, Michael (1999) 'Parliament', in: Coackley, John and Gallagher, Michael (eds) *Politics in the Republic of Ireland*, 3rd edn, London: Routledge, pp. 177–205.

Gardiner, Kevin (1994) 'The Irish Economy: A Celtic Tiger', in: *Morgan Stanley Euroletter*, 'Ireland: Challenging for Promotion', 31 August, pp. 9–21.

Garrett, Geoffrey and Lange, Peter (1999) 'Internationalisation, Institutions and Political Change', in: Keohane, Robert and Milner, Helen (eds), *Internationalisation and Domestic Politics*, Cambridge: Cambridge University Press, pp. 48–75.

Garvin, Tom (2000) 'The French are on the Sea', in: O' Donnell, Rory (ed.) (2000) *Europe: The Irish Experience*, Dublin: Institute of European Affairs.

Geary, John (1999) *Multinationals and Human Resource Practices in*

Ireland, Dublin: University College Dublin, Centre for Employment Relations and Organisational Performance.

Giddens, Anthony (1999) *Runaway World: How Globalisation is Reshaping our Lives* London: Profile Books.

Giddens, Anthony (1995) 'Living in a Post-Traditional Society', in: Beck, Ulrich, Giddens, Anthony and Lash, Scott (eds), *Reflexive Modernization: Politics, Tradition and Aesthetics in the Modern Social Order,* Cambridge: Polity Press.

Giddens, Anthony (1991) *Modernity and Self Identity: Self and Society in a Late Modern Age*, Stanford: Stanford University Press.

Giddens, Anthony (1990) *The Consequences of Modernity*, London: Routledge.

Gillespie, Paul (2002) 'Old Question of Who are We Neutral Against is Apt', *The Irish Times*, 22 June.

Glogg, Richard (ed.) (1993) *Greece, 1981–1989*, Hampshire: Macmillan Press.

Goetz, Klaus and Hix, Simon (eds.) (2001) *Europeanised Politics? European Integration and National Political Systems*, London: Frank Cass.

Goetz, Klaus and Hix, Simon (2001a) 'Introduction', in: Goetz, Klaus and Hix, Simon (eds), *Europeanised Politics? European Integration and National Political Systems*, London: Frank Cass, pp. 1–26.

Goldsmith, Edward and Mander, Jerry (eds) (2001) *The Case Against the Global Economy, and For a Turn Towards Localization*, international edition, London: Earthscan.

Goldstein, Judith and Keohane, Robert (1993) 'Ideas and Foreign Policy', in: Goldstein, Judith and Keohane, Robert (eds), *Ideas and Foreign Policy*, New York: Cornell University Press, pp. 3–30.

Gramsci, Antonio (1971) 'The Modern Prince', in: Hoare, Quentin and Smith, Geoffrey Nowell (eds), *Selections From the Prison Notebooks of Antonio Gramsci*, London: Lawrence & Wishart, pp. 123–205.

Gunnigle, Patrick and Brosnan, Kathryn (2001) 'Collective Bargaining, Employment Creation and Protection, and Competitiveness in the Republic of Ireland', paper presented at the Annual Meeting of Industrial Relations Research Associations, New Orleans, 7 January.

Gunnigle, Patrick and McGuire, David (2001) 'Why Ireland? A Qualitative Review of the Factors Influencing the Location of US Multinationals in Ireland with Particular Reference to the Impact of Labour Issues', *Economic and Social Review*, 32 (1): 43–67.

Gunnigle, Patrick, Morley, Michael and Heraty, Noreen (1997) *Personnel and Human Resource Management: Theory and Practice in Ireland, Dublin: Gill and Macmillan.

Haas, Peter (1992) 'Introduction: Epistemic Communities and International Policy Coordination', *International Organization*, 46 (1): 1–35.

Hague, Rod and Harrop, Martin (2001) *Comparative Government and Politics: An Introduction*, 5th revised edition, Hampshire: Palgrave.

Hall, Peter (ed.) (1989) *The Political Power of Economic Ideas: Keynesianism Across Nations*, New Jersey: Princeton University Press.

Hall, Peter (1989a) 'Introduction', in: Hall, Peter (ed.), *The Political Power of Economic Ideas: Keynesianism Across Nations*, New Jersey: Princeton University Press, pp. 3–26.

Hall, Peter (1989b) 'Conclusion: The Politics of Keynesian Ideas', in: Peter Hall (ed.), (1989) *The Political Power of Economic Ideas*, New Jersey: Princeton University Press, pp. 361–391.

Hall, Peter (1986) *Governing the Economy*, New York: Oxford University Press.

Hall, Peter and Taylor, Rosemary (1996) 'Political Science and the Three Institutionalisms', *Political Studies*, 44: 936–957.

Hall, Peter and Soskice, David (eds.) (2001) *Varieties of Capitalism: The Institutional Foundations of Comparative Advantage*, Oxford: Oxford University Press.

Hall, Peter and Soskice, David (2001a) 'Introduction', in: Hall, Peter and Soskice, David (eds), *Varieties of Capitalism: The Institutional Foundations of Comparative Advantage*, Oxford: Oxford University Press.

Hardiman, Niamh (2005) 'Politics and Markets in the Irish "Celtic Tiger"', *Political Quarterly*, 76 (1): 37–47.

Hardiman, Niamh (2002) 'From Conflict to Co-ordination: Economic Governance and Political Innovation in Ireland', *West European Politics*, 25 (4): 1–24.

Hardiman, Niamh (2000) 'Social Partnership, Wage Bargaining, and Growth', in: Nolan, Brian, O'Connell, Philip and Whelan, Christopher (eds), *Bust to Boom: the Irish Experience of Growth and Inequality*, Dublin: Institute of Public Administration.

Hardiman, Niamh (1988) *Pay, Politics, and Economic Performance in Ireland 1970–1987*, Oxford: Clarendon Press.

Hardt, Michael and Negri, Antonio (2000) *Empire*, Cambridge: Harvard University Press.

Harmes, Adam (2001) 'Mass Investment Culture', *New Left Review* 9: 103–124.

Hay, Colin (2004) 'Ideas, Interests and Institutions in the Comparative

Political Economy of Great Transformations', *Review of International Political Economy*, 11 (1): 204–226.

Hay, Colin (2001) 'What Place for Ideas in the Structure–Agency Debate? Globalisation as a Process without a Subject', First Press: Writing in the Critical Social Science (available at: www.theglobalsite.ac.uk/press).

Hay, Colin (2001a) 'The 'Crisis' of Keynesianism and the Rise of Neoliberalism in Britain: An Ideational Institutionalist Approach', in: Campbell, John and Pedersen, Ove (eds.) *The Rise of Neoliberalism and Institutional Analysis*. Princeton: Princeton University Press, pp. 193–218.

Hay, Colin and Marsh, David (2000) 'Introduction', in: Hay, Colin and Marsh, David (eds) *Demystifying Globalisation*, London: Macmillan, pp. 1–17.

Hay, Colin and Rosamond, Ben (2002) 'Globalisation, European Integration and the Discursive Construction of Economic Imperatives', *Journal of European Public Policy*, 9 (2): 147–167.

Hay, Colin and Smith, Nicola (2008) 'Mapping the Political Discourse of Globalisation and European Integration in the United Kingdom and Ireland Empirically', *European Journal of Political Research*, 47 (3): 359–382

Hay, Colin and Smith, Nicola (2005) 'Horses for Courses? The Political Discourse of Globalisation and European Integration in the UK and Ireland', *West European Politics*, 28 (1): 124–158.

Hay, Colin and Watson, Matthew (1999) 'The Discourse of Globalisation and the Logic of No Alternative', University of Birmingham, Department of Political Science and International Studies, mimeo (later published in: *Policy & Politics*, 31 (3), 2003: 289–305).

Hoffmann, Reiner, Jacobi, Otto, Keller, Berndt and Weiss, Manfred (eds) (2000) *Transnational Industrial Relations in Europe*, Dusseldorf: Hans-Böckler-Stiftung.

Howarth, David (2000) *Discourse*, Buckingham: Open University Press.

Howarth, David, and Stavrakakis, Yiannis (eds) (2000) *Discourse Theory and Political Analysis*, Manchester: Manchester University Press.

Howarth, David and Stavrakakis, Yiannis (2000) 'Introducing Discourse Theory and Political Analysis', in: Howarth, David, and Stavrakakis, Yiannis (eds), *Discourse Theory and Political Analysis*, Manchester: Manchester University Press, pp. 1–23.

Huntington, Samuel (1991) *The Third Wave: Democratization in the Late Twentieth Century*, Norman: University of Oklahoma Press.

IBEC (1997–2002) *Annual Review*, Dublin: IBEC.

ICTU (1997) *Unions in Action: Making Partnership Work*, Dublin: ICTU.

ICTU (1999) *Report of the Executive Council 1997–1999*, Dublin: ICTU.

ICTU (1999a) *Report of Proceedings: Biennial Delegate Conference, Killarney 1999*, Dublin: ICTU.

ICTU (2001) *Report of Proceedings: Fifth Biennial Delegate Conference, Bundoran 2001*, Dublin: ICTU.

ICTU (2001a) *Working for a Fair Society – A Sound Economy (Part I): Priorities and Strategy*, Dublin: ICTU.

ICTU (2001b) *Working for a Fair Society – A Sound Economy (Part II): Organisation and Finance*, Dublin: ICTU.

Ikenberry, John (1988) 'Conclusion: An Institutional Approach to American Foreign Economic Policy', *International Organization*, 42 (1): 219–243.

IMF (1999) *Greece: Staff Report for the 1999 Article IV Consultation*, Report No. 99/131, 8 November.

Inglis, Tom (2000) 'Irish Civil Society: From Church to Media Domination', in: Inglis, Tom, Mach, Zdzislaw and Mazanek, Rafal (eds), *Religion and Politics*, Dublin: University College Dublin Press, pp. 49–92.

Inglis, Tom (1998) *Moral Monopoly: The Rise and fall of the Catholic Church in Modern Ireland*, 2nd ed, Dublin: Gill and Macmillan.

Ioakimidis, Panayiotis (2001) 'The Europeanisation of Greece' in: Featherstone, Kevin and Kazamias, George (eds), *Europeanization and the Southern Periphery*, London: Frank Cass, pp. 73–94.

Ioakimidis, Panayiotis (1996) 'Contradictions in the Europeanisation Process' in: Kevin Featherstone, and Ifantis, Kostas (eds), *Greece in a Changing Europe*, Manchester: Manchester University Press, pp. 33–52.

Ioannou, Christos (1999) *Trade Unions in Greece*, Athens: Friedrich Ebert Stiftung.

ISTAME (2001) *Institute for Strategic and Development Studies, Andreas Papandreou* (information booklet), May.

Jacobsen, John Kurt (1994) *Chasing Progress in the Irish Republic*, Cambridge: Cambridge University Press.

Jacobsen, John Kurt (1995) 'Much Ado About Ideas: The Cognitive Factor in Economic Policy', *World Politics*, 47 (2): 283–310.

Kamaras, Antonis (2001) 'A Capitalist Diaspora: The Greeks in the Balkans', *Discussion Paper No. 4*, Hellenic Observatory, European Institute, LSE.

Katseli, Louka (1990) 'Structural Adjustment of the Greek Economy', in: Bliss, Christopher and de Macedo, Jorge Braga (eds), *Unity with*

Diversity in the European Economy: The Community's South Frontier, Cambridge: Cambridge University Press, pp. 235–309.

Katzenstein, Peter (1996) *The Culture of National Security*, New York: Columbia University Press.

Katzenstein, Peter (1984) *Corporatism and Change: Austria and Switzerland and the Politics of Industry*, Ithaca: Cornell University Press.

Katzenstein, Peter (1977) 'Conclusion: Domestic Structures and Strategies of Foreign Economic Policy', *International Organization*, 31 (4): 879–920.

Kazakos, Panos (2004) 'Europeanisation, Public Goals and Group Interests: Convergence Policy in Greece, 1990–2003', *West European Politics*, 27 (5): 901–918.

Kazakos, Panos (1999) 'The Europeanisation of Public Policy: The Impact of European Integration on Greek Environmental Policy', *Journal of European Integration*, 21: 369–391.

Kazakos, Panos (1992) 'Socialist Attitudes Towards European Integration in the 1980s', in: Kariotis, Theodore (ed.), *The Greek Socialist Experiment*, New York: Pella.

Kazakos, Panos (1992a) 'The Coordinative Role of State in Economy: Problems and Perspectives of Privatisation Policies in Greece', mimeo (in Greek).

Kazakos, Panos and Ioakimidis, P. C. (eds) (1994) *Greece and EC Membership Evaluated*, London: Pinter.

Keck, Margaret, and Sikkink, Kathryn (1998) *Activists Beyond Borders: Advocacy Networks in International Politics*, Ithaca: Cornell University Press.

King, Anthony (1994) '"Chief Executives" in Western Europe', in: Budge, Ian and McKay, David (eds), *Developing Democracy*, London: Sage.

Kioukias, Dimitris (1997) 'Interest Representation and Modernization Policies in Greece', *Journal of Modern Greek Studies*, vol. 15 (2): 303–324.

Kirby, Peader (2002) *The Celtic Tiger in Distress*, New York: Palgrave.

Kissane, Bill (2003) 'The Illusion of State Neutrality in a Secularising Ireland', *West European Politics*, vol. 26 (1): 73–94.

Kissane, Bill (1995) 'The Not-So Amazing Case of Irish Democracy', *Irish Political Studies*, vol. 10: 43–68.

Kjær, Peter and Pedersen, Ove (2001) 'Translating Liberalization: Neoliberalism in the Danish Negotiated Economy', in: Campbell, John and Pedersen, Ove (eds), *The Rise of Neoliberalism and Institutional Analysis*, Princeton: Princeton University Press, pp. 219–248.

KKE (2000) *Strengthening the Fight for Education and Life*, Perissos: KKE (in Greek).

KKE (1996) *Electoral Manifesto of the Communist Party of Greece*, Perissos: KKE (in Greek).

Knill, Christoph and Lehmkuhl, Dirk (1999) 'How Europe Matters: Different Mechanisms of Europeanisation', *European Integration online Papers (EIoP)*, vol. 3 (7): 1–24.

Kofman, Eleanor and Youngs, Gillian (eds) (1996) *Globalization*, London: Pinter.

Konidaris, Ioannis (2003) 'The Legal Parameters of Church and State Relations in Greece', in: Couloumbis, Theodore, Bellou, Fotini and Kariotis, Theodore (eds), *Greece in the Twentieth Century*, London: Frank Cass.

Krasner, Stephen (1995) 'Power Politics, Institutions and Transnational Relations', in: Risse-Kappen, Thomas (ed.), *Bringing Transnational Relations Back In*, Cambridge: Cambridge University Press, pp. 257–279.

Kudrle, Robert (2004) 'Globalization by the Numbers: Quantitative Indicators and the Role of Policy', *International Studies Perspectives*, vol. 5 (4): 341–355.

Labour Party (2002) *Our Values, Our Pledges*, Dublin: Labour Party.

Labour Party (1997) *Making the Vital Difference*, Dublin: Labour Party.

Laclau, Ernesto (2001) 'Democracy and the Question of Power', *Constellations*, 8 (1): 3–14.

Laclau, Ernesto (2000) 'Identity and Hegemony', in: Judith Butler *et al. Contingency, Hegemony, Universality*, London: Verso, pp. 44–89.

Laclau, Ernesto (1996) 'Why Do Empty Signifiers Matter to Politics', in: Laclau, Ernesto *Emancipation(s)* London: Verso, pp. 36–46.

Laclau, Ernesto and Bhaskar, Roy (1998) 'Discourse Theory and Critical Realism', *Journal of Critical Realism: Alethia*, vol. 1 (2): 9–14.

Laclau, Ernesto and Mouffe, Chantal (1985) *Hegemony and Socialist Strategy*, London: Verso.

Laffan, Brigid (2006) 'Managing Europe from Home, in Dublin, Athens and Helsinki: A Comparative Analysis', *West European Politics*, 29 (4), 687–708.

Laffey, Mark and Weldes, Jutta (1997) 'Beyond Belief: Ideas and Symbolic Technologies in the Study of International Relations', *European Journal of International Relations*, 3 (2): 193–237.

Langley, Paul (2007) 'Uncertain Subjects of Anglo-American Financialisation', *Cultural Critique* 65: 67–91.

Larsen, Henrik (1997) *Foreign Policy and Discourse Analysis*, London: Routledge.

Lavdas, Kostas (1997) *The Europeanization of Greece*, London: Macmillan.

Lee, Joseph (1989) *Ireland 1912–1985*, Cambridge: Cambridge University Press.

Lehmbruch, Gerhard (1979) 'Liberal Corporatism and party Government', in: Schmitter Philippe and Lehmbruch Gerhard (eds), *Trends Toward Corporatist Intermediation*, London: Sage, pp. 147–185.

Lijphart, Arend (1971) 'Comparative Politics and the Comparative Method', *American Political Science Review*, vol. 65 (3): 682–693.

Lockwood, Ben (2004) 'How Robust is the Kearney/Foreign Policy Globalisation Index?', *World Economy*, vol. 27 (4): 507–523.

Lockwood, Ben and Redoano, Michela (2005) 'The CSGR Globalisation Index: An Introductory Guide', *Working Paper 155/04*, CSGR, University of Warwick.

Lyrintzis, Christos (2005) 'The Changing Party System: Stable Democracy, Contested "Modernisation"', *West European Politics*, 28 (2): 242–259.

Mac Einri, Piaras (2001) 'Immigration into Ireland', paper for the project Governance Models and New Migration Patterns, Irish Centre for Migration Studies, University College Cork.

Mair, Peter (1999) 'Party Competition and the Changing Party System', in: Coackley, John and Gallagher, Michael (eds), *Politics in the Republic of Ireland*, 3rd edn, London: Routledge, pp. 127–151.

Manoilesco, Mihail (1936) *Le Siècle du Corporatisme*, revised edition, Paris: F. Alcan.

March, James and Olsen, Johan (1984) 'The New Institutionalism: Organisational Factors in Political Life', *American Political Science Review*, 78 (3): 734–749.

Marsh, Michael and O'Malley, Eoin (1999) 'Ireland', *European Journal of Political Research*, vol. 36 : 423–427.

Mavrogordatos, George (1993) 'Civil Society Under Populism', in: Glogg, Richard (ed.), *Greece, 1981–1989*, Hampshire: Macmillan Press, pp. 47–64.

Mavrogordatos, George (1988) *Between Pityokamtes and Prokroustes*, Athens: Odysseas (in Greek).

McNamara, Kathleen (1998) *The Currency of Ideas*, Ithaca: Cornell University Press.

Milliken, Jennifer (1999) 'The Study of Discourse in International Relations: A Critique of Research and Methods', *European Journal of International Relations*, 5 (2): 225–254.

MITnews (1999) 'Ireland and MIT will establish MediaLabEurope in

Dublin', 3 December (http://web.mit.edu/newsoffice/nr/1999/mle.html).

Mitsos, Achilleas and Mossialos, Elias (eds) (2000) *Contemporary Greece and Europe*, Hampshire: Ashgate.

Mouzelis, Nicos (1995) 'Enlightenment and Neo-Orthodoxy', *To Vima*, 21 May (in Greek).

Mouzelis, Nicos (1986) *Politics in the Semi-Periphery*, London: Macmillan.

Murphy, Gary (1999) 'The Role of Interest Groups in the Policy Making Process', in: Coackley, John and Gallagher, Michael (eds), *Politics in the Republic of Ireland*, 3rd edn, London: Routledge, pp. 271–293.

Mytelka, Lynn (2000) 'Knowledge and Structural Power in the International Political Economy', in: Lawton, Thomas, Rosenau, James and Verdun, Amy (eds), *Strange Power*, Aldershot: Ashgate.

NESC (1999) *Opportunities, Challenges and Capacities for Choice*, Dublin: NESC.

New Democracy (2000) *The Governmental Programme of New Democracy*, Athens: ND (in Greek).

New Democracy (1995) *The Governmental Programme of New Democracy for the Economy*, Athens: ND (in Greek).

Nicolacopoulos, Ilias (2005) 'Elections and Voters, 1974–2004: Old Cleavages and New Issues', *West European Politics*, 28 (2): 260–278.

Nicoletti, Giuseppe, Scarpetta, Stefano and Boyland, Oliver (2000) 'Summary Indicators of Product Market Regulation with an Extension to Employment Protection Legislation', *Working Paper No. 226*, OECD.

O'Clery, Conor (1986) *Phrases Make History Here*, Dublin: O'Brien Press.

O'Connor, Tom (2001) 'Foreign Direct Investment and Indigenous Industry in Ireland: Review of Evidence', *Working Paper 22/01*, project One Europe or Several, ESRC.

O'Donnell, Rory (2000) 'The New Ireland in the New Europe', in: O'Donnell, Rory (ed.), *Europe: The Irish Experience*, Dublin: Institute of European Affairs.

O'Donnell, Rory and O'Reardon, Colm (2000) 'Social Partnership in Ireland's Economic Transformation', in: Fajertag, Giuseppe and Pochet, Philippe (eds), *Social Pacts in Europe*, Brussels: European Trade Union Institute, pp. 237–256.

OECD (2004) *Employment Outlook 2004*, Paris: OECD.

OECD (1994) *The OECD Jobs Study. Evidence and Explanations. Part*

II: The Adjustment Potential of the Labour Market, Paris: OECD.

O'Hearn, Denis (2000) 'Globalization, "New Tigers", and the End of the Developmental State? The Case of the Celtic Tiger', *Politics & Society*, vol. 28 (1): 67–92.

O'Hearn, Denis (1998) *Inside the Celtic Tiger*, London: Pluto.

OKE (2000) 'The Globalisation of Trade in the Framework of WTO', *Opinion*, No. 45.

O'Leary, Brendan (1991) 'An Taoiseach', *West European Politics*, 14 (2): 133–162.

O'Riain, Sean and O' Connell, Philip (2000) 'The Role of the State in Growth and Welfare', in: Nolan Brian, OConnell, Philip and Whelan, Christopher (eds), *Bust to Boom: The Irish Experience of Growth and Inequality,* Dublin: Institute of Public Administration, pp. 310–339.

Pagoulatos, George (2003) *Greece's New Political Economy*, Basingstoke: Palgrave.

Pagoulatos, George (2001) 'Economic Adjustment and Financial Reform', in: Featherstone, Kevin and Kazamias, George (eds), *Europeanisation and the Southern Periphery*, London: Frank Cass.

Pappas, Takis (2003) 'The Transformation of the Greek Party System since 1951', *West European Politics*, 26 (2): 90–114.

Pappas, Takis (2001) 'Party System and Political Competition in Greece, 1981–2001', *Greek Political Science Review*, vol. 17: 71–102 (in Greek).

PASOK (2000) *The Governmental Programme of PASOK*, Athens: PASOK (in Greek).

PASOK (1996) *Strong and Modern Greece*, Athens: PASOK (in Greek).

Petrakos, George and Totev, Stoyan (eds) (2000) *The Development of the Balkan Region*, Aldershot: Ashgate.

Phelan, Sean (2007) 'The Discourses of Neoliberal Hegemony: The Case of the Irish Republic', *Critical Discourse Studies*, 4(1): 28–49.

Poulantzas, Nicos (1976) *The Crisis of the Dictatorships,* London: New Left Books.

Pridham, Geoffrey and Verney, Susannah (1991) 'The Coalitions of 1989–90 in Greece', *West European Politics*, 14 (4): 42–69.

Progressive Democrats (2002): *Value for Your Vote*, Dublin: Progressive Democrats.

Progressive Democrats (1997) *Real Answers, Not Idle Promises*, Dublin: Progressive Democrats.

Przeworski, Adam and Teune, Henry (1970) *The Logic of Comparative Inquiry*, New York: Wiley.

Rabinow, Paul and Rose, Nikolas (2003) 'Thoughts on the Concept of

Biopower Today', unpublished manuscript (version: 12 October 2003).

Raunio, Tapio and Hix, Simon (2001) 'Backbenchers Learn to Fight Back' in: Goetz, Klaus and Hix, Simon (eds), *Europeanised Politics?* London: Frank Cass, pp. 142–168.

Reid, Julian (2007) *The Biopolitics of the War on Terror*, Manchester: Manchester University Press.

Rhodes, Martin and Mény, Yves (1998) 'Europe's Social Contract Under Stress', in: Rhodes, Martin and Mény, Yves (eds), *The Future of European Welfare*, Hampshire: Macmillan Press.

Risse, Thomas (1995) 'Structures of Governance and Transnational Relations', in: Risse, Thomas (ed.), *Bringing Transnational Relations Back In*, Cambridge: Cambridge University Press, pp. 280–313.

Risse, Thomas (1994) 'Ideas Do not Float Freely: Transnational Coalitions, Domestic Structures and the End of the Cold War', *International Organization*, 48 (2): 185–214.

Risse, Thomas (1991) 'Public Opinion, Domestic Structure, and Foreign Policy in Liberal Democracies', *World Politics*, 43 (4): 479–512.

Risse, Thomas and Sikkink, Kathryn (1999) 'The Socialisation of International Human Rights Norms into Domestic Practices', in: Risse, Thomas, Ropp, Stephen and Sikkink, Kathryn (eds), *The Power of Human Rights*, Cambridge: Cambridge University Press, pp. 1–39.

Roche, William and Geary, John (2000) 'Collaborative Production and the Irish Boom', *Economic and Social Review*, 31(1): 1–36.

Rosamond, Ben (1999) 'Globalisation and Multi-level Governance in Europe', paper presented at the conference Globalisation and Its Implications for Europe and the US, Atlanta, 12 March.

Rosamond, Ben (1999a) 'Discourses of Globalisation and the Social Construction of European Identities', *Journal of European Public Policy*, 6 (4), (special issue): 652–668.

Rose, Nikolas (2006) *The Politics of Life Itself*, Princeton: Princeton University Press.

Rose, Nikolas (2001) 'The Politics of Life Itself', *Theory, Culture & Society*, 18 (6): 1–30.

Rose, Nikolas (1999) *Powers of Freedom*, Cambridge: Cambridge University Press.

Rose, Nikolas and Miller, Peter (1992) 'Political Power Beyond the State: Problematics of Government', *British Journal of Sociology*, 43 (2): 173–205.

Rueschemeyer, Dietrich and Skocpol, Theda (eds) (1996) *States,*

Social Knowledge and the Origins of Modern Social Policies, Princeton: Princeton University Press.

Sabatier, Paul (1998) 'The Advocacy Coalition Framework: Revisions and Relevance for Europe', *Journal of European Public Policy*, 5 (1): 98–130.

Sabatier, Paul and Jenkins-Smith, Hank (eds) (1993) *Policy Change and Learning: An Advocacy Coalition Approach*, Boulder: Westview Press.

Schmidt, Vivien (2002) *The Futures of European Capitalism*, Oxford: Oxford University Press.

Schmidt, Vivien (2001) 'The Politics of Economic Adjustment in France and Britain: When Does Discourse Matter?', *Journal of European Public Policy*, 8 (2): 247–264.

Schmidt, Vivien (2000) 'Democracy and Discourse in an Integrating Europe and a Globalising World', *European Law Journal*, 6 (3): 277–300.

Schmidt, Vivien and Radaelli, Claudio (eds) (2005) *Policy Change and Discourse in Europe,* London: Routledge.

Schmidt, Vivien and Radaelli, Claudio (2004) 'Policy Change and Discourse in Europe: Conceptual and Methodological Issues', *West European Politics*, 27 (4): 183–210.

Schmidt, Vivien and Radaelli, Claudio (2004a) 'Conclusions: Mapping the Scope of Discourse, Learning and Europeanisation in Policy Change', *West European Politics*, 27 (4): 364–379.

Schmitter, Philippe (1979) 'Still the Century of Corporatism?', in: Schmitter, Philippe and Lehmbruch, Gerhard (eds), *Trends Toward Corporatist Intermediation,* London: Sage, pp. 7–48.

Schurmann, Franz (1974) *The Logic of World Power,* New York: Pantheon.

Searle, John (1995) The Construction of Social Reality, New York: Free Press.

SEV (2000, 2001) *Annual Report*, Athens: SEV.

SEV (1996, 1998) *Apologismos 1*, Athens: SEV.

Sinclair, Timothy (2005) *The New Masters of Capital: American Bond Rating Agencies and the Politics of Creditworthiness, Ithica: Cornell University Press.

Sinnott, Richard (1999) 'The Electoral System', in: Coackley, John and Gallagher, Michael (eds). (1999) *Politics in the Republic of Ireland*, 3rd edn, London: Routledge, pp. 99–126.

Sinnott, Richard (1995) *Irish Voters Decide*, Manchester: Manchester University Press.

Smith, Nicola (2005) *Showcasing Globalisation? The Political Economy of the Irish Republic*, Manchester: Manchester University Press.

Smith, Nicola (2004) 'Deconstructing 'Globalisation' in Ireland', *Policy & Politics,* 32 (4): 503–519.

Sotiropoulos, Dimitri (2004) 'Southern European Bureaucracies in Comparative Perspective', *West European Politics,* 27 (3): 405–422.

Spanou, Calliope (1996) 'Penelope's Suitors: Administrative Modernisation and Party Competition in Greece', *West European Politics,* 19 (1): 97–124.

Stavrakakis, Yannis (2002) 'Religion and Populism: Reflections on the "Politicised" Discourse of the Greek Church', *Discussion Paper No. 7,* Hellenic Observatory, European Institute, LSE.

Stein, Arthur (1983) 'Coordination and Collaboration: Regimes in an Anarchic World', in: Krasner, Stephen (ed.), *International Regimes,* Ithaca: Cornell University Press, pp. 115–140.

Stone, Diane (1996) *Capturing the Political Imagination: Think-tanks and the Policy Process.* London: Frank Cass.

Stone, Diane and Andrew, Denham (eds) (2004) *Think-tank Traditions: Policy Research and the Politics of Ideas,* Manchester: Manchester University Press.

Stone, Diane, Denham, Andrew and Garnett, Mark (eds) (1998) *Think-tanks Across the World: A Comparative Perspective,* Manchester: Manchester University Press.

Stratos, Iason (1999) Address by the Chairman of the Federation of Greek Industries to the Annual Assembly (afternoon session). Athens, 21 June.

Sweeney, Paul (1998) *The Celtic Tiger,* Dublin: Oak Tree Press.

Synaspismos (2000) *Decide Left – Vote Synaspismos,* Athens: Synaspismos (in Greek).

Synaspismos (1996) *Electoral Manifesto 1996,* Athens: Synaspismos (in Greek).

Therborn, Goran (1995) *European Modernity and Beyond,* London: SAGE.

Tonra, Ben (2000) 'Constructing Narratives in Irish Foreign Policy', paper presented at the American Conference for Irish Studies, University of Limerick, 27 June.

Tovey, Hilary (2001) 'Sociology in Ireland', *Irish Journal of Sociology,* 10 (2): 77–85.

Triandafyllidou, Anna (2005) *Greek Immigration Policy,* Athens: ELIAMEP (in Greek).

Tsebelis, George (1995) 'Decision Making in Political Systems', *British Journal of Political Science,* 25: 289–326.

Tsoukalas, Constantinos (1993) *Social Development and State: The Constitution of Public Space in Greece,* 5th edn, Athens: Themelio (in Greek).

Tsoukalas, Constantinos (1993a) 'Free Riders in Wonderland', *Greek Political Science Review*, 1: 9–52 (in Greek).

Tsoukalis, Loukas (2001) 'Driving Forces of Integration', in: Tsoukalis, Loukas (ed), *Globalisation and Regionalism: A Double Challenge for Greece*, Athens: ELIAMEP and Hellenic Observatory, LSE, pp. 121–126.

Tsoukalis, Loukas (1999) 'Greece: Like Any Other European Country?', *National Interest*, 55: 65–74.

Wallden, Sotiris (2000) 'Greece and the Balkans: Economic Relations', in: Mitsos, Achilleas and Mossialos, Elias (eds), *Contemporary Greece and Europe*, Hampshire: Ashgate.

Walsh, Brendan (2000) 'From Rags to Riches', *World Economics*, 1 (4): 113–133.

Ward, Alan (1994) *The Irish Constitutional Tradition*, Washington: Catholic University Press.

Ware, Kallistos (1983) 'The Church: A Time of Transition', in: Clogg, Richard (ed.), *Greece in the 1980s,* London: Macmillan, pp. 208–230.

Weber, Max (1978) *Economy and Society*, Berkeley: University of California Press.

Whelan, Christopher and Layte, Richard (2004) 'Economic Boom and Social Mobility: The Irish Experience', *Working Papers No. 154*, Economic and Social Research Institute (ESRI).

Wittrock, Bjorn and Wagner, Peter (1996) 'Social Science and the Building of the Early Welfare State', in: Rueschemeyer, Dietrich and Skocpol, Theda (eds), *States, Social Knowledge and the Origins of Modern Social Policies*, Princeton: Princeton University Press, pp. 90–113.

Zavos, Alexandros (2005), 'Migration Management as a Political Necessity' in: Papademetriou, Demetrios and Cavounidis, Jennifer (eds), *Managing Migration*, Athens: IMEPO, pp. 9–20.

Index

Anglo-Saxon model 31–33, 36, 38–40

Barry, Anthony, President of IBEC (1996–1998) 119
biopolitical approach 14, 16, 18, 166
  see also biopolitics and biopower
biopolitics 14, 20, 90
  see also biopower and biopolitical approach
biopower 14, 15, 29n.4
  see also biopolitics and biopolitical approach
Butler, Judith (1956–) 16, 168

Cassells, Peter, General Secretary of ICTU (1989–2001) 56n.20, 121–2, 126, 141n.19
Castoriadis, Cornelius (1922–97) 23
CEEP *see* Centre of Employers and Enterprises providing Services
Celtic tiger 27, 43, 104, 139, 146, 148–9, 150–1
  Desmond Connell critique of 128–9, 141n.25
  Fine Gael critique of 110–11
Centre of Employers and Enterprises providing Services 84

Christodoulos (1939–2008), Archbishop of Athens and All Greece (1998–2008) 42, 72, 79, 82–3, 148, 152n.1
church 41–43, 58n.32–37, 148–9
  globalisation in Greece and 82–83, 99
  globalisation in Ireland and 128–30, 139
Coalition of the Left and Progress 52–3, 67–8, 77–9, 80–1, 99, 145
Communist Party of Greece 67, 75–7, 79, 81, 99, 145
competitiveness 85–6, 109, 111, 114, 118, 120, 124, 126–7, 164
Connell, Desmond (Cardinal) (1926–) Archbishop of Dublin and Primate of Ireland (1988–2004) 42, 128–30, 141n.24–5, 148, 150
Constantopoulos, Nicos (1942–), Party leader (1993–2004) 78–9
corporate tax cuts *see* tax cuts
corporatism 32, 38, 55n.6, 57n.21

Deleuze, Gilles (1925–95) 10, 14, 29n.1
deregulation 20, 28, 52, 78, 85–7,